Mahalla and its Educational Role

Nation-Building and Community Education in Uzbekistan

Mahalla and its Educational Role
Nation-Building and Community Education in Uzbekistan

ASUKA KAWANO

Kyushu University Press

All rights reserved. No part of this publication may be reproduced or transmitted in any form or by any means, electronic or mechanical, including photocopying and recording, or by any information storage systems, without the written permission from the publisher.

Copyright© 2015 by Asuka Kawano

Kyushu University Press
3-8-34-305, Momochihama, Sawara-ku, Fukuoka-shi, 814-0001, Japan

ISBN978-4-7985-0161-1

Printed in Japan

Explanatory Notes

1. I conformed to the following principles regarding the notation method for terms.
   a) For essential terms, Russian and Uzbek were transcribed into the Latin alphabet to be expressed along with the English language.
   b) In employing the Latin alphabet notation of local languages such as the names of places and persons, I decided to use a method in which I also took commonly used notation into account, while paying maximum possible attention to the indigenous pronunciations and notation used in Uzbekistan and Central Asia.
   Examples: Kyrgyzstan→Kyrgyz
   Nowruz→*Navro'z*
   Ramadan→*Ramazan*

2. I conformed to the following principles regarding the spellings of Russian and Uzbek words, as well as the notation, when using the Latin alphabet.
   a) Notation of relevant literatures including the author name(s), document name, publication company name, issuing organization and issuing place were based on the original texts.
   b) I exclusively followed original texts in terms of notation in quotations. When there were errors in terms, figures and others in charts, I stated the original as it was, giving a proviso in the texts or footnotes.
   c) Unless otherwise noted, the transliteration of Russian and Uzbek was based on the table of transliteration/alphabets by Hisao Komatsu, Hiroshi Umemura, Tomohiko Uyama, Chika Obiya, Toru Horikawa, eds., *Chuou Yurashia wo Shiru Jiten (Cyclopedia of Central Eurasia)*, Heibon-sha, Japan, 2005, pp. 592-593 in principle.

Map of Uzbekistan and Neighboring Countries

Republic of Uzbekistan
Capital : Tashkent
Area (Total) : 447,400sqkm
Population : 28,929,716 (July 2014 est.)

Administrative Divisions and Capital City of the Republic of Uzbekistan

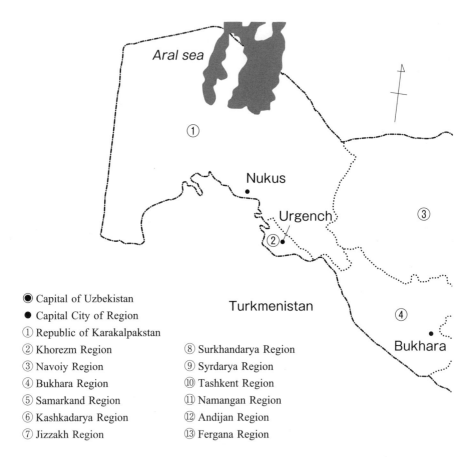

- ◉ Capital of Uzbekistan
- ● Capital City of Region
- ① Republic of Karakalpakstan
- ② Khorezm Region
- ③ Navoiy Region
- ④ Bukhara Region
- ⑤ Samarkand Region
- ⑥ Kashkadarya Region
- ⑦ Jizzakh Region
- ⑧ Surkhandarya Region
- ⑨ Syrdarya Region
- ⑩ Tashkent Region
- ⑪ Namangan Region
- ⑫ Andijan Region
- ⑬ Fergana Region

Note : Republic of Karakalpakstan (①) is an autonomous republic of Uzbekistan.
Source : Tukhliev, N., Krementsova, A., *The Republic of Uzbekistan*, Uzbekistan milliy entsiklopediyasi, Tashkent, 2003. CIA The World Factbook, Hisao Komatsu, Hiroshi Umemura, Tomohiko Uyama, Chika Obiya, Toru Horikawa eds., *Chuou Yurashia wo Shiru Jiten* (*Cyclopedia of Central Eurasia*), Heibonsha Japan, 2005.

Acknowledgments

Everyone in this world can learn whenever, wherever and from whomever they want in their whole life. Male or female, people who are living in developed countries or in developing countries, everybody has the right to learn and can receive an education and continue learning. However, in reality or fact, for many children, especially girls, it is impossible to receive education for various reasons such as tradition, culture, regional characteristics, divisions of labor by gender role, war, poverty, etc. In Uzbekistan, until the expansion of the education system under the Russian Empire, boys' education was conducted at a *maktab* or *madrasa* attached to mosques and girls' education was conducted at teachers' houses, however, nowadays a coeducational system is widespread throughout all parts of Uzbekistan from the period of Soviet Union rule. Boys and girls can receive education equally in the current school education system of Uzbekistan. However, an educational gap due to wealth disparity has materialized, regardless of male or female. In such a present world, what could allow a system where people cannot receive or continue their education throughout their lives as an educational safety net? Is it possible that schools, family and local community have the power to secure the rights of people to learn, or is something new required?

This book is an English version of *"Kyoiku" suru Kyoudoutai: Uzbekistan ni okeru Kokumin Keisei to Chiiki Shakai Kyoiku (Community "Education": Nation-Building and Community Education in Uzbekistan)* published in 2010 by Kyushu University Press. The basic research of this book would have been impossible without the warm support of many people from around the world, especially in Central Asia and Japan. For their help in making my eyes open to the former Soviet Union, Central Asia, I am grateful to Professor Akira Sakamoto, Professor Yoshiaki Katsuyama and Professor Masashi Takagi at Fukuoka University, where I was awarded my master's degree. A Professor said to me, "Studies on education in Central Asia is a yet untrodden field in Japan", I still remember when I visited Uzbekistan for the first time excitedly with that professor's words.

Also, to open the road to Uzbekistan and Central Asia I deeply appreciate the Fukuoka-Uzbekistan Friendship Association, Mr. Tatsuzen Fujino, Professor Munyuck Kim and the members of the association. Thanks to their devoted support, I could meet so many professors, teachers and friends in Uzbekistan, and research the educational situation after independence for my master's thesis with various families and at the

Tashkent State Institute of Oriental Studies.

For my doctoral dissertation, at home I benefited from the appropriate advice and encouragement of professors, in particular Professor Takeo Matsuda, my supervisor at Kyushu University, who provided the wisdom and significant perspectives of social education and social pedagogy in Japan and the Nordic countries. Furthermore, I was guided by Professor Junko Otani and Professor Takuzo Osugi through collaborative research on women's community activities in Central Asia. And above all, I especially owe thanks to Professor Nodira Egamberdiyeva, my supervisor at Tashkent State Pedagogical University named after Nizami, Uzbekistan, and professors of Sub-faculty of Pedagogy at Faculty of Pedagogy and Psychology, who guided me to *Mahalla* and real life of people in Uzbekistan, a world quite new to me.

I am also really thankful of the professors of the Graduate School of Education and Human Development at Nagoya University, who always gave me motivation and a wonderful research environment. In addition, I am very thankful to the professors of the Graduate School of Humanities and Social Sciences at the University of Tsukuba, my former workplace, who also provided me with inspired research opportunities.

Financial support for the book publishing was provided by Nagoya University, Grant-in Aid for Publication of Scientific Literature 2013. Crucial funding during the earlier stages of research and writing my doctoral dissertation, which are the base of this book, was provided by the Ministry of Education, Culture, Sports, Science and Technology, Japan "Promotion of internationalization of education in University (support for long-term studying abroad)", "Study on education and culture policies in local community and people's acceptance: Focusing on the *Mahalla* of Uzbekistan"; Kitakyushu Forum on Asian Women, Research of KFAW Visiting Researchers, "an Empirical study on community and gender in Central Asia: Uzbekistan, Tajikistan, Kazakhstan and Kyrgyz" (Research representative: Junko Otani); the Graduate School of Human-Environment Studies, Kyushu University, Research grant for overall degree 2008, "Study on the educational role of local community in Uzbekistan: *Mahalla* in Uzbekistan after independence"; Japan Society for the Promotion of Science, Grants-in-Aid for Scientific Research, Grant-in-Aid for JSPS Fellows, "Social development and local community in Central Asian countries: Examination on community view and education cooperation within the area"; Japan Society for the Promotion of Science, Grants-in-Aid for Scientific Research, Grant-in-Aid for Publication of Scientific Research Results (Scientific Literature). I deeply offer my appreciation for all financial support to my research.

I sincerely appreciate Editing Director Mr. Shunji Nagayama and the staff of Kyushu

University Press, who were patient with my quite slow writing pace and proofread my manuscript carefully.

And finally, thanks to my family, who have supported me always beside me. My mother supported me, sometimes nicely other times strictly, and my father presented me with cover photos of this book which he took in Uzbekistan. Most of all, I am glad to acknowledge my grandmother who departed from life a few weeks ago and could not see the Central Asian world. I wish this book reaches her, I dedicate this book to her.

ASUKA KAWANO

March 2015
Nagoya, Japan

Contents

Acknowledgments i

Introduction : Challenges of Education Research in Central Asia............ 1
1. Education Research in Central Asia up to Now and Research Topics 1
2. Challenges in the Local Community Education Research in Central Asia 8
3. "Mahalla" in This Study and Purpose of the Study 14

Chapter 1 Mahalla in Uzbekistan and Historical Change in Their Educational Aspect..27
1. Previous History of Mahalla in Uzbekistan 27
2. Mahalla from the End of 19th Century to the Early 20th Century 29
3. Mahalla during the Period of Russian Empire and Mahalla Policy of Russian Empire.. 31
4. Mahalla in the Period of Soviet Union and Mahalla Policy of the Soviet Authority... 32
5. Mahalla in Uzbekistan after Their Independence and Mahalla Restoration Policy of the Uzbekistan Government 36
   Conclusion 38

Chapter 2 Mahalla Structure and Learning for Adults after Independence..41
1. Systemization of Mahalla by the Nation 42
2. Activities of Mahalla as the End Institution of the Government 50
3. Community Education Activities by Mahalla Residents and Female Support.. 54
   Conclusion : How the Adult Learning in Mahalla Can Be Understood........... 61

Chapter 3 The Socialization and Cultural Succession of Children in Mahallas 67
1. Children's Life in Uzbekistan's Mahallas...................................... 69
2. Children's Rites of Passage and Islam 79

3. Becoming Socialized through Ceremonies and Rituals Conducted
   at Mahallas 84
Conclusion 91

Chapter 4 Mahalla in School Education 97
1. School System of Uzbekistan and Educational Reform after
   the Independence 98
2. The Political and Social Background of Implementing Mahalla
   in School Education : "From a Strong State to a Strong Civil
   Society", Mahalla as a Social Foundation 106
3. Mahalla's Image in School Education and Principles 107
4. The Actual Situation and Significance of Implementation
   of Mahalla in School Education 110
Conclusion 125

**Chapter 5 Raising "Citizen" Awareness in Uzbekistan through
a Combined Effort between Mahallas and Schools** 131
1. Fostering "Citizen" Awareness in Young People after the
   Independence of Uzbekistan 133
2. Fostering the Social Awareness of "Citizenship" in School
   Education in Uzbekistan 138
3. Fostering a Social Awareness of "Citizenship" by Mahallas 140
Conclusion 145

**Chapter 6 Youth Education through the Cooperative Activities
of Institutions : Examples from Mahalla, NGOs, and International
Organizations** 149
1. Position of NGOs and Youth Organizations in Uzbekistan and
   Their Activities 150
2. Cooperative Activities of Each Institutions and Mahalla 156
3. Image of Local Community for Young People in Uzbekistan and
   the Activities of Each Institution : Based on a Survey from
   Multiple Universities 157
Conclusion 168

Final Chapter : Educational Role of Mahalla in Uzbekistan *173*
   1. Relationship of the Educational Role in Each Institution *173*
   2. A Community That Educates *179*
   Conclusion—Future Views and Challenges— *180*

Selected Bibliography *183*

Introduction

Challenges of Education Research in Central Asia

1. Education Research in Central Asia up to Now and Research Topics

When a new nation is born, whether by accident or out of necessity, what is the role of education? What organizational body would a government use to communicate the ideology of a newly founded new to its citizens? If there is a "difference in education" between the people who received school education in the old system before the foundation of the new nation and people who received education now after its foundation, how can they overcome that? The study, which is the origin of this book, started from this kind of impulsive awareness of the issues.

Generally when a new nation is founded, they tend to revive the traditional and ethnical culture, as well as their ethnical history, that have been neglected and re-propose and re-create their ethnical roots. Or, they appeal to the public how their new government is superior, how they promote pioneering project that will oversee the future, and what they are doing to not repeat their past mistakes, regardless of if they were considered as mistakes or not in the old system, and then start propaganda to criticize the old system. In the educational world, it comes in the form of changing textbooks and the medium of instruction, the revision of curriculum, and the foundation of a new education system which is then taught to the "new citizens". This kind of education activity is done systematically and deliberately as well as intentionally in formal education[1] mainly at school. Then, how does government try to give new education to people who are not in school?

In order to examine the answers to questions like these in this book, I focused on "*mahalla*" (hereinafter referred as mahalla), a traditional local community in the Republic of Uzbekistan (hereinafter referred as Uzbekistan), which is one of the countries in Central Asia that became independent in 1991, and tried to clarify their educational role. To be specific, I set up the following 4 research topics and examined them in each chapter.

(1) What are the objectives of the education policy in relation to the local community called "mahalla" in Uzbekistan after their independence in 1991 after the dissolution of the Soviet Union?

(2) What are the educational activities in mahalla and what role do they take in education for children, adolescents, young adults and adults?
(3) How is the mahalla treated in school education and how do they cooperate?
(4) What are the cooperative activities between mahalla and NGO, youth organizations, and international organizations?

The results of research on Uzbekistan and other countries in Central Asia have been accumulated in the fields of history, political science, international relations, area studies, anthropology, and developmental economics. Among these researches on local societies in Central Asia, mahalla has been represented in the fields of history, urbanology, politics, and area studies. However, education research regarding Central Asia has very few remarkable achievements and, compared to other areas, it is still a sprouting area of study.

Recently, there have been some studies that dealt with the educational phenomena of the local area which targeted Central Asia and Caucasus, formerly of the Soviet Union. In those studies, however, multiple authors discuss the issue on the whole for Central Asia or a specific country from their perspective, so there has not been any full scale research that focuses on one country in Central Asia and discusses the facts of education systematically and empirically. Furthermore, the subjects of these previous researches mainly focused on the elementary, secondary, and higher education of Central Asia, so research on education outside of school, such as social education, community education or adult education, lifelong education, lifelong learning, non-formal education, or informal education in Central Asia is almost non-existent.[2]

So the purpose of this book is to focus on the 4 research tasks that were mentioned earlier and to clarify the tasks for Central Asia education research at the same time within the possible range. In order to do so, it is necessary to thoroughly organize the previous research done on local education in Central Asia and see what kind of trends are seen as well as to understand what has not been clarified in the previous research and specify what needs to be done.

Then, what has been talked about in the education of Uzbekistan and Central Asia? For example, the education for this area has sometimes been talked about as a part of life history or historical phenomena of people, or other times, it was talked about in a report or "framework" of international support organization or from the perspective of execution analysis for NGO. In other words, the education of Central Asia and Uzbekistan has been described from these standpoints, and it is desired to clarify what perspectives exist in these positions. So in this chapter, I will classify the education research in Central Asia and Uzbekistan into three categories, research on education in general, education research of Uzbekistan and Central Asia in the field of international education development, and previous education research of Uzbekistan and Central Asia in other disciplines, and clarify from what kind of standpoint the research was done.

The first study that I will introduce from the research of Uzbekistan and Central Asia from the general pedagogy is the *Summarized History of Citizen Education in Turkestan* (1960) written by Bendrikov, K. E. regarding the expansion of education and the modern educational system in the local community during the period of the Russian Empire.

According to Bendrikov, traditional education centering on religion was taught to boys in *maktab*, a school that is attached to a mosque or madrasa, a seminary, and girls learn at the teacher's house. In a *maktab*, where boys attended their elementary education, they learn how to write and read as well manners based on Islamic belief. In Samarkand before the early 19th Century when the Russian Empire advanced to Central Asia, there were *maktabs* in each local community such as mahalla and *guzar* (square), and some had *maktab* for girls. The teachers at a *maktab* were usually an *imam*, (Islamic monk and it means "model" and "instructor" in Koran)[3] from the nearest mosque.

During this time period, mahalla was a place where the non-formal education mentioned above was given, and had a role of supporting this type of learning. It can be said that the research of Bendrikov is valuable because it not only discusses the expansion of modern education in Turkestan[4] from the perspective of the government of the Russian Empire and modern school, but it also discusses it in detail from the perspective of the local community and the education activities at *maktab* and madrasa.

However, it is undeniable that this research was done from the perspective of the rulers so as to show the uncivilized area of the local community in Turkestan and how the life of local citizens is behind as well as showing how the modern school from the Russian Empire contributed to the modernization of the local citizens. In the research of Bendrikov, mahalla and mahalla residents are the receivers of the modernization strategies promoted by the Russian Empire, so independent educational activities of the people in the local community and the educational role that the local community took was not mentioned. In other words, it did not mention the rich education provided by the people in the local community and it is one of the reasons why the previous research lacks in content.

Although it is not a research specialized in Central Asia, Haruka Ebihara discussed in his research, the *Historical Research of Education Policy in the Russian Empire*, the development of educational strategy in Russia from the 17th Century under the rule of

Pyotr I to the early 19th century when it was under the rule of Alexandre I. This book mentions the foundation and development of naval school, garrison school, mining factory school, and Moscow State University under the rule of Pyotr I, "Rules of the Russian Empire Citizen's School" under the rule of Ekaterina II, and specific examples of Citizen's Education System set under the rule of Alexandre I, and discusses the intentions behind these educational strategies. Since the Russian empire invaded the south of the Central Asia and invaded Tashkent was in 1865, the time period in which this research was done is not the same time as the research done for this book. However, the educational strategy and development of the early Russian Empire discussed in this research certainly shaped the expansion strategy of modern education in the Russian Empire and Central Asia, so in that sense, this can provide various perspectives and historical material.

For the education in Uzbekistan and Central Asia during the period of the Soviet Union, there are not very many specialized studies, most of them mention about the Soviet education and educational policy of the Soviet Union in general. There is a lot literature that deals with citizen's education in the Soviet Union. Among those, *Citizen's Education in the Soviet Union 1917 to 1967* written by Prokofieva and others mentions the education of all 15 republics that made up the Soviet Union, and the promotion of education policy and the literacy rate in Uzbek Soviet Socialist Republic (Uzbek SSR) during the early soviet period. Even though it is not focused on Uzbekistan during the soviet period, it is undoubtedly a valuable material in grasping the educational situation at the time. *Schools in Soviet* (1976) written by Tomiak. J. J. translated into Japanese introduces specific information, such as that they had early childhood education facilities that could accommodate 50% to 80% of children aging from 2-3 months to 7 years old in Tashkent at the time[5] and it not only focuses the educational situation of elementary and secondary education at the time, but also introduces pre-school education to higher education, so this literature provide plentiful information. The same research by Tomiak also mentions *Oktyabryata* (October child, Little Octobrist) other than the school education, youth groups such as *Pioneer* and *Komsomol*, and adult education, so it is an important literature that considers the social education and lifelong education in Uzbekistan and Central Asia during the Soviet and post-Soviet periods.

However, similar to the research done during the period of the Russian Empire, they focus on claiming the "Educational Power of Soviet and Basis of True Success"[6] to the world, and we must be reminded that it was difficult to discuss the educational phenomena freely at the time since they had strict censorship and self-restriction. We can grasp the summary of education in the former Soviet Union, but it is no easy to read the local and micro education which lay hidden beneath. So in that sense, it painfully reminds us the necessity of material collection at site and field work.

For Japanese literature, we cannot leave out the research of Satoshi Kawanobe that systematically and chronologically considered the history of education in Soviet up to today. Although he did not mention too much about Uzbekistan and Central Asia in the *Education of Russia, Past and Future* (1996) supervised by Satoshi Kawanobe, the *Educational Reform of Soviet* (1985) edited by Satoshi Kawanobe, and the *Annual History/ Development of Post War Education in Soviet* (1991), it is an essential body of material for understanding the summary of education in Soviet Russia, which is the basis, or roots, of education in Uzbekistan today. Also, literature on the activities of *Pioneer, Summer Vacation Living School-One Month in Pioneer Camp* written by Shiro Murayama is based on his experience participating in Pioneer Camp for a month, and is a very interesting literature because it describes the image of *Pioneer* from the Japanese perspective.

The independence after the dissolution of the Soviet Union made it possible to do on site field work, which was difficult before, and various international assistance organizations and NGOs started conducting assistance activities on site, so education research that is based on the actual situation in the local area has increased drastically. Also, there are some researchers who learn the language and follow the people who are related to the educational institution to clarify the educational phenomena. As for recent related literature, *The Challenge of Education in Central Asia* by Heyneman, edited by Deyoung, covers the social, political and economic background of education in Central Asia and the basic elements in the local education such as elementary and secondary education. There is a characteristic that many of the authors of the theses are not only local researchers, but are also international cooperation institution and NGO personnel from groups such as the Asian Development Bank (ADB) and Open Society Institute (OSI) founded by George Soros. However, there are some points that are in question from the pedagogic perspective, such as higher education and university education, which are described in the area of elementary and secondary education.

Also this literature not only has education in Uzbekistan as its subject of focus, but also mentions higher education and education reform in Kazakhstan and Kyrgyz as well as the educational challenges in general in Central Asia. Needless to say, there is no discussion on social education or adult education, so it only allows a fraction of the current situation that the education system in Central Asia is facing and it does not go into detail regarding the actual situation, nor does it discuss learning from the local or micro standpoints. From the field of pedagogy in Japan, there are some studies that relate to education in Central Asia and Uzbekistan such as "Constructing the Lifelong Learning System that Promotes the Transition to a 'citizen Society'–Educational Reform in the Republic of Uzbekistan" (1998) by Yukiko Sawano, "Ethnicity, Religion, and Education in Uzbekistan –a discussion from the perspective of character formation" (2000) by Keiko Seki, "The Principle and Current Situation of Occupation Education Expansion Strategy in Uzbekistan" (2000) by Kuniko Mizutani, "Uzbekistan-Focusing on the Educational Reform at the High School Level-Human Resource Development for Moving Away from Russia" (2001) by Kuniko Mizutani, and "Living in Multi-Ethnic Society –Character Formation in the Transition Period of Russia" (2002) by Keiko Seki. These studies mention educational reform and educational administration right after the independence and reformation of the educational institution in detail so they are pioneering studies for the education research of Central Asia in Japan. It is also a ground-breaking point of these researches that they actually visited the area to do the research on educational reform sponsored by the "National Programme for Personal Training (NPPT)".

Furthermore, *Globalization and Education Reform in Central Asia* (2012) was published by Japanese and Central Asian researchers. They are examining current situation of education in Central Asian countries, and analyzing the impacts of globalization.

However, basically the research stop at the analysis of school education and the educational system and it does not discuss the educational activities in the local community, so they do not clarify the educational view of mahalla residents, the educational role of mahalla, or the specific cooperation between school and local community and its meaning.[7] Also, the data related to the present educational situation changes on a daily basis so it is necessary to collect the newest data and do field research in order to clarify the current image of education in Central Asia.

Because of these reasons, pedagogic research in Uzbekistan and Central Asia overemphasize school education, and it is understood that people's learning outside of school is not researched very well. This suggests that future, systematic, education research in Uzbekistan and the Central Asia area needs to be done on the social education and adult education that has yet to be focused on thus far.

Then how has the education research in Uzbekistan and Central Asia been done in the field of international education development? One of the recent studies, *How NGOs React: Globalization and Education Reform in the Caucasus, Central Asia and Mongolia* (2008) by Silova, I. eds., is similar to the "Challenges in Education in Central Asia" mentioned before, and it is a collection of the endeavors of OSI activists in countries in Central Asia. In countries in Central Asia after independence, there are various non-governmental organizations and non-profit organizations, such as NGO and NPO, which are active in various areas such as education, health and sanitation, and environmental problems. The subject of this book is the meaning of the activities of NGO, mainly OSI in Central Asian countries after their independence, and discusses the education situation in Central Asia, empirically based on the practice of NGO.

However, it has a tendency to talk about the education in Central Asia with an overemphasis on OSI activities, such as the thesis that discussed the topic of Uzbekistan "Quarter for Quota: Mainstreaming the Value of Open Society". It is true that there are "government type" NGOs in Central Asia and Uzbekistan that people wonder whether they can call them NGO. It is unfortunate that the image of NGO education is slightly blurred because it is focused on the NGO's activities. In other words, it is necessary to be careful about including various NGO activities in the future.

Various reports by international organizations, such as by United Nations Children's Fund (UNICEF) and United Nations Educational, Scientific and Cultural Organization (UNESCO), and United Nations Development Program (UNDP), provide valuable materials to know about the current education situation of Uzbekistan. For example, a national report related to the UNESCO international adult education conference (CONFINTEA), hosted by UNESCO every 12 years, reports the current situation for adult education, lifelong learning and their future plans in each country. In the national report of Uzbekistan, the importance of mahalla for adult education and the adult education policy was reported and explained in the summary of "Tashkent Call to Action" which was suggested in adult education conference for the Central Asia held in Tashkent in 2003, which allow us to grasp on the adult education in Uzbekistan and Central Asia comprehensively.[8]

Although it is not a literature from the field of pedagogy, the *History of Samarkand* (1969) edited by Muminov. I. M. recorded in detail that school and mahalla was one of the largest bases for enforcing the Soviet ideology and the formation of the citizen of the Soviet Union, along with the agitator[9] and a specific number of teachers.

However this book claimed how the agriculture, urban manufacturing, cultural activities, citizen education, and scholarly activities of Samarkand in Marxism and Leninist propaganda in Uzbekistan contributed to the modernization of Uzbekistan, so it's goal was to reflect the communist policies and ideology. These writings had the role of strategic propaganda for the political powers that be at the time, but on the other hand, it mentions the actual implementation situation for citizen education strategy in Samarkand from the early Soviet era to 1960s and the actual number of students and schools as well as advertisement activities in mahalla. It provides beneficial information to help understand the school education of mahalla at the time, and it also can be compared to the present situation.

Literature by Muminov shows that mahalla played a role in turning the citizens into "citizens of Soviet", and they used the traditional framework and the provided education aimed at the modernization and Sovietization of citizens that include the ideology of Soviet government.

I have discussed the previous research on education in Uzbekistan and Central Asia from the views of general pedagogy, the field of international education development, and fields other than pedagogy. What I found from these was the definite lack of perspective in social education and adult education.

As it was mentioned, the educational reform to renew the educational system during the Soviet period in Uzbekistan, but it is projected that there will be an "education gap" between children who received school education during the Soviet period and children now. For this reason, exploring what has been happening in the social education and local community by subjecting various generations will lead to the exploration of important aspects of the education in Uzbekistan. So in the next section, I will discuss the social education of local communities in Central Asia.

2. Challenges in the Local Community Education Research in Central Asia

(1) Theory of Social Education and Mahalla

For the education research on Uzbekistan and Central Asia, the research on the educational role of the local community and education activities in the local community, the main topic of this book, has been done mainly in the field of social pedagogy and educational sociology. Here, we will clarify the position of this book in pedagogy, especially social pedagogy and educational sociology upon the examination of previous research.

Social education in Japan has had various discussions and practice reports, mainly in social pedagogy and educational sociology. Generally speaking, however, it stops at the practice report on local social education focusing on specific areas, and there have not been very many full-scale discussions on what the social education in the local community is or what the correlation between the local area and education is.

On this point, Yoshiyuki Kudomi mentions that "the problem is that they have the attitude of researching one example of the type in many investigational studies, but lack the intention of theorizing or generalizing the results".[10] Based on this, Kudomi classified the area of educational sociology area into 3 categories relating to "local area and education", "character formation in the local area (theme area A)", "what schools mean to the local area (theme area B)" and "what the local area means to the school (theme area C)".[11] Furthermore, it was divided into 3 periods after the war, causing the discussion on how the research the "local area and education" has changed over time.

Period I (up to 1959): During this time, the education system was decentralized with a trend for community schools, so investigational research of farming, mountain, and fishery villages were mainstream and it was the trend of the academic society.

Period II (1959 to 1973): With the high growth of the economy fully in progress, there was an advancement of centralized education, education to prepare for academic advancement, and separation from the local area and life. During this time steady research subjecting the local area was decreased.

Period III (after 1975): The dreams of the flourishing Showa-period were crushed due to the Oil Shock, and social injustice erupted. There was the reviewing of the education's ability to prepare for academic advancement, and the emergence of the concept of "Regionalism". Local areas and community buildings were reviewed in education again during this period.[12]

Kudomi narrowed down the research area to "local area and education" in educational sociology and discussed the matter, but as a result he claims that "the problem of the school system is that the education society formed within the school (teacher culture) is being separated from the local society (residents, parents, and children) where the school is based" is still unsolved and being left alone. In order to overcome this problem, he concluded that it is necessary to deepen the "schoolization", "school system" and "teacher society and teacher culture", which are included actively in the field of educational sociology, theoretically, historically, and substantially. Also in the local area, he emphasized that "it is necessary to research the matter in the combination of school system and characteristics of teacher society".[13]

For previous research, Kudomi has discussed mainly on the relationship between school and local community, but he has not discussed much on the formation of education power in the local society, nor he has pointed out the danger of love for their home town or how personal identification centering on the community could lead to a uniform identity of integrated citizens and nation lead by the government.

On the other hand, Takeo Matsuda researched the re-examination of the community's value in social education in the field of social pedagogy. He mentions the following about the role of social education in a community.

Social education is the education world that is rooted in society, especially in local society = community. Through the free independent educational activities by residents and citizen, they promoted the growth of their self-realization as well as developing new abilities. They contributed to the sharing of "common goods" and the creating of self-government, and have developed an education practice for restoring, constructing, and activating the community.[14]

The perspective of social education pointed out by Takeo Matsuda can supplement the discussion of Kudomi on "Local Area and Education" mentioned before. Matsuda discusses the relationship between local social education with the formation of social capital, and this perspective can be applied to mahalla.

Matsuda proposes the danger of social capital; that "models and values in social capital can restrict the freedom of an individual in the community and can be a factor in promoting intolerance. Individuals belonging to the community based on these models lead to the nurturing of attitudes such as "public spirit" and "love for the nation and hometown" and we cannot deny the possibility that it can connect to demanding uniform belonging to the nation".

Switching from a sense of belonging and love for their hometown to a sense of belonging to a nation and patriotism is often seen as a part of the local government and education strategy in developing nation. In order to nurture the human resources who have loyalty to a nation, which is unrealistic to citizens, it is easier and quicker to nurture loyalty to their close communities which they can see and are real to them. Promoting citizens to belong to the community that they live in and promoting participation in the activities in the community and nurturing their loyalty for their community, which leads to the enhancement of their awareness as citizens is a strategy trend that is often seen in developing nations right after their independence.

Such indications made by Matsuda are the base of the subject that is suggested in the conclusion of this book "switching the love for the hometown centering on mahalla to patriotism centering on Uzbekistan" in the current Uzbekistan. Since Japan has similar challenges as Uzbekistan, it is significant to examine the modern challenges that mahalla provides in Uzbekistan from the perspective of social pedagogy in Japan.

On the other hand, the research example related to the local social education in Japan recently is a research on education that is based on local community such as *aza* (village) in Okinawa.[15]

Various theories try to clarify why there is an increased number of village community learning centers (*Shuraku Kominkan*) in Okinawa and active local social education activities are developed. Bunjin Kobayashi pointed out that by "Having the historical experience of war, occupation, and military and having various challenges that occur in the modern period as opportunities and living the same area and village, they have repeated activities to renew the government and culture of the village and build a new relationship with social community (*yuimaru*)".[16]

When we examine mahalla in Uzbekistan by applying the indications of Kobayashi, we can find various similarities such as "factors that can come to reality because it is the project done in a special area called mahalla", "member of the mahalla committee, people who are in charge of the projects, such as mahalla activists, the creation of the power to overcome the challenges in life are promoted by the involvement in mahalla activities and social cooperation", "practice is becoming an opportunity to reconsider the independence and life of the members of the mahalla committee, mahalla activists, and the local residents", "They have the common memory and historical experience of having the mahalla, local culture, religious rituals being oppressed during the period of the Soviet Union, and it is currently becoming the motivational power to restore mahalla".

The difference between the practice of *aza* in Okinawa and mahalla in Uzbekistan is that although mahalla is positioned as a basis for the construction of new nation and activities to nurture the independence of the community is promoted, there is an internal question that mahalla is involved in the formation of Uzbekistan citizens. This point is related to the social integration that is based on the multi-ethnic aspect of mahalla. On the other hand, the practice of *aza* in Okinawa and the self-governing function that *aza* has as a community is not necessarily leading to citizen formation or national integration, but it is solely emphasized on the local government and town development, promoting the activity of the local area, and the reconstruction of local culture.

For this point, Chiaki Yamashiro uses the example of town development in Yomitan-son (son=village) and "several of *aza*'s plot" and mentions about the creative and independent self-government of the residents as "it is a practice of 'local democracy' of Yomitan village who believed that 'energy for the town's development is created within the community of people who center on *aza*'".[17] While group activities functioning as cooperative self-government carried out by the residents of each village are developed, various unique villages are created naturally and the local identity called "*aza* character" and self-identity of the residents that centers on the local community for the citizens is thus constructed. She claims that small society is constructed through these activities and that those groups are developing the individuality of Yomitan-son.[18]

As it was mentioned, *aza* of Okinawa was discussed as an example that relates to the self-governing function of a community in the social pedagogy filed in Japan. Among those, the indication of Kobayashi that relates to *aza* is directly linked to the foundation of social education and the social education and self-governing functions of a community that a locality has, and the importance of education in local community through *aza* is emphasized again. The self-governing function of a local community is common in the *aza* of Okinawa and the mahalla of Uzbekistan, so we can find significance in the discussion about mahalla in Uzbekistan based on the local social education theory for social pedagogy in Japan. Furthermore, in research of local social education in Asia, there are studies related to community education in China and lifelong education in Korea.[19]

Other studies that discuss the cooperation of school and social education in Japan are those conducted by Yasuaki Ohashi.[20] Ohashi took a look at the activities of the Izumigaoka citizen's public hall (*Kominbunkan*) in Toyonaka-shi (shi=city), Osaka, and discussed the history of the cooperation and its challenges from the perspective of the indirect effect of the cooperation, and considers a new method of cooperation between school and social education.

In this research as the first effect that is created in cooperation by both parties, it mentions the "direct and short term effects" that "from the cooperation of social education and school teachers to support the lessons at school, the academic ability of the children improved and adults in local community and parents who are not enthusiastic about their children's education were involved in the education activities." As the second effect, it suggests "indirect and long term effects" that "through the educational activity that accompanies mutual interaction, children and adults are related as well as preventing the collapse of the family as well as the spread of crime by the relationship between teachers and adults in the community".[21]

At the end of the discussion, Ohashi mentions some challenges such as the lack of an active approach from schools to the citizen's public hall, the lack of key people to bridge the gap between schools and the citizen's public hall, the experience and ability of the citizen's public hall, and ensuring the place of activities.[22]

The two effects that Ohashi suggested were often seen in the activities with the concept of "cooperation among families, mahalla, and school in the mature generation's development" promoted mainly by the Ministry of Public Education after the independence of Uzbekistan, and it is also a goal of the cooperative activities between school and mahalla in the present Uzbekistan.[23]

What was mentioned above is the summary of main bodies of previous research in social pedagogy and educational sociology. Based on this, the significance of this book in pedagogy, especially social pedagogy, is considered as the following.

(1) It discusses not only the school education, but also the educational role of educational activities of mahalla in the present Uzbekistan in the context of social education (Discussion of educational role of mahalla from the perspective of social education).
(2) While mahalla is clearly controlled by the nation, it discusses the educational practice of mahalla while they have various ethnic views of mahalla. (Discussion of the educational role of mahalla from the perspective of nation and local society).
(3) It expresses the suggestion to study mahalla in Uzbekistan based on the accumulated results of social pedagogy in Japan (Discussion of educational role of Mahalla from the perspective of accumulated research in Japan).
(4) It is a local society education study in a community (mahalla) that has an Islamic element, which has not been studied before (Discussion of the educational role of mahalla from the perspective of local society and religion).

For (1), it is referred in Chapter 2 about the structure of mahalla after the independence and the actual situation of education activities, with references from the study of *aza* in Okinawa mentioned earlier. Specific examples are support for socially vulnerable people in excursions and events with residents and sports promotion activities.

For (2), it is discussed mainly from the perspective of educational policy in Chapters 3, 4, and 5 about the view of mahalla in each ethnicity and the relationship between school education and mahalla, which is the root of the viewpoint of the nation and local community.

For (3), modern challenges of mahalla were discussed in each chapter based on the perspective that "individuals belonging to the community will lead to the nurturing of 'public spirit' and 'love for their nation and hometown', and there is a possibility that these will connect to demand the standard belonging to the nation" which was pointed out by *aza* in Okinawa and Matsuda's research.

Lastly for (4), it attempts to examine the educational role of mahalla from the perspective of local society and religion in a community (mahalla) that include

Islamic elements, which has been studied before, with the example of socialization of children based on the religious mannerism mentioned especially in Chapter 3.

(2) Common Ground Between Development and Social Education

So far, I have discussed the accumulation of local education studies in Central Asia and their challenges. In learning that is rooted in the local area, local residents are actively, and continuously, involved in the local community they live in. Through interaction among various generations and activity practices, not only children, but also adults learn and grow. This kind of initiative for community building is considered to be directly connected to the nation building and social development.

In the field of social education, community building and learning rooted to the local area is discussed as a method for promoting local activities, especially in the area of local social education.[24] However, the viewpoint of "development" was rarely a mediator, and local social education is not often discussed from the perspective of development theory. When discussing local social education in developing countries such as Central Asia, education such as learning in a local area, job training courses, and female education will naturally lead to the development of the local area as well as the society as a whole.

In the national report from the 6th international adult education conference submitted to UNESCO by the Uzbekistan Government in 2008, which was mentioned in detail in the previous section, mahalla was mentioned and it was emphasized that mahalla is positioned to be something that supports the local development and local people.[25] This book examines the possibility of the connecting point or union of development and social education in the latter chapter.

3. "Mahalla" in This Study and Purpose of the Study

(1) What is "mahalla"?

In this section, I would like first define the word "mahalla", which is the subject of this study. Mahalla is an Arabic and Farsi language which has been defined in various ways in previous research. In one discussion, mahalla is defined as "neighborhood community"[26] and in others, it was defined as a "block of an 'Islamic city'" (basic living space for the citizens of Muslim city)[27] or "cell that supports the society and economy for the whole city"[28] as well as a "traditional local community of Uzbekistan"[29]; there have been various definitions for mahalla. On the other hand, the Uzbekistan government defines mahalla as "a unique model of national self-government in the dwelling area and has a function of important educational organization to support tradition, customs, and rituals from a long time ago".[30]

In this book, "mahalla" is defined as a unit of local society that exists in Muslim societies such as Central Asia that is closely related to their lives and is formed from the street that supports the lives of residents. In the present Uzbekistan, mahalla means simply a street, block, or district as well as local executive institution called the mahalla committee, or its office. In this book, "mahalla" is defined as a unit (local community) of local society that consists of a mutual relationship of people, so when it means mahalla committee or office of mahalla, it is indicated when it applies.

Also in this book, the main subject period is after the independence of the Republic of Uzbekistan in 1991 until present. However, mahalla itself has been in Uzbekistan for a long time, and has been a local community in the society until now, even though their activities have changed. Therefore, mahalla and the educational aspects in its foundation, the Russian Empire period, and the Soviet period is dealt as the previous history.

In the following, previous research regarding mahalla is categorized into 3 periods, the Russian Empire period, the Soviet period, and after independence, and is discussed with examples of research results, both in and outside of Uzbekistan.

In Central Asia, people used to form small communities in cities and rural areas based on their occupation, religious sect, and ethnicities. In the 20th century Bukhara, for example, people who had occupations related to metal or cleaners of dead bodies lived in their own district and those areas were their houses as well as their workplaces.

Study related to the local society of the Soviet Union, research on Bukhara by Sukhareva, O. A. is well known. Especially *Bukhara from 19th century to early 20th century* (1966), and *Local community of Bukhara after the feudalism related to the district history* (1976) mention that the city of Bukhara at the time was divided into mahalla which were structured based on ethnicities and occupations. This provides valuable information for discussing the structure of mahalla and its formation process.

On the other hand, the Soviet government used the traditional system and function of mahalla to change the way of thinking for the residents into a more "Soviet style" and in line with communism, thus forming "Soviet citizens". A specific example of this policy is the *choykhona*, which was a place for interaction for residents as well as a place to prepare weddings and traditional festivals. The Soviet government change *choykhona* into "Red *choykhona*", and tried to use this place to deepen the understanding of the Soviet government.

In Uzbekistan after independence, the government promoted the emphasis of mahalla as a foundation of the new nation's construction, so many books on mahalla were published in Uzbekistan.

On the study of mahalla in Tashkent, there are studies by Arifkhanova, Z. H., *Modern Life of Traditional Mahalla in Tashkent* (2000) and *Mahalla in Tashkent-Tradition and Modernization* (2002) also edited by Arifkhanova. Also in 2005 a few researchers, including her, published a collection of theses called the *Ethnic Cultural Change Today of Mahalla in Tashkent*, which discusses the daily lives of residents in a mahalla in Tashkent from the perspective of cultural anthropology.

Furthermore, after the dissolution of the Soviet Union, it became easier to do mahalla research in Uzbekistan and access to the related literature on mahalla study in and outside of Uzbekistan increased drastically.

For mahalla study in Japan, there are "Notes on the mahallas of Bukhārā: based on the ethnographical material collected by O.A.Sukhareva" (1978) by Hisao Komatsu and *The Customary Economy and Economic Development: The Community-based Structure of a Mahalla in Uzbekistan* (2008) by Masato Hiwatari, but the exemplary study is *The Actual Image of Mahalla-Change in Tradition in the Society of Central Asia (Mahalla)* (2006) by Dadabaev, T. Dadabaev hypothesized that there are two types of present mahalla mainly in Uzbekistan: one is "formal mahalla" and the other is "traditional mahalla". He conducted an empirical study by clearly describing the view of mahalla from residents and the typical mahalla image. There are other studies such as the *Targetting Social Assistance in a Transition Economy: The Mahallas in Uzbekistan* (1998) by Coudouel et al., "The Uzbek Mahalla" (2003) by Massicard, E. and Trevisani, T., *Uzbekistan's Mahalla: From Soviet to Absolutist Residential Community Groups Associations* (2002) by Sievers, E. W., and "Between Women and the State: Mahalla Committees and Social Welfare in Uzbekistan" (2004) by Kamp, M.

(2) Research Purpose

In order to answer the 4 research topics that were set up in earlier in this book (page two), I will clarify the historical changes of mahalla and their educational aspects as the first topic. However, the formation of mahalla is considered to be closely related to the city structure at the time. In such cities, mahalla was structured according to their ethnicity, religion, and occupation, and mahalla executives took various educational roles. Non-formal education during this period was changed to modern education during the Russian Empire period, and this was when educational role of mahalla was changed drastically. During the Soviet period, the role of mahalla got attention for the construction of the Soviet nation, and educational activities that had political propaganda were actively conducted inside of mahalla. In the present Uzbekistan

Republic after their independence, mahalla is in charge of various educational activities along with the mahalla restoration policy by the government. In the first topic, I would like to discuss the matter with the change of mahalla and their educational aspects that change along with the transition of their political situation (Research topic (1)).

Next for the second topic, I will clarify the structure of mahalla after the independence and the actual situation of their educational activities from the perspective of local educational activities in social pedagogy.

Before the independence of the Republic of Uzbekistan, the systemization of mahalla was promoted by the Russian Empire and the Soviet Union. So, in order to get out of the system of the Soviet Union, the systemization of mahalla is done by the Uzbekistan government. These are especially seen in the specific examples of the activities of mahalla as the smallest unit of the government such as (1) residents management system and family support by mahalla committee, (2) self-warning activity of *Posbon* team (vigilante team within mahalla) and the instruction of youth, and (3) local social education activities by women's committee and female support. Of the examples of the independent and subjective activities of mahalla residents against the government-led systemization, there are (1) excursions for the residents of mahalla, (2) events in mahalla to support the socially vulnerable people, and (3) sports promotion activities in the facilities of mahalla. In the second topic, I will focus on the practice of community education in mahalla and develop the discussion of whether it is possible to have both "integration" with the nation and "self-governing" of local residents in mahalla in the current Uzbekistan, based on the perspectives of both government and residents (Research topic (2)).

Next for the third topic, I will clarify the socialization and cultural inheritance for the children in mahalla.

In Uzbekistan, the support from mahalla is essential in traditional rituals such as circumcision and ritual for birth. For example, the mahalla committee provides monetary and labor support for poor families to have the celebration of circumcision. On the other hand, they limit the celebrations of rich families so as not to let them be too luxurious. In this aspect, it can be said that mahalla is both a "supporter" and "intervener". For the third topic, I will clarify the involvement of mahalla in the socialization and cultural inheritance for children while taking a look at two filed work examples for *ramazan, kelin salom* (ritual for greeting bride), and *kelin kordi* (observation for bride) related to Islam, based on the life of children and growth ritual of mahalla and Islam in the period of Russian Empire, the period of Soviet, and after independence (Research topic (2)).

For the 4th topic, I will clarify education related to mahalla in school education.

In the current school education in Uzbekistan, mahalla is implemented in school education through textbook, classroom format and school events as "traditional space", "fundamental space for the integration of citizens" and "space for mutual assistance." In the background, there was the plan of the government to get out of Soviet system, integration of ethnicities in the country and Central Asia, and expansion of new national system. There was the goal of making the government's plan a reality by permeating the ideas of traditional aspects of mahalla and governmental aspect of mahalla after the independence into the students through the implementation of mahalla in school education. For the fourth topic, I will try to clarify the concept of "cooperation among families, mahalla, and school in the mature generation's development" brought by the national system of continuous education standards in Uzbekistan and Ministry of Public Education by using the participatory observation results from classrooms and school events. Also, using the textbooks on "Foundation of Spirituality", "The Alphabet of National Constitution", and "Courtesy" and school event of "memorial day", I will clarify the nurturing of the awareness as a "citizen" through the cooperation of mahalla and schools (Research topic (3)).

For the fifth topic, I will clarify the actual situation of youth education in the cooperative activities of organizations and its significance.

Currently, mahalla is cooperating with various organizations such as youth organizations, domestic and international NGOs, and international organizations to plan and implement education activities. Here, I will focus on (1) the youth social cooperation central council "*Kamolot*", (2) the youth initiative center "Voice of the Future", and (3)NANNOUz (Natsional'noi assotsiatsii negosudarstvennykh nekommercheskikh organizatsii Uzbekistana, Uzbekistan non-governmental non-profit organization), (4) international organizations-UNICEF, UNDP, and UNAIDS (Joint United Nations Program on HIV and AIDS) to discuss the examples of cooperation activities of each organization and mahalla. In addition, I will clarify the view of local community for the youth of Uzbekistan and activities of each institution based on the qualitative analysis of survey research conducted by multiple universities (Research topic (4)).

(3) Research Method and Structure of the Book

Discussions on the construction of a new nation in the present Uzbekistan and educational reform and mahalla policy during that process as well as the political and social background is starting to be done in various areas such as history, politics, international relations, area studies, sociology, cultural anthropology, development studies, international cooperation, and pedagogy.

Therefore, the research method used in this book was a mahalla study done in Uzbekistan centering on area studies and politics, research on school education in Uzbekistan after its independence that are promoted mainly in the comparative education, and research methods used in the research of community education in social pedagogy in and outside of Japan.

To be specific, for the cooperation of mahalla and school education, participatory observation in school events and classes as well as interviews with school personnel and the mahalla committee is done based on the discussion of previous research in comparative education, social pedagogy, and educational sociology. For the socialization of children and cultural inheritance in mahalla, record of participatory observation in *ramazan, kelin salom* with multiple families in Tashkent were analyzed based on the knowledge of sociology and cultural anthropology. Furthermore, for the discussion of cooperation between mahalla and each institution is done using previous research in social pedagogy, public administration, and development study as well as survey research subjecting university students in Tashkent.

In this book, the subjected levels of education are pre-school education, elementary education, secondary education, higher education for school education, and social and adult education as outside of school education. Because of this consideration of discussion from various perspectives instead of analyzing the educational role of mahalla in a single level of education.

This book is consisted of the following research results as well as the result of field research done in Central Asia mainly Uzbekistan.

1) Investigations of the educational institutions, departments of city education, UNDP, NGOs, and multiple families in Tashkent from July 23rd 2004 to August 30th (participatory observation and interview research).
2) Investigations of the educational institutions, Ministry of Public Education, Ministry of Higher and Secondary Specialized Education, governmental institutions, NGOs, mahalla, medical institutions, international organizations, and multiple families in Tashkent, Urgench, Angren, and Nukus in Republic of Karakalpakstan from March 9th to June 5th, 2006 (participatory observation and interview research).
3) Research in Uzbekistan done with the support of the "international promotion program in university education (assistance in long term study

abroad)" (September 2006 to August 2008) supported by the Ministry of Education, Culture, Sports, Science and Technology, Japan based on the theme of "research on education and cultural policy in local society and acceptance of the citizen: focusing on mahalla in Uzbekistan — " (participatory observation, interview research, and survey research).

4) Research on the local societies of Uzbekistan, Kazakhstan, and Kyrgyz, Tajikistan and the community activities of women from "an Empirical study on community and gender in Central Asia: Uzbekistan, Tajikistan, Kazakhstan, and Kyrgyz" assisted by the Kitakyushu Forum on Asian Women (representative: Associate professor, Junko Otani, Osaka University in the year of 2007 to 2008) (participatory observation and interview research).

5) Research on cooperative activities with local societies, medical institutions, and international organizations in the capital of Tajikistan, Dushanbe, mahalla in Isfara in Sughd Province, and *jamoat* (local community in Tajikistan) based on the internship (April to March 2008) in UNICEF Tajikistan office (participatory observation and interview research).

6) Research on mahalla in Uzbekistan relating to the "social development and local community in Central Asian countries: Examination on community view and education cooperation within the area" supported by the Japan Society for the Promotion of Science Grants-in-Aid for Scientific Research (Financial Incentive for JSPS Research Fellowship for young scientists) (2009) (participatory observation and interview research).

When starting the field research, the author first went to U mahalla located in the central part of the capital Tashkent and Z mahalla in a mining town of Angren in the Tashkent region (*Obrast*), which is about a 2 hour drive from Tashkent to conduct the interview research for the related personnel for the mahalla committee (research in Tashkent was done in March 2006, research in Angren was done in March 2006). When I first started the research I was supposing three frameworks of comparison of multiple mahallas in Tashkent, comparison among 13 regions in Uzbekistan as well as Karakalpakstan, which is a republic, and comparison of mahalla in urban and farming areas. However, after getting the research results from pilot research in two cities as well as moving forward with the interview on mahalla in other cities, there were large differences in the characteristics and aspects of mahalla, as well as people's views on mahalla, between mahalla that was traditionally there such as in Tashkent, Samarkand,

Bukhara, and Fergana and mahalla was set up artificially in the process of the construction a new nation after independence such as in Karakalpakstan.

Also, mahalla in the areas that have group housing in the city and mahalla in the areas that have traditional houses have different neighborhood relationships and levels of participation in the events that are held in mahalla. Furthermore, this difference was significant not only in the urban area and farming town, but also in the old and new districts of Tashkent.

Table 1 Mahalla that was research subjects

Tashkent City	
G mahalla (Mirzo Ulugbek)	F mahalla (Sergeli)
A mahalla (Mirzo Ulugbek)	U mahalla (Mirobod)
O mahalla (Mirobod)	O mahalla (Shaykhontohur)
C mahalla (Shaykhontohur)	S mahalla (Shaykhontohur)
Tashkent Region	
U mahalla (Tashkent, Kibray)	
Z mahalla (Tashkent, Angren)	

So in order to explore the educational role of mahalla in the present Uzbekistan, long term field work was mainly done in Tashkent and its suburbs (strictly speaking, the suburban area mainly in Tashkent region) where mahalla existed for a long time and has elements of both the new and old. One of the reasons for electing Tashkent is that in the present when the emphasis of government policy in mahalla is more prominent, mahalla in Tashkent, where the capital of Uzbekistan is, has more thorough government policy and it was considered to be better suited to examining how the mahalla resident accept it. Research on mahallas that were located in different cities or states was done periodically to supplement the comparison with the mahallas in Tashkent.

From this process, the 10 mahallas that were selected as research subjects are listed in Table 1. Research was also conducted in mahalla and local society outside of Uzbekistan, educational institutions in Uzbekistan, governmental institutions, international organizations, and NGO.

For research on mahalla, we requested the cooperation of people in various positions such as university staffs, staffs in elementary and secondary education, university students, NGO staffs, corporate staffs, staffs in governmental institution, representative of mahalla, staffs in mahalla committees and related personnel were contacted.

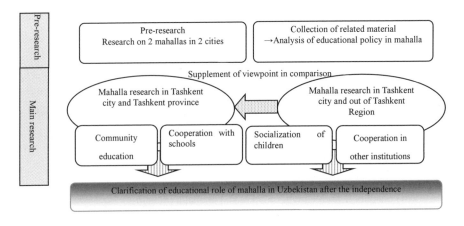

Figure 1 Figure for research in Uzbekistan

To be specific, the methods of visitation and interview for mahalla, participation in the events held in mahalla, interviews for mahalla representatives while participating in school events were used for this research. For research institutions, class observation and participation in class as a guest teacher, participation in school events, interviews with school personnel, and survey research of university students were conducted. Furthermore for governmental organizations, international organizations, and NGOs, mainly interview research, participatory observation of events that were held by these organizations, and analysis of reports given by the representatives of the organization when participating in international conferences were done (Figure 1).

In this book, I will first clarify the historical change of mahalla and its educational aspects in Chapter 1 in order to discuss the educational aspect of mahalla in Uzbekistan. The researched time period was before the period of Russian Empire, during the occupation of Russian Empire, the period of the Soviet Union, and after the independence of Uzbekistan.

In Chapter 2, I will discuss the structure of mahalla after independence and the actual situation of education activities. To be specific, the excursions of residents, support for socially vulnerable people in events, and sports promotion activities were researched.

In Chapter 3, how mahalla is influencing the socialization of children and cultural inheritance is discussed. Here, mahalla's function as "supporter" and "intervener" was clarified using the specific examples of *ramazan* and *kelin salom* and how the social customs are carried out in celebrations and rituals in mahalla.

In Chapter 4, how mahalla is implemented in the educational policy and school education as well as their purposes are is discussed. Government policy on emphasizing mahalla is discussed for the political and social background for implementing mahalla in school education. Analysis is conducted using "the national standard of Uzbekistan" and related concepts to see how the mahalla image and principle is manifested in school education.

In the next Chapter 5, school education and cooperative activities with mahalla are discussed. To be specific, how mahalla cooperates with schools and how they nurture awareness as "citizens" are discussed.

In Chapter 6, youth activities where NGO, international organizations, and mahalla cooperate, which are more active recently, is discussed. In order to clarify the position of NGO, youth organizations, and international organizations and their actual activities, the activities of the youth social cooperation central council "*Kamolot*", youth initiative center "Voice of the Future", NANNOUz, and international institution-UNICEF are researched. In addition to the discussion of the example of cooperative activities between each institution and mahalla, the image of local society held by the youth of Uzbekistan is described and the view of local society held by youth and the activities of each institution are discussed based on the survey conducted in multiple universities in Uzbekistan.

Finally in the last chapter, to summarize this research, the educational role of mahalla in Uzbekistan is clarified and future development and challenges are discussed.

Notes

[1] From the point of embodiment, education is divided into three; formal education, non-formal education and informal education. Formal education, like school education, consists of educational activities which have systematic and planned features.

[2] In reference to previous studies, there are *How NGOs React: Globalization and Education Reform in the Caucasus, Central Asia and Mongolia* (2008) and *The Challenge of Education in Central Asia* (2004).However, these studies focused on elementary, secondary and higher education in Central Asia. There is not much research on social education in Central Asia.

[3] *Imam* means "Model" or "Instructor" in the Koran, but after a while the meaning of *Imam* was changed to the coryphaeus of a Muslim group in Arabic context. *Imam* is; 1) Instructor of group worship, 2) Caliph of Sunni, 3) the top leader of Shia, 4) an eminent scholar. Nihon Islam Kyokai (Japan Islam association), *Islam Jiten (Encyclopedia of Islam)*, Heibon-sha, Japan, 1982.

[4] Turkestan is the historical area name after the Turkization of Central Asia. The Russian Empire invaded the Khanate of Kokand in the late 19th century, and established the Government-General of Turkistan in Tashkent in 1867. The Russian Empire invaded still more

and their territory was expanded from the west of the Tien Shan Mountains, the Pamirs to the eastern Caspian Sea, and the borders of Iran and Afghanistan. Depending on the establishment of the Russian Turkistan (West Turkistan), Xinjian under the Qing dynasty reign was called East Turkistan. In addition, northern Afghanistan was regarded as the Afghan Turkistan. Hisao Komatsu, Hiroshi Umemura, Tomohiko Uyama, Chika Obiya, Toru Horikawa eds., *Chuou Yurashia o Shiru Jiten (Cyclopedia of Central Eurasia)*, Heibon-sha, Japan, 2005, p.388.

[5] Tomiak, J. J., *Soviet no Gakkou (Schools in Soviet)*, Meiji Tosho, 1976, p.64.

[6] Tomiak, J. J., *op. cit.*, 1976, p.5.

[7] *Kokasasu to Chuou Ajia no Ningen Keisei (Character of Caucasus and Central Asia)*, Akashi Shoten, 2012 by Keiko Seki argued on Mahalla and "outside of school" education, however, disquisitions about mahalla and its educational role still have not been published in the world.

[8] *CONFINTEA VI National Report*, Uzbekistan, *Tashkent Call to Action*, 2008.

[9] Agitator means communist or member of *Komsomol* who actively promotes the Soviet ideology in this context.

[10] Yoshiyuki Kudomi, "Chiiki to kyoiku (Local Community and Education)", The Japan Society of Educational Sociology, *Kyoiku Shakaigaku Kenkyu (The Journal of Educational Sociology)*, No.50, 1992, p.71.

[11] Yoshiyuki Kudomi, *op. cit.*, 1992, p.68, p.70.

[12] Yoshiyuki Kudomi, *op. cit.*, 1992, p.69. Kudomi's research to relies on Shun Yano, *Chiiki Kyoiku Shakaigaku Josetsu (Introduction of Local Educational Sociology)*, 1981, where he highlighted Yano's division of three periods according to the restoration period after World War II, period of rapid growth and post-period of rapid growth.

[13] Yoshiyuki Kudomi, *op. cit.*, 1992, p.82.

[14] Takeo Matsuda, "Shakaikyoiku ni okeru community teki kachi no saikentou—Shakai kyoiku gainen no saikaishaku wo tooshite (Reexamination of Community Values in Social Education: Through Reinterpretation of the Concept of Social Education)", Japanese Educational Research Association, *Kyoikugaku Kenkyu (The Japanese Journal of Educational Research)*, Vol. 74, No.4, 2007, p.93.

[15] Takeo Matsuda, *Gendai Shakai kyoiku no Kadai to Kanousei —Shougaigakushu to Chiiki Shakai (Challenge and Possibilities of Current Social Education: Lifelong Learning and Local Society)*, Kyushu University Press, Japan, 2007, Chiaki Yamashiro, *Okinawa no "Shima" Shakai to Seinenkai Katsudou ("Shima" Society and Activities of Youth Association in Okinawa*, Eidell Institute, Japan, 2007.

[16] Bunjin Kobayashi, Masatoshi Shimabukuro, eds., *Okinawa no Shakai kyoiku —Jichi ·Bunka · Chiikiokoshi (Social Education in Okinawa: Autonomy, Culture, Promotion of Local Community)*, Eidell Institute, Japan, 2002, p.18.

[17] Chiaki Yamashiro, *op. cit.*, 2007, p.114.

[18] Chiaki Yamashiro, *op. cit.*, 2007, p.115.

[19] "Tokushu: Kankoku 'Heisei Gakushu' no atarashii doukou (The New Movement of the South Korean 'Life-long Education')", "Chugoku no shougai kyoiku·shaku kyoiku (Life-long and Community Education in China)", *Higashi Ajia Shakai Kyoiku Kenkyu (The East Asian Journal for Adult Education and Community Studies)*, Volume 12, 2007.

[20] Yasuaki Ohashi, "Gakkou kyoiku to shakai kyoiku no kyoudou—Koumin bunkan katsudou wo jiku ni (Collaboration between School Education and Out-of-school Education: A case study of activities as a citizen's public hall)", The Japan Society for the Study of Adult and Community Education, *Nihon Shakai Kyoiku Gakkai Kiyou (Bulletin of the Japan Society for the Study of Adult and Community Education)*, No. 37, 2001, pp.51-59.

[21] Yasuaki Ohashi, *op. cit.*, 2001, p.54.

[22] Yasuaki Ohashi, *op. cit.*, 2001, p.56.

[23] Interview with Minister of Public Education of the Republic of Uzbekistan, August 19, 2008.

[24] Katsuko Sato, *Shougai Gakushu to Shakai Sanka —Otona ga Manabu Koto no Imi (Lifelong Learning and Social Participation: The Meaning of Adult Learning)*, University of Tokyo Press, 1998.

[25] *CONFINTEA VI National Report*, Uzbekistan, 2008.

[26] Timur Dadabaev, "Chuou ajia shokoku no gendaika ni okeru dentouteki chiiki shakai no arikata to yakuwari—Uzbekistan no 'mahalla' wo chushin ni (Ideal existence and Role of Traditional Local Community in Modernization of Central Asian countries: Focusing on 'mahalla' of Uzbekistan)", *Toyo Bunka Kenkyusho Kiyou (The Memoirs of the Institute for Advanced Studies on Asia)*, Vol.146, 2004, p.100.

[27] Hisao Komatsu, "Kashgar no Andijan ku chousa houkoku (Field Work Report of Andijan District of Kashgar)", Kosuke Shimizu eds., *Islam toshi ni okeru gaiku no jittai to minshu soshiki ni kansuru hikaku kenkyu (A Comparative Study of the Islamic City Quarters "Mahalla" and Popular Organizations)*, Tokyo University of Foreign studies, 1991, p.46.

[28] Chika Obiya, "Mahalla no kurashi—Muslim no nichijou to kinjo zukiai (Everyday Life in Mahalla: Daily Life and Interactions with Muslim Neighbors)", Tomohiko Uyama eds., *Chuou Ajia wo Shirutame no 60 shou (60 Chapters for Understanding on Central Asia)*, Akashi Shoten, Japan, 2003, p.160.

[29] Masato Hiwatari, "Uzbekistan no kanshu keizai: Mahalla no kyoudoutai teki kinou no kentou kara (The Customary Economy in Uzbekistan: A Study of the Community Function of Mahallas)", Japan Association for Asian Studies, *Asian Studies*, Vol.50, No.4, October 2004, p.82.

[30] *Ideya natsional'noi nezavisimosti: osnovnye ponyatiya i printsipy*, Tashkent: O'zbekistan, 2003, s.67-68.

Chapter 1

Mahalla in Uzbekistan and Historical Change in Their Educational Aspect

In Chapter 1, mahalla in Uzbekistan before the Russian Empire, during the occupation of the Russian Empire, period of the Soviet Union, and after independence and historical changes in their educational aspects are clarified in order to discuss the educational aspects of mahalla in Uzbekistan. In the end, educational reform and the mahalla restoration policy after the independence of Uzbekistan is discussed and educational aspects of mahalla are clarified.

1. Previous History of Mahalla in Uzbekistan

(1) City Structure of Uzbekistan and Central Asia, and Mahalla

Mahalla is originally an Arabic and Farsi word, and as it was mentioned earlier, it is defined in many ways, such as a "'neighborhood' type community that is formed based on the district where people live"[1] and "block of 'Islamic city'".[2] When those are integrated, it can be said that a mahalla is a unit of local community that exists in a Muslim society such as Central Asia[3] and is close to the lives of residents and street that support their lives.[4]

There are various claims as to the origin and formation process of mahalla such as "it used to be a residential area for relatives but then expanded over time"[5], and some claim that "the origin of mahalla is a formation of a small scale community where people with the same occupation, religious sect, or ethnicity were living close in a city or farming town with large population".[6] Also, Yasushi Sanada explains that mahalla was made from *uy* (houses) that were built by the canal that branched from a large canal and made small groups.[7]

Back in the days in Central Asia, small scale communities based on occupation, religious sect, or ethnicity were formed in the cities and farming towns.[8] This type of community was called mahalla in Tashkent and people formed and maintain the awareness as being a mahalla resident through participation in the rite of passage and other important ceremonies, cooperation in cultural heritage, use of water, and mutual assistance. During that time, there were many mahallas surrounded by large walls in the city.

As it was mentioned, in Uzbekistan and Tajikistan, where settled agricultural people lived, traditional local communities like mahalla emerged and continued, and they had various educational activities there. On the other hand, in Kazakhstan, Kyrgyz, and Turkmenistan where nomadic people lived had, no such settlement culture existed so local communities as they are seen in Uzbekistan and Tajikistan did not develop.[9]

(2) Educational Role of Mahalla Executive and Lives of People

As mahallas formed, mosques and mausoleums were constructed and they started to become a place for entertainment and information exchange. People started to participate in the rites of passage and important ceremonies, cooperate in the use of water, and helped each other to maintain the sense of belonging. If there is some trouble or if a conflict occurs in mahalla, an elder, called *oqsoqol* (meaning an elder or white beard), would intervene with the conflict and mediate the conflict. As it shows, mahalla became an important local unit to process the problems of people as it was seen in Bukhara from late 19th century to early 20th century.[10]

From this period, *oqsoqol* and the female leader who had the role of assistant, and the other people in charge of miscellaneous duties existed within the community, and if there was a conflict among residents, the elder would mediate the fight. Other than this duty, the elder prepared the ceremony out of his own pocket and looked after orphans and widows. Also the elder was essential in the rituals of local residents. He determined the participating members, the number of people in the rituals beforehand and led the event.

As it was mentioned, the elder of mahalla at the time had authority in various areas of mahalla, and the mahalla residents trusted the elder and left the management of the area up to him.

At this point, the organization that exists in the current Uzbekistan, such as committees, did not exist. However, the important system in managing and operating mahalla such as *poykkor*[11] who assist the elder and *kaivoni* who support the activities related to women are already formed. In other words, sprouting organizations like the mahalla committee that is functioning in the current Uzbekistan had already existed at the time. Furthermore, as the role of the elder for looking after the orphans was mentioned so it was considered that the elder had the role of social security, currently conducted by the mahalla committee. For the educational aspects of the residential life, the elder had a strong leadership.

(3) Educational Institutions in the City and Mahalla

Until the Russian Empire occupied Central Asia in the late 19th century, children's education was done privately or in part of religion in mahalla or *guzar*. Especially for boys, education was mainly done in a *maktab* or madrasa attached to a mosque. On the other hand, traditional education for girls was mainly the religious teaching taught at the teacher's house.[12]

Until the Russian Empire started their occupation and modern education was established, religious and non-formal education was done in mahalla and *guzar*. The character formation of children was done through human interaction between mahalla residents in their daily lives surrounding the children in places such as mosques in mahalla. "Education power of the local community" and "Character formation power of local community" mentioned by Yoshiyuki Kudomi in the field of educational sociology can be seen in the education conducted in mahalla at that time. "Formation and education power of the local community" as pointed out by Kudomi that "needless to say, school is an educational facility that exists in the local area, but it is undoubted that 'Formation and education power of the local community' existed before historically and even for the life history of the individual" existed in mahalla at the time.[13]

2. Mahalla from the End of 19th Century to the Early 20th Century

In Section 2, I will discuss the educational activities in mahalla according to ethnicity, religion, and occupation from the 19th century to early 20th century.

(1) Mahalla Structured according to Ethnicity, Religion, and Occupation

Sukhareva, O.A. who is known for the study of local community in Bukhara in the 19th century to 20th century classified the *guzar* in Bukhara in the following 6 categories.

(1) Name of a famous person or historical figure
(2) Name of *mazar* (grave mausoleum)
(3) Name of specific ethnicity or tribe
(4) Name of the occupation that the resident had
(5) Name that indicates local characteristic
(6) Name that is unclear[14]

According to Sukhareva, in the early 20th century in Bukhara, for example, people who had jobs related to metal and people who washed dead bodies lived in their separate districts. In those districts, they are places of living as well as working. In Bukhara at the time, they could use ethnicity, grave mausoleum, building, and the occupation of the people in the area from the name of their mahalla. The name of mahalla represented the originality of mahalla and it is presumed that it represented the symbol of the people who lived there and pride of the area. Mahalla could provide an opportunity to teach children in that area about the origin of the name of their mahalla, the ethnicity that composes the mahalla, occupation, and originality of the area passively as well as actively. They learn many things informally by seeing, listening, and being in contact with the job of the mahalla in their daily lives.

(2) Educational Activities in Mahalla Community Facility

As it was mentioned before, until the education system of the Russian Empire expanded, boys were taught in *maktabs* and madrasas attached to a mosque and girls were taught traditional and religious teaching at the teacher's house. In a *maktab*, boys from 6 to 16 years old (or 5 to 15 years old) learned how to read and write and education that had the core of the spirit of Islamic belief was taught. Until the Russian Empire advanced to Central Asia, there were *maktabs* in each local community such as mahalla and *guzars* in Samarkand and there were *maktabs* not only for boys, but also for girls. Usually, *imam* (refer to the Introduction) from the mosque in the mahalla acted as a teacher and taught children how to read and write and the teachings of the Koran.[15]

On the other hand, the community facility for residents that existed in mahalla had various activities. Especially, the mosque that is located in mahalla had an extremely large role. Mosques are a place of praying for the residents as well as a place of interaction. Ritual prayers given 5 times a day were done systematically in front of children. Also in religious holidays, it was an important opportunity where the customs of families and society were most obvious.[16]

Other than that, mahalla had various tools used in weddings and funerals. Mahalla residents participated in the rite of passage and life rituals done for children in mahalla. They also helped with the labor and funding for the ritual and supported the family that was conducting the ritual from various directions.

As it was already mentioned, children learned the prayer ritual in mosque, had the opportunity to be close to the jobs that were related to their mahalla, and had opportunities to learn about their ethnic culture in mahalla. By living in mahalla, children could learn about the religion, jobs, and their ethnicity that are close to them.

Mahalla in this time period was a place to have informal education such as "learning that is built into their daily lives" mentioned above, and they had the role of supporting such learning. As the education in *maktabs* and *madrasas* expanded, they had the role of supporting this type of non-formal education.

3. Mahalla during the Period of Russian Empire and Mahalla Policy of Russian Empire

Next in Section 3, I will clarify the modern education expansion policy and activities in mahallas during the period of Russian Empire.

(1) Non-Formal Education in Mahalla and Modern Education Expansion Policy by the Russian Empire

During the period of the Russian Empire, mahallas were divided clearly for the formation of the city. Due to the occupation of Central Asia by the Russian Empire, "old city" where mahalla is formed based on the unpaved roads and European style "new urban area" that was planned were constructed so the ruler and local residents started to live separately.

The Russian rulers during the period of the Russian Empire actively collected information on how the social life of the local residents were and put their effort into expanding their ruling of the local people. However, they lacked in manpower to conduct the local government due to financial difficulties. So what got their attention was the traditional communities and their representatives. Mahalla was positioned as something that supports the occupation of Russian Empire from the bottom, and was expected to take that role. However, unless they directly affected the benefit or damaged the Empire's ruling, they took the position of no intervention for the general life of the local residents.[17] Therefore, even in the period of the Russian Empire, mahalla was formed based on their occupation and ethnicity so it is presumed that education was done in the range centered on the place. In other words, children had the opportunity to learn about religion, jobs, and ethnicity that were close to their life by living in mahalla.

While the Russian occupation was expanding to the whole Western Turkestan, the expansion of modern education that followed the standard of the Russian Empire was focused on. In the education policy of the Russian Empire at the time, improving the educational level of residents in the undeveloped area was focused on so the education in mahalla tended to be looked at lightly. Due to this kind of policy, the opportunities for *madrasa* in mahalla and non-formal education at home kept decreasing as the modern school system was implemented.

(2) Modern Schools and Mahalla

During the period of the Russian Empire, mahalla was viewed as the end unit to support their occupation. The systemization of education was started and the first Russian school with both boys and girls were opened in Tashkent in 1866.[18] Also in March 1871, Seid-Azimbay Mukhammedbaev, who was a merchant of Tashkent, criticized the previous *madrasa*, and made a report to suggest opening a new type of Muslim schools to Kaufman, the governor-general of Russian Turkestan at the time. In June 1871, based on this suggestion by Muhammedvaev, Terenchieva, who was the captain of the cavalry, became the head of the committee in order to prepare the construction of a new school in Ishankul Madrasa.[19] During this period, they demanded new changes to the educational facility that existed before, such as *madrasa*, as the modern school by the government of the Russian Empire was prepared. However, as the modern school increased and children learned more there, the education in *madrasa* lessened.

As it was mentioned, learning in the living world for children in mahalla was gradually systematized before and after the period of the Russian Empire. During the period of the Russian Empire, informal learning in mahalla was continuing the same as it had before, the maintenance of non-formal education in *maktabs* and *madrasas* and the transition to the Russian Empire style of public education separated the three clearly.

4. Mahalla in the Period of Soviet Union and Mahalla Policy of the Soviet Authority

In Section 4, I will discuss the modern education expansion policy during the period of Soviet Union and activities of mahalla.

(1) Mahalla for Construction Soviet Nation

During the Soviet period, the Soviet government tried to unify the Soviet Union that consisted of various ethnicities and promoted the policy to form "Soviet Citizens". As part of the program, the conversion from *madrasas* to Soviet schools, teacher training for soviet schools for Muslims, and the expansion of Soviet school areas were promoted.

In the constitution of Russia in July, 1918, it was already defined that "church and nation, and school and church, are separated and that the freedom of religious preaching and anti-religious preaching is recognized for all citizens", and financial assistance was given from Soviet government to construct Soviet schools.[20] However, due to the termination of financial assistance from the later government, the government of Turkestan Republic had to close large part of the elementary education, so they changed the policy to recognize *madrasa* as well as to supervise and regulate it in July 1922. So other areas continued to train teachers for Soviet schools for Muslims and promoted the expansion of the Soviet school area.

On the other hand, double policies of the Soviet government were started in mahalla. Before the period of Soviet Union, Mahalla had the court system with laws based on customs, as well as roles, functions, and influence on traditional systems such as mosques. So abolishing mahalla quickly in order to diffuse the ideology of the Soviet government and form "Soviet citizens" was considered to be a possible trigger of strong resistance from the Uzbek people. Therefore, the Soviet government started the following double policies for mahalla.

- By using the traditional system and functionality of mahalla, change the residents' way of thinking to "Soviet type" communism and form "Soviet citizens". For one of the policies, an elder that agreed with the Soviet government and strongly supported communism was set up in each mahalla and made policy to influence the youth in mahalla through that elder.

- While carrying out a policy of using mahalla they tried to weaken the power of mahalla slowly and change the function of the traditional base to one more geared towards Soviet communism. They will be supported more than the Soviet national institutions but the system of mahalla, which was respected, will be eliminated slowly.

In order to implement the double policies mentioned above, the Soviet government made scholars and intellectuals, as well as elders and residents, try to use mahalla to diffuse the ideology of the Soviet communist nation.[21]

The specific policy of the Soviet government for mahalla was the *choykhona* that existed in each area already. *Choykhona* has the meaning of "tea room and room for drinking tea", it was a place where men gathered and exchanged information with people who lived in the same area. They also had weddings, traditional rituals (*Navro'z*, spring festival, and New Year's festival by Zoroastrianism), and the celebration of the end of fasting for Islam. Soviet government changed this *choykhona* to "Red *choykhona*" and tried to use this place for deepen the understanding for the Soviet government. According to Dadabaev, T., "Red *choykhona*" had small libraries as well as a place for drinking tea and talking.[22] There were magazines and books as well as posters that were written in multiple languages. Since the beginning of 1960s, as the permanent place for instigation, schools invited teachers and technicians who were mahalla residents, *Komsomol* (The All-Union Leninist Young Communist League), promoters of scientific intellect, and representatives of parties and national organizations, and had lectures.[23]

In the same way, the soviet government positioned mahalla as a place of constant advertisement and education for communism, promoting the policies to diffuse the government's ideology.

It has been pointed out that the policy of forming "Soviet citizens" by the government resulted in the end of principle of nomadism, customary system of court and law held by Uzbek people and traditional system of Uzbekistan such as mosques.[24] As it was mentioned, there were some parts of the old systems and functions of mahalla in Uzbekistan that started to deteriorate.

Also, the evaluation of mahalla education by the Soviet government during the Soviet period was extremely low. The government rated children who lived and grew up in mahalla negatively as "raised in mahalla". The government policy of "Red *choykhona*" was expected to compensate for the low standards of mahalla.

(2) Establishing School Education during Soviet Period and Mahalla

Although the informal learning in the life of residents was continuing, the educational role of mahalla started to include a more systemized part as the systemization of education centering on the establishment of school education and activities of teachers expanded through the period of Russian Empire and the Soviet period.

Also, because of the change in social structure included in mahalla, the lives of children who live there changed drastically. During World War II, an education department for children who were fleeing from the war was set up by the committee at republic, state, city, and district levels. During the same period, orphanages and learning facilities for minors were set up.[25] In this period, kindergarten teachers were active and played a large role in early childhood education. In Samarkand, 2,435 children were educated in 43 facilities in 1950, but 3,823 children were educated in 49 kindergartens in early 1957.[26]

The basic policy of education in the Soviet Union was determined in the party convention of communist party, the Central Committee of the Communist Party and in cabinet meetings, and then implemented through various laws. The basic policy for education in 1970s was determined in the 24th party convention (1971) and the 25th party convention (1976), but their largest issue was the complete implementation of secondary education as compulsory education. In the new constitution of the Soviet Union which was established in 1977, article 45, it said "all citizens of the Soviet Union have the right to receive education. This right is warranted by the various types of free education, implementation of standard compulsory secondary education for the youth, vocational education based on the combination of learning, practical life, and production, development of a wide range of secondary specialized education and higher education, provision of national scholarships and privileges for students, possibility of learning in native language in schools, and establishment of conditions for self-learning"[27] and clearly indicates the specific contents of "right to receive education". Here, the "learning in native language" was indicated specifically, but there were only a limited number of schools that people could learn in the native language of their ethnicity. Parents also believed that schools taught in Russian had a higher level of education, so the education in native language was limited.

(3) Educational Activities in Mahalla and Political Propaganda during the Soviet Period

During the Soviet period, the Soviet government tried to unify the Soviet Union which consisted of various ethnicities, and promoted policies to form "Soviet Citizens". The government positioned mahalla as a permanent place for advertising and educating communism, and aimed for the diffusion of their national ideology.

At the time, the Soviet government tried use the traditional system and functions that mahalla had for a long time to change the resident's way of thinking to a more "Sovietified" and communist view, forming "Soviet citizens".[28] Mahalla had the role of transforming the residents into "Soviet citizens", and the education provided there was aimed to modernize and Sovietify the residents to have the ideology of the Soviet government. Through the literatures that were placed in the library of the "Red *choykhonas*" and meetings that were often held there had the purpose of expanding the communist ideology. At the time, mahalla took the role of new non-formal education that was different from *maktab* and *madrasa*.

Although the informal education in the lives of residents was continuing, the educational role of mahalla included parts that started to be systemized through the systemization of education, which mainly included the establishment of the modern school education in the periods of the Russian Empire and Soviet Union.

The Soviet government focused on the organizing ability to communicate the intention of the government, and they gave the operation department of mahalla the role to report the situation of residents to the government and implemented the "Sovietification of citizens" all over Uzbekistan.

5. Mahalla in Uzbekistan after Their Independence and Mahalla Restoration Policy of the Uzbekistan Government

Lastly in Section 5, I will clarify the educational aspects of mahalla by focusing on the educational reform and mahalla restoration policy after the independence of Uzbekistan.

(1) Government's Campaign for Mahalla Restoration—2003 the "Year of the Mahalla" Policy

In December 2002, the President Islam Karimov gave a speech during the 10th anniversary of the constitution that "I declare that 2003 in the Republic of Uzbekistan is the 'Year of the Mahalla' to enhance the role and importance of the self-governing institution by the mahalla residents, enhance the value and tradition of our ethnicity and humanity with the mutual affection, and increase the authority".[29] Based on the declaration of the president, the specific action plan for the "Year of the Mahalla" was publicized at the same time.[30]

To collaborate with the mahalla restoration campaign, Ministry of Public Education publicized the concept of "cooperation among families, mahalla, and school in the mature generation's developmnt" and promoting the cooperation of those three.

As it was mentioned, mahalla is positioned by the government as a place for economic development, maintenance of infrastructure, social insurance and health promotion for mahalla residents and children. In order to do those activities, the authority of self-governance by the residents themselves is expanded. However, in the specific action plan, there was a "Uzbekistan type" domestic NGO founded by the governmental institution and president's order, as a person in charge for the activity implementation and fund for the activity so a large part of the activity was led by the government. If the funding and control is done by the government as it was mentioned before, it might be difficult to freely conduct activities that suites the life and demand for mahalla residents.

Also, when promoting the integration of ethnicities in Central Asia while holding up Islam in the culture of everyday life such as mahalla is an extremely convenient, so I want to point out that it is why the government is promoting the renovation policy.

(2) Objective of the Establishment of Mahalla Related Organizations and the Actual Activity Situation The Establishment of Fund "Mahalla"

In the presidential decree in September, 1992, the President Karimov mentioned the establishment objective of mahalla renovation and Fund "Mahalla".

Respecting the nation and the spiritual values, and emphasizing those values consistently will form history. The most wonderful custom and tradition of the citizens are popularized. Therefore, the purpose is to place the cultural activities in the center of mahalla in the republic, and enhance the social economic problem solving strategies in mahalla.

1. The residents of Uzbekistan are demanded to actually organize the mahalla fund for conducting various proactive activities in mahalla.
2. Registration of Fund "Mahalla" and the indication of activity details is prescribed in the law of Uzbekistan.
3. Basic role structure for the newly established fund:
   To support the respect and enrichment of the organization, customs and traditions of Uzbek residents from various aspects;
   Appeal the principle of humane interaction of people and affection for families, socially vulnerable people, orphans, and seniors living alone who are provided with the fund;
   Support the development of mahalla to socio-economical and cultural beings in the market economy.
4. Ministers under the president of the Republic of Uzbekistan must structure the organization for Fund "Mahalla" and discuss the rules for the method to create environment necessary for proposing the activity for the fund.[31]

Fund "Mahalla" is an independent self-governing organization, and their activity include various supports in mahalla, supports for improving the standard of living for mahalla residents, and activities for Fund "Mahalla" in each area. Among the 102 activity plans mentioned later, Fund "Mahalla" is the organization in charge for up to 52.

The policy for the fund is determined during a conference that is held every 5 years. Also, the fund acts as a supervisor in the conference of the representatives of mahalla, and has the role of supervising and instructing all mahallas in the Republic of Uzbekistan such as hold meetings for all mahallas in the district.[32] However the role of Fund "Mahalla" is not just within the country. Mahalla has an external role such as receiving donation from funding organizations abroad. Various funds are positioned by the government as an executive institution for stockpiling international support funds and donation from the private companies within the country, and the mahalla fund is no exception.

The characteristics of Fund "Mahalla" itself are unique. Officially, Fund "Mahalla" is included in the realm of NGOs that are "non-government and non-profit", and are therefore not a governmental institution. However, the fund was established by the order of the president. The active member of mahalla call Fund "Mahalla" "local government" so it is pointed out that they view the fund to be on the government side.[33]

Conclusion

In this chapter, the historical formation of mahalla was discussed based on the topic of clarifying the historical change of mahalla from the educational aspect.

There are many theories on the origin of mahalla in Uzbekistan and the true origin is not clear. However, the formation of mahalla is closely related to the city structure at the time. In that city mahalla executives had various educational roles, structured according to the ethnicity, religion, and occupation.

During the period of the Russian Empire, it changed from non-formal education to modern education, so the educational role of mahalla changed drastically in this period. During the Soviet period, the role of mahalla was getting attention for constructing the Soviet nation and educational activities that had political propaganda were actively conducted during that period. In the present, after the independence of Uzbekistan, various educational activities are moved to mahalla because of the mahalla restoration policy of the government.

The change in the educational aspects of mahalla is closely related to the change of policy accompanied by the change of the political situation, so the evaluation of mahalla and their educational role has changed drastically with the change in political situation. Especially, the difference between the educational role of mahalla during the Soviet period and the educational activities that are based in the mahalla after the independence of Uzbekistan are quite large. As it was mentioned earlier in this book, it is considered that the difference between the educational roles during the Soviet period and after independence has to do with the criticism from the prior government in power so in any period, mahalla had the role of nurturing citizens who supported their government. That point is still the same today and the nurturing of "Uzbekistan citizens" is strongly promoted in mahalla as well as school.

Notes

[1] Timur Dadabaev, *Mahalla no Jitsuzo: Chuou Ajia Shakai no Dentou to Henyou (Mahalla)*, University of Tokyo Press, 2006, p.1.
[2] Hisao Komatsu, "Kashgar no Andijan ku chousa houkoku (Field Work Report of Andijan District of Kashgar)", Kosuke Shimizu eds., *Islam toshi ni okeru gaiku no jittai to minshu soshiki ni kansuru hikaku kenkyu (A Comparative Study of the Islamic City Quarters "Mahalla" and Popular Organizations)*, Tokyo University of Foreign Studies, 1991, p.46.
[3] Mahalla also exists in Turkey, Egypt, and India as Mahalle, El-Mahalla El-Kubra, Mohalla respectively, and it does mean neighborhood.
[4] On other works, see, Sukhareva, O.A., *Kvartal'naya obshchina pozdnefeodal'nogo goroda Bukhary: V svyazi s istoriei kvartalov*, Moskva: Nauka, 1976, Abdullaev, Sh.M., *Sovremennye etnokul'turnye protsessy v makhallyakh Tashkenta*, Tashkent: Fan, 2005.; E.W.Sievers, "Uzbekistan's Mahalla: From Soviet to Absolutist Residential Community Associations", *The Journal of International and Comparative Law*, Vol.2, 2002, pp.91-158.
[5] Rizwan Ablimit, "Uighur no kodomo no hattatsu ni okeru mahalla (chiiki kyoudoutai) no yakuwari (The Role of the *Mahalla* in the Development of Uighur Children)", The Japanese Society of Life Needs Experience Learning, *Seikatsu Taiken Gakushu Kenkyu (The Journal of Life Needs Experience Learning)*, Vol.1, 2001, p.40.
[6] Masaru Suda, "'Shimin' tachi no kanri to jihatsuteki hukuju—Uzbekistan no mahalla (The Control and Voluntary Subjection of "Citizens": Uzbekistan's *Mahalla*)", The Japan Association of International Relations, *Kokusai Seiji (International Relations)*, Vol.2004, No.138, 2004, p.44.
[7] Yasushi Sanada, "Toshi・Nouson・Yuboku (City, Village, Nomadism)", Tsugutaka Sato eds., *Kouza Islam 3 Islam ・Shakai no Shisutemu (Lectures on Islam 3 Islam and Social System)*, Chikuma Shobo, 1986, pp.116-117.
[8] Sukhareva, O.A., *Bukhara XIX- nachalo XXv*, Moskva: Nauka, 1966, s.325-326.
[9] Related to nomadic tribe Turkmen early leaded seminomadic life and semisettled life. Agriculture became popular not only to Turkmen, but among the Kazakh and Kyrgyz people in the period of Russian Empire as well. In the Soviet era, the settlement promoted by the Soviet government more actively, however, nomadic life was also continued into 1930s and 1940s. Hisao Komatsu, Hiroshi Umemura, Tomohiko Uyama, Chika Obiya, Toru Horikawa, eds., *Chuou Yurashia wo Shiru Jiten (Cyclopedia of Central Eurasia)*, Heibon-sha, Japan, 2005, pp.517-518.
[10] Hisao Komatsu, "Bukhara no mahalla ni kansuru noto—O.A.Sukhareva no Field work kara (Notes on the mahallas of Bukhārā: based on the ethnographical material collected by O.A.Sukhareva)", *Journal of Asian and African Studies*, No.16, 1978, pp.178-215.
[11] Timur Dadabaev, *op. cit.*, 2006, p.47.
[12] Bendrikov, K.E., *Ocherki po istorii narodnogo obrazovaniya v Turkestane (1865-1924gg.)*, Moskva: Akademiya Pedagogicheskikh Nauk RSFSR, 1960, s.27-60.
[13] Yoshiyuki Kudomi, "Chiiki to kyoiku (Local Community and Education)", The Japan Society of Educational Sociology, *Kyoiku Shakaigaku Kenkyu (The Journal of Educational Sociology)*, No.50, 1992, p.67.
[14] Sukhareva, O.A., *op. cit.*, 1966, s.271-291.
[15] Muminov, I.M. i dr, *Istoriya Samarkanda*, Tom pervyi, Tashkent: Fan, 1969, s.293.
[16] Bendrikov, K.E., *Ocherki po istorii narodnogo obrazovaniya v Turkestane (1865-1924gg.)*, Moskva: Akademiya Pedagogicheskikh Nauk RSFSR, 1960, s.28.
[17] Masaru Suda, *op. cit.*, 2004, pp.46-50.

[18] Bendrikov, K.E., *op. cit.*, 1960, s.61.
[19] Bendrikov, K.E., *op. cit.*, 1960, s.69-70.
[20] Hidesuke Kimura, Satoshi Yamamoto, *Sekai Gendaishi 30 Soren Gendaishi II (World Contemporary History 30 Soviet Contemporary History II)*, Yamakawa Shuppansha, 1979, pp.118-119.
[21] Timur Dadabaev, "Chuou ajia shokoku no gendaika ni okeru dentouteki chiiki shakai no arikata to yakuwari—Uzbekistan no 'mahalla' wo chushin ni (The Ideal Existence and Roles of the Traditional Local Community in the Modernization of Central Asian Countries: Focusing on 'mahalla' of Uzbekistan)", *Toyo Bunka Kenkyusho Kiyou (The Memoirs of the Institute for Advanced Studies on Asia)*, Vol.146, 2004, p.258.
[22] Timur Dadabaev, same as above, 2004, p.259.
[23] Masaru Suda, *op. cit.*, 2004, pp.46-50.
[24] Uzbekistan's Mahalla: From Soviet to Absolutist Residential Community Associations, Eric W. Sievers, *The Journal of International and Comparative Law at Chicago Kent*: Vol.2 2002.
[25] Muminov, I.M. i dr, *op. cit.*, 1969, s.227.
[26] Muminov, I.M. i dr, same as above, 1969, s.295.
[27] Ministry of Education, Culture, Sports, Science and Technology, Japan, *Attached document (1) II Recent Trends of Educational Policy of Major Countries the Soviet Union*, http://www.mext.go.jp/b_menu/hakusho/html/hpad198001/hpad198001_3_188.html (May 20, 2010 browsed).
[28] Timur Dadabaev, *op. cit.*, 2004, pp.257-258.
[29] Oʻzbekiston Mahalla xayryya jamgʻarmasi, *Mahalla*, Toshkent, 2003, b.29-39.
[30] Oʻzbekiston Mahalla xayryya jamgʻarmasi, *op. cit.*, 2003, b.200-236.
[31] Oʻzbekiston Respublikasi Prezidentining Farmoni, Toshkent shaxri, 1992 yil 12 Sentyabr', PF-472 son.
[32] Masaru Suda, *op. cit.*, 2004, p.52.
[33] Masaru Suda, *op. cit.*, 2004, p.52.

Chapter 2

Mahalla Structure and Learning for Adults after Independence

In Chapter 2, I will discuss the structure of mahalla and education activities after independence.

The purpose of this chapter is to clarify the contradiction of the citizen formation function of mahalla, which systemization is promoted by the nation, and the self-governing function, and to clarify the learning for adults that is done there.

The Republic of Uzbekistan became independent after the dissolution of the Soviet Union in 1991 so they had to quickly arouse and create their citizen's awareness as being "Uzbekistanis" for the construction of a new nation. So the government adopted the policy to restore the traditional culture and Uzbek language, their ethnic language, as their public language and nationally symbolize the old hero, Amir Timur in order to heighten the citizen awareness and promote citizen formation.

Among those, the government developed various national construction policies for mahalla, which had already been there for a long time. The government positioned mahalla as the end organization for the government and promoted the resident's awareness for self-governing by, among other things, electing *oqsoqol* (elder, see Chapter 1), who take leadership in mahalla by the mahalla residents.[1] Also, they positioned mahalla as the core for the channel to distribute subsidy for underprivileged families and a place of education for the youth. At the same time, mahalla is a place for various assistance activities from international organizations such as NGOs in Uzbekistan as well as international NGOs. For example, UNICEF is promoting the activities for informing about basic education, health issues for the youth, and HIV/AIDS titled "Five Year Country Programme Action Plan (CPAP 2005-2009)" in cooperation with the Uzbekistan government, United Nations, and other organizations based on the "Convention on the Rights of the Child" of the UN.[2] These kinds of activities by UNICEF are done in cooperation with NGO and governmental organizations called *Kamolot* (the Republic of Uzbekistan Central Council for Youth Social Activities) and Fund "Mahalla".[3]

In this Chapter, I will clarify the contradiction between the function of citizen formation done by the nation and the function of self-governing by the citizens in mahalla where various actors are developing activities. So, I will first discuss the systemization, structure, and function of mahalla based on the mahalla policy of the nation, and then analyze the activities of mahalla as the end institution for the government. Lastly, I will discuss the community education activities and support for females by mahalla residents, and discuss the contradiction of the function of citizen formation done by the nation and the function of self-governing by the citizens.

1. Systemization of Mahalla by the Nation

In Section, I will discuss the systemization of mahalla by the current Uzbekistan government structure and the function of current mahalla mainly focusing on the mutual relationship between mahalla, families, schools, and mosques.

(1) Historical Development of Mahalla Systemization

Prior to the period of the Russian Empire, small scaled communities called mahalla in Tashkent and Fergana area managed the mosque, mausoleum, and tea house, which were central to the life of people, and they also formed and maintained the community by participating in the rites of passage, inheriting the tradition, and having the sense of belonging by communizing the water and cleaning the community together.[4]

During the period of Russian Empire, mahalla was clearly divided because of the city formation. The occupation of Central Asia by the Russian Empire started at the end of the 19th century, and they also occupied the area that Uzbekistan is currently located[5], and the "new city" with an European style was planned and constructed by the conqueror. During this process, the conquerors and the local residents lived separately in the "new city" and mahalla ("the old city").

Until the period of the Russian Empire, political intervention for mahalla was relatively few, and character formation was done based on the interaction between residents. In the community operation from the leadership of the elder accomplished character formation and social security of the residents, and the community was a self-governing organization through the interaction of residents.

During the period of the Soviet Union, mahalla had to go through rapid systemization because the Soviet Union promoted the policy to form "citizens" who had the identity as being part of the Soviet Union in order to integrate all of the Soviet Union, which consist of various ethnicities.

The soviet government tried to form "citizens" by changing the way of thinking for the residents into "Sovietified" and communist by using the traditional system and function of mahalla. As a policy, they recognized elders who agreed with the soviet government and strongly supported the socialism and communism of the Soviet Union for each mahalla and tried to influence the youth through the elders.[6]

Furthermore, while the government promoted the policy using mahalla, they tried to weaken the influence of mahalla slowly as they tried to change its function, which is based on tradition, into a community that is based on Soviet socialism. They promoted the policy that uses the only the framework of what is supported more than the national institutions, and tried eliminate the respected influence mahalla had over the residents.[7]

Because of these facts, it is understood that the Soviet government positioned mahalla as a permanent place for the advertisement and education for communism, and were promoting the policy to diffuse the ideology through mahalla. The government gave mahalla the role of forming "Soviet citizens" from the local residents, and the education done there was aimed to modernize and Sovietify the hesitant residents. The old system and function of mahalla in Uzbekistan had some parts that were starting to deteriorate.

As the importance of the institution that was based on the previous system deteriorated along with the dissolution of the Soviet Union, the national policy for mahalla changed drastically, and support for mahalla increased. Also, in order to remove the system of the old Soviet Union, the restoration of tradition, values, and culture of each ethnicity increased and the socio-political base for mahalla was enhanced during that process.[8]

Recently, the government declared that 2003 was the "Year of the Mahalla" and repeatedly publicized the slogan "mahalla is a socio-political mirror of ourselves" and promoting a campaign that claims the importance and tradition of mahalla. As a part of the project, the government explained and provided information relating to the importance of mahalla committees, and publicized the practice examples through "mahalla newspapers" published every week by the committee.[9] Furthermore, mahalla is treated as the foundation of the spirit of Uzbekistan citizens in the subject of school education such as "Homeland Consciousness" and as a "Foundation of Spirituality".[10] Not only those, but the government also issued a regulation with the concept of "Cooperation among families, mahalla, and school in the mature generation's development" and are trying to enhance this cooperation.[11]

In addition, "entrusting the educational department to local government (*hokimiyat*) institutions (Article 27)" of the laws of the Republic of Uzbekistan "On Education" that was revised in 1997 determined that the local government provides the life security for children for the development of local area.[12] Because of this, mahalla, which is under the leadership of the local government, has provided support for socially vulnerable people since 1994, and for children since 1997.[13]

Based on these, it can be said that the current mahalla is determined to be an end organization for the government and is positioned to have the role of transforming mahalla residents into "Uzbekistan citizens" on top of being an institution for providing social security.

The characteristic of this positioning by the government is that unlike the Soviet period, they aim for the formation of "Uzbekistani" by promoting the restoration of mahalla and by emphasizing the traditional parts of mahalla. Also, another characteristic is that mahalla's role in social security expanded publically after independence because of the new political position given by the government. Although the political position and role of mahalla changed along with the transition of political power from the Russian Empire to the Soviet Union, then to the current Uzbekistan government, it remains the same that the government understands mahalla to be a place to form their citizens. After independence, various rights were determined by the order of the president and regulations, and given to mahalla compared to the Soviet period. At the same time, mahalla not only has the political element, but also has the traditional spirit of mutual help with neighboring residents and aspects of the place of traditional culture where rites of passage and important ceremonies take place. And these two aspects of mahalla started to become more prominent when the citizen formation from the nation and self-governance from the inside of mahalla collided.

(2) Legal and Administrative Construction of Mahalla by the Nation after the Independence

According to the new law established in 1992; "local self-governing institution of mahalla in urban residential district, farming village, and *aul*[14], must elect the chair in the residential meeting and their term limit is 2 and half years. Their authority is determined by their local self-governing institution based on the law (Article 105)", so mahalla was determined to be a self-governing institution. According to Dadabaev, T., the function of the mahalla committee as a governmental committee is determined in "On Self-Governing Organization of the Citizens" in the law of the Republic of Uzbekistan as; 1) to play a role in crime prevention (including making a list of people with criminal records, members of prohibited religious groups, and mother-and-child families), 2) provide financial assistant for poor families and unemployed people, 3) expand the interaction between mahalla and educational institutions and nurture the youth, 4) make a list of people who wish to make a pilgrimage to Mecca, and select pilgrims, 5) support the employment of the district residents and eliminate unemployment in the district, 6) establish, abolish, and revise the small companies that are useful to the daily lives of the district residents, 7) get volunteers together and promote labor with no cost that enhances the district, 8) explain to residents the methods of using resources in environmentally friendly ways such as saving water and electricity, 9) manage the land usage within the district, 10) manage the environment and sanitary condition of the district that could influence the health of the residents, 11) manage the fire prevention and how to take care of animals (livestock), 12) select assistants among the residents in case of natural disaster.[15]

Based on the regulation, it shows that there is an influence of the mahalla committee as a governmental organization in various areas of the residents' lives. The mahalla committee is evaluated as a function that promotes the development of resources for citizens such as the nurturing of youth in cooperation with schools and environmental education. On the other hand, the committee has a legal function in forming citizens that can operate local community buildings by themselves by, for example, getting together a volunteer organization among the district residents and asking for restoration assistance in natural disasters. What supports the function of mahalla committee is the local network that is made up by the mutual relationships and trust between mahalla residents.

In December 2002, the President Karimov gave a speech during the 10th anniversary of the constitution where he mentioned that "I declare that 2003 in the Republic of Uzbekistan is the "Year of the Mahalla" to enhance the role and importance of the self-governing institution by the mahalla resident, enhance the value and tradition of our ethnicity and humanity with the mutual affection, and increase the authority"[16] and declared that 2003 would be the "Year of the Mahalla".[17]

Because of the declaration of the president, the actual activity plan for the "Year of the Mahalla" was published at the same time. Regarding this, they mentioned 6 goals "I. Development of the organization of mahalla activities and base for the law", "II. Enhancement of the plan in mahalla and construction of the position of new activities for the small business department that does not limit to the development of labor and market department", "III. Develop the social infrastructure in mahalla", "IV. Improvement of social security for the families and promotion of the nurturing of young families", "V. Giving rights to senior citizens and the enhancement of support", and "VI. Improvement and provision of medical facilities and rest homes for mahalla citizens and the development of sports for the children", and a total of 102 activities were planned.[18]

As it was mentioned, mahalla is positioned by the government to promote economic development, establish social infrastructure, and promote social security and health enhancement for the residents and children. Also, in order to conduct those activities, their rights as a self-governing institution by the residents were expanded. However, in the actual activity plans, there are NGOs that were established by the president's order, outer shells of the government as the designated organization in charge or funding source for the activities, so a large part of the activities are led by the government.

It is characteristic of the NGOs in Uzbekistan that there are a few organizations that were established by the order of the president. For example, the previous Fund "Mahalla" was an independent, self-governing, organization that was established by the order of the president, but they must proceed with their activity based on the constitutions, laws of Uzbekistan, and international standards, and must be registered with the Ministry of Justice.[19] There are various funds, such as *Kamolot*, mentioned before that were established by the order of the president as NGOs, but those funds are positioned as the institution that stocks the donation from international assistant funds and private companies within the country and execute their policy using the fund as well as their earned income.[20] In December 2003, President Karimov gave a speech that it is getting close to stopping the exploration of assistance from abroad and domestic resources should be spent for the development of the independent nation. It is pointed out that the President Karimov's speech was the beginning of the national pressure placed on the NGO sector, and there were various conditions in the details; assistant funds from the international assistant organization must be received by the special committee, activities done by the international assistant organization must get permission prior to the event, all international NGOs must be registered by the Ministry of Justice, and they had to open an account in both the National Bank of Uzbekistan and Asaka Bank in the NGO's name. As a result, most of the international NGOs had to stop their activity or left the country, and over 60% of the domestic NGOs that had been active had to close their organization.[21] When we discuss the NGO activities in Uzbekistan we have to pay attention to the fact that NGOs are active in an environment that is strongly influenced by the intentions of the government and are controlled by the strong initiative of the government. As it was mentioned, if the fund and control is from the government, NGOs can receive support from the government constantly, but the usage and activity is limited and it may be difficult for NGOs within mahalla committees to freely conduct the activities that suite the lives and demands of the mahalla residents.

(3) Structure and Function of Current Mahalla: Mutual Relationship of Mahalla, Family, School and Mosque

Currently, mahalla in Uzbekistan consists of a mutual relationship between mosques, schools, residential meetings, representative mahalla, mahalla committee, use of common facilities such as office and ceremony hall, *posbon* (self-protection group), and families of mahalla. As a standard for mahalla, the government requires the residence of over 500 households. The representative of the mahalla is elected and a wage is paid by the government. Also, they have various activities such as solving problems of family issues, re-construction of the finances of mahalla and ensuring support, and mahalla operation, specific activities are different depending on the personal history of the representative and their domestic situation.[22] For example, the mahalla that the author conducted the research on, the mahalla representative provided some funds and promoted sports for children and youth strongly. The representative was enthusiastic about this and mentioned that "Sports is the originality of this mahalla".[23]

Photo 1 All mahallas have the office of mahalla committee.
(Photo is taken by the author in March 2006).

Photo 2 Chart showing the presence of the mahalla representative,
posbon, and a person in charge for the women's
committee posted at the entrance of mahalla committee office.
(Photo is taken by the author in June, 2007.)

Each mahalla has a mahalla committee[24] that conduct specific activities as a governmental institution and a lower committee is placed under it. In the lower committee, there are different departments such as "ethics and education", "women" and "social security" and each department conducts various activities.[25]

As the function of mahalla according to Dadabaev, there are 4 functions of mahalla: 1) function to give the unit of identity for the people in the local society, 2) function as an institution that is part of the government system, 3) function as an institution for living assistance and support, and 4) function as a peaceful solution for social conflicts and collisions between ethnicities.[26] Furthermore, he indicates that there are 2 types mahalla currently in Uzbekistan; the "traditional mahalla that has been there historically (="informal mahalla", informal network of people)" and "mahalla as administrative organ which bears a part of nation building (= formal mahalla)".[27] According to this, "traditional mahalla that has been there historically" has lived through the Soviet period as one traditional culture and has the function of people's interaction and mutual assistance in the current Uzbekistan. On the other hand, the aspect of mahalla as a governmental institution is becoming complicated, and it is not only the inside of mahalla, but is also positioned as the place of activities for domestic NGOs such as Fund "Mahalla" and governmental institutions such as local government.

Although the restoration of mahalla was part of returning to their own culture, there were two aims in the background. One was to get rid of the old Soviet system by emphasizing their own culture, and the other is to use the framework of mahalla as the foundation for construction the new nation.

When the functions of citizen formation and self-government of mahalla is categorized according to the "formal" and "informal" categories pointed out by Dadabaev, the "formal mahalla" is significant in the function of citizen formation and specific examples are support for socially vulnerable people and the education of patriotism done by mahalla committee. Also, the "informal mahalla" (= informal network of people)" has the function of self-governance by the residents and mutual support among mahalla residents, interaction of residents in *choykhona*, and independent learning on the issues of the local area at the mahalla committee are considered as such.

Table 2 Total number of mahalla in Uzbekistan

№	Name of region (Region, City, District)	Number of village			Number of mahalla			Number of households		
		Total	Including		Total	Including		Total	Including	
			Rural areas	Urban areas		Rural areas	Urban areas		Rural areas	Urban areas
	Total of Republic	1,470	1,459	11	8,190	6,520	1,670	4,746,167	4,168,553	577,614
1	Republic of Karakalpakstan	141	141		241	184	57	247,931	216,641	31,290
	Region									
2	Andijan	94	94		875	785	90	506,200	433,200	73,000
3	Bukhara	121	119	2	426	342	84	348,334	282,389	65,945
4	Jizzax	100	100		194	160	34	151,662	136,707	14,955
5	Qashqadaryo	147	147		491	429	62	440,140	426,178	13,962
6	Navoiy	55	55		290	247	43	200,737	145,851	54,886
7	Namangan	99	99		772	690	82	417,597	369,873	47,724
8	Samarkand	125	125		1,084	821	263	557,232	490,649	66,583
9	Surxondaryo	114	114		709	679	30	373,461	348,813	24,648
10	Sirdaryo	69	66	3	265	237	28	124,541	115,100	9,441
11	Tashkent	146	146		1,014	841	173	410,479	369,590	40,889
12	Fergana	161	155	6	860	648	212	701,456	598,295	103,161
13	Xorazm	98	98		494	457	37	266,397	235,267	31,130
14	Tashkent city				475		475			

*This data obtained through reports by local government.

Source: Fund "Mahalla", Informatsiya o kolichestve skhoda grazhdan, makhalli i domov po Respublike Uzbekistan (Information of number of villages, mahallas and households in Republic of Uzbekistan), January 23, 2015. The map of Uzbekistan and the surrounding area in the beginning of this book indicates Jizzax as Jizzakh, Xorazm as Khorezm, Qashqadaryo as Kashkadarya, Surxondaryo as Surkhandrya, Sirdaryo as Syrdarya.

2. Activities of Mahalla as the End Institution of the Government

In Section 2, I will discuss the activities of mahalla as the end institution for the government after the independence. Specifically, I will analyze the example of residents' management system by mahalla committee and family support system.

(1) Residents Management System and Support for Socially Vulnerable People by Mahalla Committee

The law on mahalla determines that it is the duty of the mahalla committee to protect and ensure individual freedom and promotes the systemization of mahalla to enhance its execution power as a governmental institution. The local network built by the mutual relationship between the residents in mahalla is utilized in that situation. Here, I will use the example of the support of socially vulnerable people by *posbon* and mahalla committee on violation of human rights, which is a big issue when mahalla committees support and ensure the freedom of mahalla residents.

Posbon is a safety management organization of mahalla and laws on mahalla *posbon* determine the organizational structure and activity contents. Members of *posbon* are selected from the local residents for the most part. It has the background of supervising mahalla residents by the *posbon* member from the same area, and suppresses the resistance for residents' supervision.[28] However, it has been pointed out that the policy of the committee to protect the freedom of its residents through the self-protection group is, in reality, triggering a violation of human rights in the area.[29] Among those, what are considered as malicious are; 1) the action of the committee, whose authority was enhanced in order to represent police in the local society to prevent crime, is invading the privacy of the residents, 2) register the affairs of the areas statistics (statistics of population, unemployment, mother-and-child families, "poor" families, people with criminal history, alcohol and drug dependent people, rebellious youth) and provide it to the police as necessary, 3) check foreigners and people who came from a different area (and rent a place) who live within the local area, and 4) mahalla take no measures against domestic violence (DV) and prevent divorce when the women wish to do so.[30]

For those actions mentioned above by the mahalla committee and *posbon*, they explained that such activities are conducted to maintain public safety and reduce crime in the local society. It is true that the safety management of the area by the local residents gives the right of self-government to the residents, and has the advantage to conduct the activity smoothly by using the local network that has been built. Also, by having the residents walk around and see their own area, it will have them recognize that the local area is close to them. On the other hand, it means that supervision is all over the people's daily lives in the area, and this type of over supervision has a danger of triggering the invasion of human rights. Also for young people who would not participate in the military service, leaders of *posbon* coach them to participate in military service and take young people to Ministry of Defense and coach them on the importance of military service with the staff of Ministry of Defense.

Other than *posbon*, for the national policy of utilizing the local network, there is an example of support for socially vulnerable people by mahalla committee.

The government started the support for socially vulnerable people through the mahalla committee of 1994. 0.6% of GDP was budgeted for the activities and the budget for the support for socially vulnerable people is provided to mahalla from the local government, instead of the central government. To determine the poor class, the number of children in a household, existence of disabled people, condition of the residence, health condition, and income or pension receiver are used.

What is characteristic in the support of mahalla committee is that the committee is the one who targets the poor people using the traditional knowledge and local network as well as public evaluation standards determined by the Ministry of Labor and Social Security. It is considered that it has the advantage of being able to support socially vulnerable people efficiently with a low budget and bear the possibility of self-government by the residential organization providing the social support. However, local area and ethnic structure, occupation structure, and distribution of generations are different among mahallas and it has the possible disadvantage of having trouble maintaining a consistent monitoring.[31] Resident assistants and the self-governing of residents with territorial bonds make it easy to reflect the demand of the resident, but the method and evaluation of the activities is locally oriented and is therefore difficult to generalize.

Similar to *posbon* mentioned before, the support of socially vulnerable people by the mahalla committee is the local network of mahalla. This network is rooted in the relationship of local people and is the mutual relationship of resident and trust that were cultivated by the interaction of people at traditional *choykhona*. The advantage of providing support for the socially vulnerable people through mahalla is that they can utilize the human network of "people who know each other well" in the local residents of the same mahalla. Instead of researching sporadically, constant research allows quick assistance to the family that was not poor before. Also, they can reduce the assistance to the family that is no longer poor, and can thus provide efficient support for socially vulnerable people. The problem is that the private information of a resident is used in the area that is not intended by the government, causing the invasion of privacy. According to Iwane Takahashi, the private information of residents is used to reveal criminals related to terrorism.[32]

In mahalla in current Uzbekistan, there is a collision between the national policy and self-government of residents in various scenes and it is contradicting the self-governance of mahalla.

The President Karimov mentioned the following as the role of mahalla in citizen formation.

> The best way to prevent erosion (crime) and spoilage is the high level of ethics for citizens and internal immunity for criminal behavior. All ethical education in schools, labor unions, mahalla, public opinion, mass media, and church must instruct citizens that criminal activity will be criticize severely.[33]

> The system of orderly local government cannot be though about without the core of self-governing institution of residential meetings (mahalla).[34] These institutions were created with the historical tradition and spirituality of the citizens. The position of mahalla used to be a self-governing institution. Mahalla played a large role in the creation of good neighbors, respect and humanity in human relationships. They protected the social benefit and the residents and provided support for the poorest population. At the same time, the situation now is required to add more new content in the function of mahalla.[35]

The words of the president mentioned the role and value of old mahalla as well as "adding new content to the function of mahalla". In other words, it is to emphasize the addition of new governmental function that mahalla did not possess before. This was also to symbolically express the system of mahalla that has been promoted after independence.

Also for the 102 activities planned for in the "Year of the Mahalla" mentioned previously, there was a plan with the objective to publicize TV programs with the theme of "mahalla is a wonderful home country", "patriotic awareness", "improvement of the position of mahalla in children's education and responsibility"[36] planned by person in charge of Uzbek TV & Radio Company (UzTV), Fund "Mahalla", Religious activity committee, Women's committee, "Ethics and education" center, *Kamolot,* and

"Patriotism" organization. The specific activity is to enhance the authority of mahalla in the education of the youth and families in mahalla. In other words, this plan was to create patriotism in the children of mahalla and to reform citizens into being "Uzbekistani".

While this kind of citizen transformation progressed systematically, they have been forming interactions among generations and forming human characteristics in the local community scale through the cultures that are close to their lives such as traditional songs sang in rituals, folktale, and sayings.[37] Recently, however, there has been a report that "they are instructed by the national government to 'reduce' the traditional customs and rituals of Uzbekistan while keeping the 'format' the same".[38] The background of the government giving such instruction is projected that they are aiming to create, and awaken, the awareness as citizens and patriotism by contacting with the traditional culture instead of making the citizens learn the traditional culture and customs of Uzbekistan. The extension of the creation of mutual help of mahalla lead by the nation is the formation of Uzbekistan citizens.

Furthermore, the relationship mentioned above is systemized in the law and governmental framework. The law relating to mahalla is positioned as it is the duty of mahalla committee to protect and ensure the freedom of individual and promote the systemization of mahalla in order to enhance the execution power as a governmental institution. And the local network consist of the mutual relationship of citizens in mahalla is used for those activities.

(2) Right to Learn of the Residents and Social Educational Activities in the Local Community

As it was mentioned, mahalla in current Uzbekistan corresponds with various problems in the daily lives of mahalla residents and has a role of finding solutions with the residents. In other words, the current mahalla has the challenge of grasping the local issues accurately and creating a social education environment to satisfy the demand of the residents in community building and learning.

A similar situation was seen in Japan during the period of rapid economic growth. During that rapid change in social environment, they held the position that the local issues of the local residents in Japan were their own problem, and proclaimed to the local self-governing organization that they want to participate in overcoming the issues, community building, and development of their local area. At the same time, local residents' campaign was started to aim the development of community education on the national and local scale. Because of this, the Japanese government and self-governing organizations expanded the opportunities for citizens to participate in the re-construction of the infrastructure and social education environment mainly in the civic hall (*Kominkan* or *Kokaido*).

The educational rights of the citizens in social education were clearly indicated in "*Hirakata These*"[39] in the 1960s.

"*Hirakata These*" of Japan clearly mentions that social education, especially the social education in the local area, is the basic rights for each resident. Also in the 4th UNESCO International Adult Education Conference held in Paris France in 1985, UNESCO "Declaration of the Right for Learning" was adopted and the right for learning is the essential human rights of human, and defined it as "The right to learn is: the right to read and write; the right to question and analyse [sic]; the right to imagine and create; the right to read one's own world and to write history; the right to have access to educational resources; the right to develop individual and collective skills".[40] On the other hand, the Uzbekistan Constitution and in the law of the Republic of Uzbekistan "On Education" guarantee the "The rights to receive education" but it has not gotten to the point of clear indication of the educational rights of residents or guarantees of the freedoms of residential activities. In other words, the right of education for the residents of a local community is not established yet.

However, as the legal and governmental establishment is delayed, the sprout of independent learning, mainly done by residents and mahalla committee, can be seen through various examples in mahalla. In Section 3, I would like to discuss the adult learning in Uzbekistan using the actual examples in mahalla.

3. Community Education Activities by Mahalla Residents and Female Support

Females in Muslim society in Central Asia were placed in polygamy, early marriage, segregation, mandatory dressing of veil before the Russian Revolution. However, during the Soviet period, the women's liberation movement was promoted mainly by the women's department of the communist party. During this period, there was a Soviet Women's Committee, which was the only female organization active nationwide and their headquarters was located in Moscow.

In 1924, the first women's club in Central Asia was created in Tashkent, and women learned the knowledge of medicine and law. This women's liberation movement was aimed to relieve women from religion and gain women as a labor force, but because of this change in social structure, they were forced to have long hours of labor as well as housework and childrearing. Although the social progress of women was promoted, there was sexual discrimination in the advancement of position, so most of the managerial jobs and mission-critical works were done by men. This tendency is continuing now after the dissolution of the Soviet Union.[41]

Even after the promotion of women's liberation movement by the Soviet Union, the view of the sexual roles in the traditional and patriarchal system is still deeply rooted and many people believe that women should do the housework and childrearing in the present. On the other hand, there is an increase of prostitution and commercialization of sex in the urban areas recently. Also, globalization, becoming an information-oriented society due to the diffusion of cell phones and internet, and the change of family structure changed their life styles drastically after independence. Because of this, various sexual views are formed currently that does not fit in with the framework model religious views and customs.

In the current situation of women in Uzbekistan mentioned above, domestic violence from husbands is becoming a big issue. As an actual problem, a few hundred cases of suicide of women who suffered from the violence from their husbands are reported yearly.[42] In Central Asia, a counseling service that responds to such problems and shelters to protect females are still in progress[43], domestic violence is secretly processed within the family and mahalla.[44]

Also, there are some problems related to domestic trouble and divorce. For this, Kamp pointed out that the "family protection" policy of Uzbekistan is making it difficult to get a divorce these days.[45] In addition, people cannot start the divorce process unless it is approved by the mahalla committee in the current system of Uzbekistan, so there are various complicated problems.[46]

The representative organization of female activities in mahalla is the women's committee under the mahalla committee. The women's committee exists in most of all mahallas, and they deal with various activities such as taking care of children with problem behavior, employment courses for unemployed women, and mediating domestic troubles such as divorce and domestic violence. Also, because of the order of the president, there are various measures to assist the activities of the women's committee.[47]

Furthermore, the women's committee cooperates with the schools that children in mahalla attend, and their deep connection can be read from the school events and yearly plan, reports written by students on the "Year of the Mahalla" in 2003, and the list of mahalla data of students gathered from research called passport.[48]

Then, what kinds of activities are conducted by the women's committee in mahalla specifically? In the following, I will discuss the community education activities of mahalla and female support in mahalla in Tashkent focusing on a) opening of mahalla office for female in mahalla and activities of women's committee in A mahalla, b) mediation activities of the head of women's committee in F mahalla for domestic troubles, and c) excursion for female in F mahalla.

(1) Female Support in Mahalla
Various ethnicities live in A mahalla located in the Mirzo Ulugbek district in Tashkent. It was called a different name before, but it was changed to A mahalla recently. Here, I will introduce two example cases; the activity of women's committee for children with problem behaviors and opening of office for females in mahalla.

The first one is the example of cooperative activity between the mahalla women's committee and school that was researched by the author in March 2006. Many of the children in this mahalla attend school in either the Uzbek language or in Russian (referred as A school later) and there was a girl in the second grade that always has problem behavior. She never listens to the teacher during class and she would go somewhere if the teachers didn't keep their eyes on her. During the school year, teachers took care of her, but during a long holiday, it was very difficult for only the family to take care of her. So the members of women's committee took turn watching her and prevented her from going somewhere alone.

Also, if there are any children who have problem behavior at school, the school would write to the women's committee of the mahalla where the children live, and ask for advice and cooperation. Children feel that it is shameful for people in the same mahalla to know that they have problem behavior and they often change their behavior.[49] Also, the women's committee coaches childrearing to women with children living in the mahalla.

The second example is the opening of the mahalla office to women. The mahalla office is open to the public so residents can gather, talk and play simple sports such as table tennis every day. In the office there is an individual room where the committee chair of the women's committee works containing books on the "History of Uzbekistan", "Legal operation", "Family" and so on. The chair of the women's committee said that women in mahalla come in to the office and read those books enthusiastically. Also, at the meeting room in the office building, there are magazines and newspaper for women such as "mahalla" and "family", and women gather there and read them freely. Also, there are posters with the labels of products, whose factory is located in the mahalla to show them what kinds of companies or factories are in mahalla and provide a valuable opportunity to show them opportunities for employment.[50]

Enlightenment activities are promoted for female in mahalla. Some mahallas, including A mahalla, periodically have competitions for single women. Among those, women perform a play with a theme of mahalla. Many of them have a theme that "many women these days go abroad to make money. For the development of our country, we should stay here instead of going abroad" and have an aim to promote self-restriction for women to go abroad.[51]

Photo 3 Office of the committee chair of women's committee in mahalla with various books and magazines. (Photo taken by the author October 2007)

Photo 4 Poster of the label of products whose factories are located in the same mahalla. It is handmade by the chair of the women's committee.
(Photo taken by the author on October 2007)

As it was mentioned, the women's committee of mahalla supports problems regarding children and provides support, and opens the mahalla office to promote enlightenment activities. The mahalla office is a place for "interaction" and "gathering" for women as well as a place "to get to know their own mahalla", "to gather information from newspaper and books" and "to learn".

Female support and community education activities are done in mahallas other than A mahalla.

F mahalla is located in Sergeli district, a suburb of Tashkent. The former chair of the women's committee in this mahalla had 15 years of experience working at the women's committee. Of those, 6 years were as a chair, and 9 years as vice chair. Here, I will focus on examples of mediation for domestic trouble by the chair of the mahalla's women's committee and excursions for women.

The first one is the mediation for solving domestic troubles in mahalla. The story of the former chair started from a young woman visiting the office. Her story was that her husband had not come home and she assumed that he made a lover somewhere else so he did not come home. She cried that "I cannot continue my life", but the former chair first researched what kind of living condition she was in.

What was surprising when she visited her was that her house was very dirty and was not organized at all. There was dirty laundry in the washer and bathroom and toilet were not cleaned. There were dirty dishes, tea leaves, and coffee everywhere in the kitchen. Children were dirty and did not look like they ate proper meals. The woman's hair was dirty and undone, she was not wearing makeup, and her clothes were dirty. The former chair thought that she fist need to improve her appearance and lifestyle. So she told her, "First, wash your hair. Keep your nails trimmed and put on *Usman* (eyebrow makeup in Uzbekistan)". Put on some make up. Keep your house clean. Do the laundry periodically and put on clean clothes for your children. Clean your kitchen, bathroom, and toilet. Cook three times a day and feed it to your children. If you can do those, your husband will come back".

After a while, the husband came home all of a sudden. He came into the house and surprised that it was neatly cleaned, and felt like it was not his house. The house was organized and warm meal is cooking. Soon after that, the husband formally came back to the family.

Because of this example of solving domestic trouble, the chair of women's committee in mahalla not only gave some advice to the women from the mahalla office, but actually went into their life to help them out. The chair of women's committee not only acts as an adviser, but also becomes part of their life as an actor and provides support activities.

The former chair of the women's committee in F mahalla mentioned above on the divorce problem between married couples also planned a small excursion for women and took them to Tashkent. The former chair mentioned the following for the various excursions for women in mahalla.

> We rented a bus and went to Hamza Theater because some of the women said that they wanted to go to the theater. That time, 38 women participated. In the theater, they bought and had juice and snacks, but among those women, there were a few who looked uncomfortable. I asked what is wrong, and they said that they didn't have the money to buy snacks and drinks. So I told them to use this, and gave them a *Som* bill. It is not just food and drink. I had paid my own money to rent a bus and if they could not buy a ticket, I bought it for them. I usually carry about 5000 *Som* and if I saw a woman who was in trouble I would always give her money. I take the women to the theater about once a month. I also have taken women to Lake Chorvoq. For that trip, I did a lot of things such as arranging a bus, *Kazan* for *Plov*,[52] and meal preparation.[53]

Also in this case, it shows that the chair of women's committee in mahalla responds to various requests of women and provides various supports. What should be focused on in this example is that the bottom-up type of activities such as excursions requested by the women in mahalla instead of the top-down type from the women's committee to women in mahalla. The close human relationship of mahalla from the human network can grasp the requests and needs from women and respond to them in kind.

From these two examples in mahalla, the following can be considered as the role of women in mahalla.

In most of mahalla, trouble of women, problem that women have, and family problems are categorized into the women's committee. Because of the religion and ethnic spirituality, it is difficult for women to express their problems externally, so the women's committee clarified those buried problems by visiting their homes. They give a sense of security by being the same sex as the women in mahalla and convey their problems to the mahalla committee. The women's committee in mahalla is a mediator of domestic troubles and educator of children as well as a pipeline that connects women to the mahalla committee and, eventually, the society. In other words, the women's committee is providing support for women by utilizing the human network in mahalla.

On the other hand, women in mahalla who are not part of the committee have a role in supporting the activities of the women's committee and communicating the situations in mahalla to the women's committee. Here, mutual help between the women's committee and women in mahalla is done in the local perspective that they are all women. In the process of mutual support, women in mahalla are expected to play the role of a mahalla citizen who can be part of the future women's committee.

However, it has been pointed out that "mahalla does not take measures against domestic violence and prevents divorce even when the women wishes to do so"[54] in the background of these activities. Also, it is true that divorce between married couples is not possible without the permission of the mahalla committee. There are some cases where they solved the domestic trouble and the couple did not have to get divorced in the mahalla that the author researched. In situations such as this, it is essential to clarify what was promoted, and how the women accepted the promotion. The women's committee should be the supporter of women in mahalla, not an illegitimate intervener to the family.

Furthermore, the women's committee should not be contacted only when there is a problem such as the domestic trouble that was showed in the example, but it is necessary for being a place for expressing opinion, requests, and suggestions for community building from women such as in the example of the excursion. The important part is the exchange of opinions between women who receive support and those who provide it. And it is necessary for the chair of the mahalla women's committee to have the ability to extract the opinion of those women and communicate it to the mahalla committee and Uzbekistan society. Promoting the community activities of women in Uzbekistan is up to whether the women in Uzbekistan can speak up and everyone around them can listen to them.

(2) Sports Promotion Activities in the Facilities of Mahalla

Each mahalla in Uzbekistan maintains and owns various facilities. The contents are versatile, and there is a mahalla with an office with a computer room and others have the Tashkent Islamic University[55] within the area of mahalla.

One of the mahallas that the author conducted research on had a large sports complex. This mahalla, located in the Shaykhontohur district in Tashkent, had various sports projects for the youth provided mainly by the representative of mahalla.

For example, this mahalla holds sports events such as soccer and gymnastics. They formed a few soccer teams and had them participate in the tournament held in Tashkent and have many events that make young people enthusiastic about sports. The representative of mahalla mentioned the following for this reason.

Young people are interested in many things and sometime it leads to a deviant behavior. We put their interest towards sports so they don't go toward the deviant behavior. If they release their stress through sports, they won't do bad things. We have a few soccer teams in our mahalla and one of the teams won the tournament held in the city. Our mahalla is one of the most enthusiastic mahalla for sports among the more than 40 mahallas in Shaykhontohur.[56]

As it was mentioned, the unique activities of each mahalla are different depending on some elements, such as the character, education, and current occupation of the mahalla representative. In other mahallas, when the representative of the mahalla is a professor at a university and is knowledgeable in computers, he created the database for the residential information of the mahalla and managed that information. This tendency can work effectively using the knowledge and specialty of the mahalla, but the activity of the mahalla is largely influenced by the resignation of the representatives so there is a disadvantage that when there are a few representatives with short terms, the activities of mahalla could change frequently.

Photo 5 Resident management using computer by the representative of mahalla. (Photo taken by the author on March 2007)

Conclusion: How the Adult Learning in Mahalla Can Be Understood

As it was mentioned, mahalla's structure and characteristics, and activities in mahalla were discussed in order to discuss the citizen formation function by the nation and self-governing function of mahalla.

In mahalla, the self-governing function of mahalla was cultivated for a long time via the interaction among residents in *choykhona* and the relationship among residents called *gap*, mutual assistance, and traditional rituals. The current government of Uzbekistan added the citizen formation function to mahalla with such a function.

The creation of Fund "Mahalla", expansion of the authority held by mahalla committee, and mahalla restoration campaign seen in the "Year of the Mahalla" were policies aiming to promote the smooth formation of the national citizenry. Therefore, it was necessary to expand the legal authority of mahalla in order to use the governmental framework for mahalla committee and Fund "Mahalla", and as such it was expanded based on the law. It is certain that the possibility of self-government for mahalla residents increased. For example multiple mahallas in Tashkent have unique projects that correspond to the needs of mahalla's residents.

This movement can be accepted as the sprout of self-government by mahalla residents. However, this policy in mahalla includes the citizen formation so the centralization of authority by the nation corresponding to the formation of mahalla residents to citizen formation is concerned. Mahalla that went through the oppression under the Soviet government is in the critical stage now after the independence of Uzbekistan.

The important element of adult learning is pointed out that how they select the opportunity for learning for themselves and independently decide on how to learn what is based on the internal demand and necessity.[57] Acquiring the knowledge and information through literature placed in the mahalla committee office and the request from the women in mahalla "to want to go to the theater" for the excursion in mahalla discussed in this chapter as an excellent example of the participatory request in the place of learning for adults in mahalla. However, the independent demand for learning by the residents is not at the level of determining the selection of learning opportunities for the resident themselves and plans and contents for the learning. It is still left as one of the issues in adult learning in mahalla.

The citizen formation and self-governing function of mahalla mentioned in this chapter are contradicting functions at first glance, and the self-government of the current Uzbekistan is converged by the citizen formation and national integration function. However, the actual situation for the place of learning for adults is done through the discovery of local issues and solutions found by the residents and community building through participating in the planning of the local activities, which leads to the possibility of self-governing. In the future, the development of local social education that ensures the rights to learn for all residents is desired and mahalla is expected to take the important role in linking the consensus of the mahalla resident and mahalla activities.

Notes

[1] *Konstitutsiya Respubliki Uzbekistan*, Tashkent: O'zbekisotn, 2003.
[2] "Report: New Country Programme for 2005-9 signed in Tashkent", Uzbekistan UNICEF HP: http://www.unicef.org/uzbekistn/media_2091.html (October 23, 2005 browsed).
[3] "Report: New Country Programme for 2005-9 signed in Tashkent", Uzbekistan UNICEF HP: http://www.unicef.org/uzbekistn/media_2091.html (October 23, 2005 browsed).
[4] Masaru Suda, "'Shimin' tachi no kanri to jihatsuteki hukuju—Uzbekistan no mahalla (The Control and Voluntary Subjection of "Citizens": Uzbekistan's *Mahalla*)", The Japan Association of International Relations, *International Relations*, Vol.2004, No.138, 2004, p.44.
[5] Namio Egami eds., *Chuou Ajia Shi Sekai Kakkoku Shi 16 (History of Central Asia The World History 16)*, Yamakawa Shuppansha, 1987, pp.650-652.
[6] Timur Dadabaev, "Chuou ajia shokoku no gendaika ni okeru dentouteki chiiki shakai no arikata to yakuwari—Uzbekistan no 'mahalla' wo chushin ni (The Ideal Existence and Role of the Traditional Local Community in the Modernization of Central Asian Countries: Focusing on 'mahalla' of Uzbekistan)", *Toyo Bunka Kenkyusho Kiyou (The Memoirs of the Institute for Advanced Studies on Asia)*, Vol.146, 2004, p.257.
[7] Timur Dadabaev, same as above, 2004, pp.257-258. As a policy over the concrete Soviet Government's mahalla, the example of *"Choykhona"* which had already existed in each area is given. *"Choykhona"* was a word with the meaning of "the tea room", and was a place in which male's mainly living in the same area gathered for exchange. It was also a place that made preparations for wedding ceremonies or traditional festivals. The Soviet Government changed this *"Choykhona"* to "The red *Choykhona"*, and they tried to use the spot in order to foster a deeper understanding of the Soviet Government and Soviet ideology. Depending on the Dadabaev, there may also have been a small bookroom, except in the place where people drink tea or talk in "The red *Choykhona.*" Timur Dadabaev, same as above, 2004, p.259.
[8] Timur Dadabaev, same as above, 2004, pp.254-255.
[9] Massicard, Elise, Trevisani, Tommaso, "The Uzbek Mahalla", *Central Asia: aspects of transition*, edited by Tom Everett-Heath, London, 2003, p.206.
[10] Asuka Kawano, "Uzbekistan no gakkou ni okeru chiiki kyoudoutai (mahalla) no kyoiku— Seihu no mahalla seisaku tono kanren de (Community Education in Uzbekistan in Relation to the Mahalla Policy)", Japan Comparative Education Society, *Hikaku Kyoikugaku Kenkyu (Comparative Education)*, No.35, 2007, p.173.
[11] O'zbekiston, Mahalla xayryya jamg'armasi, *Mahalla*, Toshkent, 2003, b.333.
[12] *Barkamol ablod-O'zbekiston taraqqietining poydevori, Sharq nashriet- matbaa kontsernining Bosh tahririyati*, Toshkent, 1997, b.28.
[13] Japan International Cooperation Agency (JICA), *Central Asia (Uzbekistan, Kazakhstan, Kyrgyz) Report of Research Group on Aid, Present Data Analysis*, Part II Uzbekistan, Chapter 13 Poverty, 2001, pp.102-103, http://www.jica.go.jp/activities/report/country/2002_02_02.html. (November 15, 2004 browsed).
[14] *Aul* (village) is an administrative unit of rural area in Uzbekistan.
[15] Timur Dadabaev, *Mahalla no Jitsuzo: Chuou Ajia Shakai no Dentou to Henyou (Mahalla)*, University of Tokyo Press, 2006, p.124.

16 O'zbekiston , Mahalla xayryya jamg'armasi, *Mahalla*, Toshkent, 2003, b.29-39.
17 O'zbekiston Respublikasi Vazirlar Mahkamasining Karori, Toshkent shahri, 2003 yil 7 Fevral', 70 son.
18 O'zbekiston , Mahalla xayryya jamg'armasi, *Mahalla*, Toshkent, 2003, b.200-236.
19 Tukhliev, Nurislom, Krementsova, Alla, eds., *The Republic of UZBEKISTAN*, Tashkent, 2003, pp.173-174.
20 Yukiko Sawano, "'Shimin shakai' heno ikou wo unagasu shougai gakushu taikei no kouchiku —Uzbekistan kyowakoku no kyoiku kaikaku (The Formulation of a Lifelong Learning System towards a "Civil Society": Education Reform of the Republic of Uzbekistan)", *Roshia・Yurashia Keizai Chousa Shiryou (Vestnik ėkonomiki ĖKS-SSSR, Russian-Eurasian economy)*, No.798, 1998, p.6.
21 Silova, Iveta, eds., *How NGO React: Globalization and Education Reform in the Caucasus, Central Asia and Mongolia.*, Kumarian Press, 2008, p.232.
22 Timur Dadabaev, *op. cit.*, 2006, p.9, 232, 242.
23 Information obtained through Interview with representative of C mahalla, Shaykhontohur District, Tashkent (May 24, 2006).
24 Mahalla committee is similar to *Chonaikai* (neighborhood association) or *Jichikai* (residents' association) in a Japanese local community.
25 Timur Dadabaev, *op. cit.*, 2006, p.125. Information obtained through Interview with adviser of women's committee of G mahalla (April 15, 2006), Interview with representative of A mahalla (April 26, 2006).
26 Timur Dadabaev, *op. cit.*, 2004, p.261.
27 Timur Dadabaev, *op. cit.*, 2006, p.103.
28 Timur Dadabaev, "Uzbekistan no chiiki shakai 'mahalla' kara mita jinken no hogo・kakuho (Protection of Human Rights from perspective of Uzbekistan's Local Society *Mahalla)*, Slavic- Eurasian Research Center, *SRC Occasional Papers East Europe and Central Eurasian's Modern Period and Nation III*, 2004, p.35. According to laws on mahalla's *posbon*, the *posbon* was regarded as assistant of the police, and the number of *posbon* members differs depending on scale of the mahalla. For instance, 4 members are working in a mahalla which about 3,000 people are living. However, there can be 9 members working in a mahalla in which about 4,000 people are living.
29 Timur Dadabaev, *op. cit.*, 2004, pp.35-36.
30 Timur Dadabaev, *op. cit.*, 2004, pp.35-36.
31 Japan International Cooperation Agency (JICA), *op. cit.*, 2001, p.102, 108.
32 Iwane Takahashi, *Uzbekistan Minzoku・Rekishi・Kokka (Uzbekistan Nation・History・State)*, Soudosha, 2005, p.121.
33 Islam Karimov, *21 Seiki ni Mukau Uzbekistan(Uzbekistan on the Verge of the 21 Century, Uzbekistan na poroge XXI veka, in Japanese)*, Japan Uzbekistan Committee of Economy, 1999, p.49.
34 Islam Karimov, same as above, 1999, p.75. Mahalla was written to mean "residential meeting" in this book, it is important that we keep notes on how mahalla has various meanings. For example, people say "to go mahalla", which is sometimes used to express the same meaning as "to go the mahalla committee office". On the other hand, people say "my mahalla" in informal terms for the entire area of their own mahalla.
35 Islam Karimov, same as above, 1999, p.75.
36 O'zbekiston , Mahalla xayryya jamg'armasi, *Mahalla*, Toshkent, 2003, b.200-236.
37 Hiroki Sakai, *Chuou Ajia no Eiyu Jojishi Katari Tsutawaru Rekishi (Heroic Epic of Central Asia- Transportation History)*, Eurasia Booklet, No.35, Toyoshoten, 2002, pp.5-9.
38 Iwane Takahashi, *op. cit.*, 2005, p.139.
39 "*Hirakata These*" is report "Social Education for all Citizen" of Hirakata City's (Osaka

Prefecture) Education Board's social education committee, *Kominkan* governing council. In the report, six points were recommended as bellow by committees; 1) the subject of social education is the citizen, 2) social education is the peoples' right, 3) essential quality of social education is the learning of constitution, 4) social education became power for the residents' autonomy, 5) social education is the educational aspect of a grassroots movement, 6) social education educates and protects democracy. Hirakata City Education Board, *Social Education of Hirakata*, No.2 ("Social Education for all Citizen"), 1963.

[40] UNESCO, "The Right to Education", March 29, 1985, CONFINTEA IV, Paris. "Declaration of the Conference" http://www.unesco.org/education/uie/confintea/paris_e.pdf (February 28, 2015 browsed)

[41] Hisao Komatu, Hiroshi Umemura, Tomohiko Uyama, Chika Obiya, Toru Horikawa, eds., *Chuou Yurashia wo Shiru Jiten (Cyclopedia of Central Eurasia)*, Heibon-sha, Japan, 2005, pp.224-226.

[42] Hisao Komatu, Hiroshi Umemura, Tomohiko Uyama, Chika Obiya, Toru Horikawa, eds., *op. cit.*, 2005, p.226.

[43] Kyoko Katsuki, "Tajikistan ni okeru josei ni taisuru bouryoku no genjou to NGO no torikumi −Crisis center kara shelter katsudou he (Current Situation of Violence to Women in Tajikistan and NGOs' Efforts: From Crisis Center to Shelter Activities)", Kitakyushu Forum on Asian Women, *Ajia Josei Kenkyu*, No.15, 2006, pp.109-111.

[44] Hisao Komatu, Hiroshi Umemura, Tomohiko Uyama, Chika Obiya, Toru Horikawa, eds., *op. cit.*, 2005, p.226.

[45] Kamp, Marianne, "The retreat of the state: Women and the social sphere. Between women and the state: Mahalla committees and social welfare in Uzbekistan", *The transformation of Central Asia: Sates and societies from Soviet rule to independence*, edited by Pauline, 2004, pp.29-58.

[46] In Uzbekistan, next year's slogan is declared by the president on Constitution day, December 8 of every year. Divorce prevention activities by mahalla committees started since 1998 was declared the "Year of Family". Timur Dadabaev, *op. cit.*, 2006, p.262.

[47] Ukaz Prezidenta Respubliki Uzbekistan, O dopolnitel'nykh merakh po podderzhke deyatel'nosti Komiteta Zhenshchin Uzbekistana, Sobranie zakonodatel'stva Respubliki Uzbekistan, 2004g., No.21, s.251.

[48] Data of A school, Mirzo Ulugbek district, Tashkent City, Report of the "Year of Mahalla in 2003".

[49] Information obtained through Interview with a representative of A mahalla (April 26, 2006). For details, see Asuka Kawano, Takuzo Osugi, Junko Otani, "Women's Community Activities in Central Asia from Gender Perspectives", Kitakyushu Forum on Asian Women, *Journal of Asian Women's Studies*, Vol.17 (Welfare and Gender), 2008, pp.70-81.

[50] Information obtained through Interview with the chair of the women's committee of A mahalla (October 4, 2007).

[51] Women compete with each other in a variety of contests, like the presentation of mahalla's history, composing and reading poems, cooking, dancing etc. Information by Interview with the representative of A mahalla (April 26, 2006).

[52] *Plov*, or sometimes *osh*, is a traditional dish of the Uzbek people. *Plov* is cooked vegetables, mutton, rice, etc. in a cauldron called a *Kazan*. They not only eat *plov* daily, but people of Uzbekistan eat it at various events, such as the congratulations of spring festival *Navro'z*, wedding ceremonies and circumcisions. In particular, at the wedding ceremony, the courtesy of treating relatives and mahalla residents is performed, and they are offered *plov*. Support of mahalla committee or mahalla residents is indispensable to the preparation and a reception of visitor's, as well as cleaning up afterwards. Although *Kazan*, which is a thick iron pan, has various sizes, some homes are without large-sized *Kazan*s. In order to cook a *plov*, or whatever

is needed, at an event in mahalla, each mahalla office is equipped with a large-sized *Kazan*.

[53] Information obtained through Interview with a former chair of the women's committee of F mahalla (October 10, 2007).

[54] Timur Dadabaev, *op. cit.*, 2006, p.262.

[55] Tashkent Islamic University was established in April 7, 1999. They explain how the goal of the University is to prepare selfless, dedicated, highly qualified specialists as bachelors and masters who have deeply mastered the basics of religion, research principles, the history of Islam and philosophy, issues related to its role in the life and development of society, are capable of solving theoretical and practical problems facing religious institutions which embodies a high cultural, training, moral and aesthetic level of perfection, as well as training existing staff. They have three faculties; the Faculty of Islamic Law, Economy and Natural Sciences, the Faculty of History and Philosophy of Islam and the Faculty of Retraining and Professional Development. Tashkent Islamic University site http://www.tiu.uz/en/site/page/4 (January 23, 2015 browsed).

[56] Information obtained through Interview with the representative of C mahalla in Shaykhontohur district in Tashkent (May 24, 2006).

[57] Katsuko Sato, *Shougai Gakushu to Jumin Sanka —Otona ga Manabu Koto no Imi* (*Lifelong Learning and Social-Participation: The Meaning of Adult Learning*), University of Tokyo Press, 1998, p.7.

Chapter 3

The Socialization and Cultural Succession of Children in Mahallas

From the moment they are born, children in Uzbekistan experience various rites of passage and traditional festivals as they grow up. Most of these rituals are based on Islam.

For example, *sunnat toʻy*, the circumcision of Muslim boys living in mahallas are celebrated on a large-scale comparable to wedding ceremonies. Before and after a circumcision, relatives and neighbors are invited to a banquet and the whole mahalla is required to participate.[1] In their neighboring country Kazakhstan, circumcisions are performed for hygienic reasons, and this is considered to be an important ritual for boys to become Muslim men.[2]

As such, children grow up by undergoing a circumcision, a naming ceremony, an after-birth ceremony and many other rituals to become adults in their own rights. However, rituals such as the naming ceremony, *beshik toʻy* (a cradle ceremony), and circumcision are performed by the parents, relatives and the people in the community to wish the children healthy growth and a happy life. These rituals also act to maintain the social status within an area and are, therefore, "rituals dictated from above and given by adults". Obviously, there is no initiative by the children in these childhood rituals. As such, children grow up by participating in the rituals of their brothers, sisters, and the children of their relatives and neighbors, rather than by participating in their own rituals.

In contrast to these childhood rituals, the religious rituals and events such as weddings, funerals, *ramazan* (*ramazon*, ramadan), *ramazan hayit* (*ruza hayit*, post-ramadan festival) and *qoʻrbon hayit* (Feast of Sacrifice), are opportunities for children to learn the social and traditional customs of Islam voluntarily and independently. Children learn not only about their religious and traditional customs through these various rituals within the community, but also about appropriate rules and customs as well as how to relate to other children and adults.

The process of learning the social rules and values of one's own community and culture is called socialization, and the social structure, religious traditions, traditional culture and the natural environment have an enormous impact on the socialization process. In the communities of Uzbekistan, the socialization process of children is based on the religious traditions and unique culture of the country. In addition, the social structure centering on the mahalla affects important social and cultural factors and influences the socialization process of children.

Unlike with every day chores at home, the rules and values based on Islam have various social restrictions regarding gender, ethnicity, age and the time in which we live which more clearly manifest themselves in children's behaviors during these special times of rituals. At the same time, children's behaviors are also influenced by external factors such as the restriction placed on lavish feasts by order of the president, the introduction of ceremonies including circumcisions, *ramazan*, the spring festival *Navro'z*, and the traditional Uzbek wedding in mahalla into school education and children learn traditional culture, and the holding of meetings and summer courses to promote Cultural Revival by NGOs in Uzbekistan as part of the government's cultural and educational policies.

In the third Chapter, I would like to clarify the following points by considering the cultural and religious background, and the social structure, of Uzbekistan by discussing the different aspects of children's lives which are based on the traditional customs and Islam in a mahalla such as: (1) the process of socialization and cultural succession that children undergo especially at religious rituals such as *kelin salom* (bride's greeting), at *ramazan hayit* and *qo'rbon hayit*, (2) the mahalla's involvement in children's socialization and cultural succession through religious rituals.

Firstly in this Chapter, children's lives within a mahalla in Uzbekistan will be discussed over three time periods: the former being under Imperial Russian rule when the modern education system started to be supplemented by the informal education in a mahalla, then under the Soviet Union rule when the mahalla was used as a vehicle for building a socialist state, and lastly after independence was gained and the current state's reconstruction policy of emphasizing the role of the mahalla.

Secondly I will discuss the children's learning process through socialization and cultural succession in rituals such as *kelin salom*, *ramazan hayit* and *qo'rbon hayit*, which are mostly conducted in the same way and when friends and relatives are most likely to be in the area. This will be done through fieldwork at the time of *ramazan*, conducted in a family setting, in the city of Tashkent. I will also discuss how mahallas have become involved in each ritual.

Lastly, I will try to clarify how children's socialization and cultural succession are conducted in mahallas through these rituals, the role that mahallas play as a "supporter" and "intervener" in the process, and any future challenges and issues.

These rites of passage and the culture of Islamic culture will be the main part of this chapter, and will consist of case studies recorded mainly by Sukhareva, O.A. from the late 19th century and the early 20th century in Bukhara, case studies edited by Muminov on Samarkand, research conducted by Bendrikov, K.E. in the early 20th century on Tashkent, more up-to-date literature, participant observation of families and mahallas, and interviews.

The research method will be an analysis of this literature, interviews with members of a mahalla committee and other related groups, participant observation of religious rituals with families with children in elementary and lower secondary school, and interviews with parents.

1. Children's Life in Uzbekistan's Mahallas

In Uzbekistan, children are socialized through participation in activities organized and implemented by national educational institutions, such as kindergartens, elementary and secondary schools, various other social groups, and by their mahalla and home environment.

How the life of children in mahallas has changed over history will be reviewed here during three different time periods: (1) the time of Imperial Russia (1865- 1917), (2) the time of the Soviet Union (1917 – 1991) and (3) after the independence of Uzbekistan (1991 - present).

The word *Mahalla* is derived from Arabic meaning "a 'neighbourhood' type community based in an area", "a block of an 'Islamic city'" or "a community formed by settlers in the Central Asian region a long time ago and is a form of local government within a social structure" (refer to Introduction). Combined with these various definitions from past research, mahalla has been defined as a local community within the Muslim society of Central Asia, which is both closely attached to, and formed in relation to the roads which support the life of people.

After the demise of the USSR, and in order to break away from the ideology of communism and the state system of the former Soviet Union, a movement to return to traditional values of individual ethnicities was actively pursued. At the same time, government support for mahallas increased and the practice of using them as the base of a social government was strengthened.

Through the promotion and modernization of mahallas, they have re-emerged as an active support body to the state government.[3] In 2002, by order of the president, the government decided to name 2003 as the "Year of the Mahalla", and a campaign was waged to promote the importance of the mahalla with slogans such as "We were all born in a Mahalla" and "The Mahalla is our social and political mirror".[4]

Currently, a mahalla in Uzbekistan consists of public facilities including a mosque, schools, a multifunctional hall for residents' meetings, an office for the mahalla committee and representative, and as a place for weddings, funerals and the neighborhood watch; with the interaction of all families living in the mahalla. Under a government regulation, a mahalla is required to have more than 500 families. Mahalla representatives are elected and they receive an income from the government. They have various jobs including solving family feuds, restoring finances and securing support, operating and developing each facility within the mahalla. The configuration of the specific activities depends on the representative's experience and each family's situation.[5]

Structure of Mahalla (Local community in Uzbekistan)

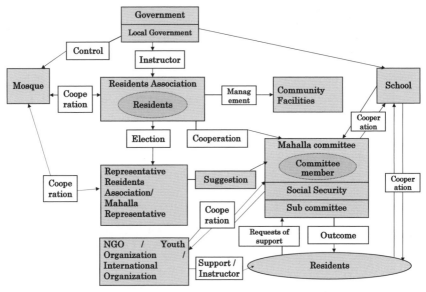

Figure 2 Structure of mahalla and organizations
Source: Timur Dadabaev, *Mahalla*, University of Tokyo Press, 2006, p.125. Depends on Dadabaev's research, author arranged figure.

For example, at the mahalla that the author visited, a mahalla representative was paying out of his own pocket to promote children's and young people's sports. He was so passionate that he said that "Sport is the essence of this mahalla". At another mahalla, a representative who used to teach Information Science and Information Technology at university had created a computer database of the mahalla's residents to

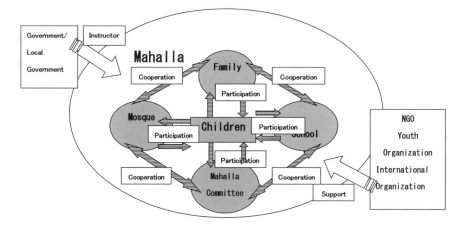

Figure 3 Correlation diagram of children in mahalla

be used for the mahalla's operation. In his database, he registered mahalla's and residents' data including the names of streets, number of households on the street, the head of family, family structure, name of residents, the date of residents' birth, sex, age and so on in detail.[6] Each representative made good use of their own specialties and skills for managing the mahalla.

Each mahalla has an active committee which carries out specific activities as an administrative body with sub committees that act beneath it. Sub committees such as "Ethics & Education", "Women" and "Social Service" implement various activities in their area of responsibility.[7]

In order to characterize the society and culture of mahallas, Dadabaev, T. who has been conducting empirical research on the mahallas in Uzbekistan, identified two factors: "Traditional Mahalla ('informal' human network)" and "'Formal' Mahalla".[8] He also points out that although mahallas during the time of the Soviet Union played a role in instilling a socialist ideology in their people, they also kept some traditional aspects from ancient times. Moreover, Komatsu, H. suggests that as well as maintaining these traditional aspects, a new aspect of mahallas to act as a bridge to receive support from international organizations and NGOs has emerged.[9] This is a common theory shared by researchers into the function of present day mahallas and can be seen in their writing and analysis of mahalla culture; this is also an important social/cultural factor for characterizing children's lives in mahallas during the times before the Russian Empire, under Soviet Union rule, and to the present day.

Following is a historical perspective on how children's rites of passage and lives have changed in mahallas within the contexts of Islamic traditions, culture, and the education system.

(1) Under Russian Empire Rule (1865-1917)

In the old days, people lived in small communities in cities and rural villages in Central Asia based on their occupation, ethnicity and religion.[10] For example, in the early 20th century in Bukhara, metal workers and body-washers lived together in their own areas and these areas served as both their residence as well as their place of business. These communities were called "Mahalla" in Tashkent and the Fergana region, and *"Guzar"* in Bukhara and Samarkand.[11] Each mahalla had a mosque/holy temple and people participated in rites of passage, weddings, and funerals within the mahalla to which they belonged, they also co-operated in the use of the local water well, and helped each other to create and maintain an awareness of being part of the same mahalla. When any trouble or arguments occurred within the mahalla, the mahalla's elderly, called *"oksokol"*, would act as mediators. As seen in Bukhara between the late 19th century and the early 20th century, these mahallas were important units to solve issues in people's lives.

Until the expansion of the education system under Russian Empire, boys' education was conducted at a *maktab* or *madrasa* attached to mosques[12] and girls' education was conducted at teachers' houses[13], and it consisted mainly of traditional education based on their religion. Islam at that time in Central Asia was greatly influencing the customs of families and the society, along with the adults' and children's interpretation of the world. 5 times-a-day prayers at the mosque in the mahalla were repeated in front of children and religious days were an opportunity to also clearly express the customs at home and in society.[14]

Boys went to the *maktab* for elementary education between the ages of 6 and 16 (or 5 and 15) and learned reading and writing as well as the disciplines based on the spirit of Islamic faith. Before the beginning of the Russian Empire's invasion into Central Asia in the late 19th century, there were *maktabs* in each local mahalla and *guzar* in Samarkand, as well as some *maktabs* for girls. The teachers at the *maktabs* were mostly *Imams* from the nearest mosque.[15] Bendrikov describes the relationship between teachers, pupils and families, and their activities in relation to religious days at *maktabs* at that time as follows:

On religious days, especially on boy's festival days of circumcision, teachers were given Muslim turbans, scarves and sometimes jackets by the pupils' parents. Because of this, most teachers taught the children of rich families with enthusiasm.[16]

Religious celebrations were held at *maktabs* and children did not have normal classes for the preparation.[17]

He also mentioned that meetings and debates with famous poets, scholars, and a comic group called "*Majilis*", were held at the *madrasas*, people's homes, shops, workshops and Bazaars.[18]

As such, children had the opportunity to learn within the mahalla about the rituals of praying at a mosque, the jobs associated with their mahalla, and about their ethnic heritage. By living in a mahalla, children were able to learn about the religions and occupations pertinent to their lives, as well as acquire knowledge about their ethnicity and gain a self-awareness of being a member of society. At that time, mahallas were places where informal education, as mentioned above, was constantly being implemented and mahallas played a role in supporting this learning. With the expansion of education at *maktabs* and *madrasas*, mahallas became places to support such informal education.

Under Russian Empire rule, mahallas came to be seen as places to support its governance at the grass-roots level. Education was being standardized and the first Russian co-education school was opened in Tashkent in 1866.[19] Also, in March 1871, a Tashkent merchant Seid-Azimbay Mukhammedbaev presented a report that criticized the existing *madrasas* and requested Kaufman, the Russian Turkestan general at that time, to open a new type of Muslim school. In response to Mukhammedbaev's plea, and in order to prepare for building a new school in the Ishankul *Madrasa*, Terenchieva, who was the captain of the cavalry became the chairperson in June 1871.[20]

As such, gradually before and after Imperial Russia, it was a time when children's learning within mahallas started to become formalized. During the rule of the Russian Empire, informal education at mahallas was continued, but with the standardization of education at *maktabs* and *madrasas* undergoing a change to be more in line with Imperial Russian-type public education, the differences between these three systems was becoming more apparent.

(2) Under the Soviet Union Rule (1917 – 1991)

Under the Soviet Union rule, the Soviet Union government attempted to use the traditional systems and function of mahallas to change the residents' way of thinking to be more "Soviet-ized" and socialistic in order to make them "Soviet citizens".[21]

As a specific example, there was a place called *choykhona* where people got together to prepare weddings and traditional festivals. It is known that the Soviet government changed the name from *choykhona* to "Red *choykhona*" to utilize this place as a means of deepening the understanding of the Soviet government.[22] In the book "*History of Samarkand*", edited by Muminov, it describes the situation that many school teachers participated in activities for fostering "Soviet citizens" as follows:

> Teachers from the Soviet devoted their energy and knowledge into educating future leaders of communism. Teachers provided highly-charged lessons at school and constantly endeavored to incite the general public at the "Red *choykhona*", clubs and mahallas. During the 1946 election of the Supreme Soviet of the Soviet Union, out of the 3,000 agitators[23] of Samarkand, approximately 500 were school teachers.[24]

From the above, it can be seen that school teachers were important members for the propaganda of communism and Soviet ideology. Teachers taught the idea of communism to children who would shoulder the future communism at school, and they propagated same idea in people out of school in places such as *choykhona*, clubs and mahalla. These activities attempted to disseminate the Soviet ideology and uplift the people's consciousness of being members of the Soviet Union, and finally the children and residents to be "Soviet citizens".

The book highlighted how farming and urban industry, cultural activities and education under the Soviet government, together with the activities of the scholars in Samarkand with Marxism-Leninism ideology, contributed to the modernization of Uzbekistan and reflected the policies and ideology of the communist party at that time. Although books like this were obviously a part of the political propaganda of the government, it is quite interesting to read in detail about the implementation of the national education policy, numbers of students, numbers of schools, and the advertizing activities at mahallas from the early Soviet time to 1960.

From books by Muminov and others, it can be seen how the responsibility to change people into "citizens" through the educational content, and traditional framework of mahallas was placed on them in order to modernize and "Soviet-ize" the people to assimilate the ideology of the Soviet government. At that time, unlike at the *maktabs*, *madrasas* or the Russian schools that were being expanded during the Imperial Russian rule, the mahallas became responsible for a new informal education.

Although the everyday informal education in the lives of the people continued, due to the standardization of an education system centered on the development of a school education, and the expansion of teachers' activities under Imperial Russia and the Soviet Union rules, the mahallas' role in education also began to contain more standardized components.

Due to the change in the social structure surrounding mahallas, the life of the children who resided there changed accordingly. During World War II, guidance divisions were established for evacuated children by committees at each level; community, city, state and republic. Also at the same time, orphanages and learning facilities for youth were established.[25] At that time, preschool education facilities were established and expanded, and kindergarten teachers contributed greatly by playing a key role in preschool education. In Samarkand, there were 2,435 children educated at 43 institutions in 1950, and by 1957 the number had increased to 3,823 children at 49 kindergartens.[26] Children lived the greater part of life in mahalla so far, after that they spent their time and learned in formal education institutions as place of formal education.

It was not only public education which affected children's lives greatly. Under the Soviet Union rule, extra-curricular activities were also being expanded, and social education facilities such as the *Pioneers* Palace became places for children's activities.

Tomiak, J. J. considers about youth organization in Soviet Union that "it is connected to extra-curricular activities of school, and organization's activities are integrated and come together with general education of youth".[27] In other word, he highlighted that youth education must be conducted not only at school, but organizational activities in society.

The youth organization of the Soviet Union consisted of *Oktyabryata* (October Children) for children under 10 years old which were derived from the Russian Revolution, *Pioneer* for children 10-15 years old, and *Komsomol* for young adults 15-28 years old. *Oktyabryata* is attached to each group of *Pioneer* which active in every school, and children of elementary school could affiliate. The main mission of *Oktyabryata* was to promote strong intentions like "I want to participate in *Pioneer*" in small children, and at same time, to be recognized in general provisions of action such as "*Oktyabryata* love school. *Oktyabryata* respect superiors. *Oktyabryata* work hard". Children who affiliated with *Oktyabryata* put on the badge uniform of the school, and went to the countryside. When they went on an excursion, the *Oktyabryata* group would hoist a small red flag. The responsible person of group of *Oktyabryata* group was a member of *Komsomol* or senior member of *Pioneer*.[28]

The official name of *Pioneer* was the All Soviet Union *Pioneer* organization named after Lenin. *Pioneer* conducted a variety of activities under the general instruction of the Soviet Communist Party as "a popular organization that children, as bearers of the state and society, receive the required preparatory education under the Soviet Communist Party's instruction".[29] Regarding the aim, *Pioneer* expressed "Spirituality of love and devotion for the homeland, friendship between other countries, fostering children through the spirituality of proletarian internationalism, subjective attitude towards learning, love of labor, development the spirit of inquiry of children, fostering children as being subjective, healthy, brave, joyous of life, never fearful of difficulties, and wholly developed individuals".[30]

Concrete activities of *Pioneer* were activities in hobby club and circle, sports, games, various competitive sports, festivals, exhibitions, participation in events, about three weeks of *Pioneer* camp during the summer holiday, participation in trips and excursions, performing theater and music concerts by children. In addition, supports for the elderly and sick people, work services for schools, cities and local communities are also promoted by the government. These activities were held in school, *Pioneer* Palace, *Pioneer* House, children engineer station, children natural scientist station, excursion and trip station, and the number of activities expanded eventually.[31] At the palace, children studied and also learned singing, dancing, sports and various other things. During summer holidays, children participated in a 3-week camp and learned about nature and how to work together with other children of the same age.

The beginning of the establishment of *Pioneer* was the resolution "Activities of Russia Young Communist League between children" which were carried out in the Third Conference in 1920, and the decision by Second All Russia Council of the Russia Young Communist League for the establishment of the *Pioneer* organization as an independent system on May 19, 1922.[32] At first, *Pioneer* had 4,000 members, however, this rose to 170,000 members in 1924, 4370,000 members in 1931, 13 million in 1949, 15 million in 1960, and finally 24 million in 1970. *Pioneer* developed into a huge organization, and Krupskaya, N. K, theoretically supervised *Pioneer* from the period of establishment. She highlighted not only school education, but education undertaken outside of school from perspective of guaranteeing the children's whole development. Krupskaya explained the fundamental idea regarding the establishment of *Pioneer* as follows bellow through letter to *Pioneer*s;

> I wrote a letter to *Komsomol* in January 1922. I indicated that *Komsomol* must put under control of *Komsomol* our children, boys and girls, support them to organize,

and foster them as thrifty successors. Boys and girls are not babies, they have sharp interests surrounding all things, they have substantial initiative, and they want to do physical and intellectual labor, I wrote. I indicated *Komsomol* has to learn to organize initiative, teach to children act friendly, conduct social activities and also work systematic in intellectual labor. I wrote they must educate children to be true Leninists.[33]

From the above, children's activities outside of school were organized systematically, from *Oktyabryata* to *Pioneer*, and on to *Komsomol*. Children participated in activities of *Oktyabryata* and contacted with *Pioneer* as leaders and youths of *Komsomol*, and children increased longing for *Pioneer* and *Komsomol* and senses of duty like "I want to be a member of *Pioneer* and *Komsomol*", "I want to take part in a variety of activities". Eventually, those children's consciousnesses were integrated into the homeland consciousness, patriotism and citizen awareness of a "Soviet Citizen".

The main difference in children's lives between the times of Soviet Union and Imperial Russian rule, was that under the Soviet Union, national and public development was extended to include children's activities outside of school. Until the time of Imperial Russian rule, the main focus was on the development of school education and the government did not intervene much into children's lives outside of school. However, under the Soviet Union rule, children's domains shifted from the mahallas and the traditional *choykhonas* to incorporate the Soviet's "Red *choykhonas*" and activities at the Pioneers Palace.

Specifically due to policies based on atheism, the education at mosques was reduced. Children under Soviet Union rule heard teachers talking about the ideology of communism at school, at the "Red *choykhonas*" within their mahallas after school, and during long holidays where they participated in activities at the Pioneers Palace.

In addition, the religious rituals and festivals such as circumcision, post-*ramazan* festivals, the Feast of Sacrifices, and traditional Uzbek weddings were either banned or restricted; instead, "*Komsomol* Weddings" or "Red Weddings" were introduced as "new rituals".[34] In the process of socialization, learning space which children could experience their own community's traditional culture and religious customs actively and passively changed drastically to introduce the Soviet's ideology and fostering of "Soviet Citizen". These strategies to change the people to be more "Soviet-ized" and become "Soviet citizens" with a socialist view became deeply rooted in children's everyday lives.

(3) After the Independence of Uzbekistan (1991 – present)

The factor which had the most impact on children's life after the independence of Uzbekistan was the great transformation of the education system and the curriculum. The school system was changed from an 11-year combined elementary/secondary schooling to a 12-year elementary/lower secondary/upper secondary separate schooling. Compulsory education is for 12 years and afterwards students can go to university by passing the entrance examinations. Skipping grades is also quite normal, and it is a special feature of education in Uzbekistan.

Regarding the language policy, Uzbek became the official language under the "National Language Law" in 1989, for new entrants at elementary schools in 1996, and the written form of Uzbek changed from the previous Cyrillic alphabet to the Latin script so that now almost all the textbooks at the elementary and secondary school level are written in the Latin alphabet. Reform in the school curriculum has proceeded and the Uzbek language became a compulsory subject in 1999. However, not all schools teach students in Uzbek. Many schools in the cities teach only in Russian and some teach in both Russian and Uzbek.

Due to this change in the writing system, a problem arose in that some students were unable to read the Cyrillic script which they needed for studying at university. Also, as most signs and billboards in the towns are still written in Cyrillic, this is causing a divide between people who can only read the Cyrillic script and people who can only read the Latin script.[35]

The aim of the classroom content to highlight the traditional Uzbek culture is prominent. As part of re-valuing their history, heroes, and traditional culture, oral literature such as the epic about the hero "*Alpamysh*", the history of the Amur/Timur Empires, using traditional musical instruments, playing traditional sports (*kurash*: the traditional sport of Uzbekistan which is similar to the Japanese *Sumo*), the role of mahallas and the spring festival *Navro'z* are taught in class.

One of the children's rites of passage, the cradle ceremony, is also included in a children's textbook. Children learn themes including "Family Tradition" and "Tradition – its Role in the Development of Nationalism and Patriotism".[36] Islam and courtesies are also taught at moral education.

After the independence of Uzbekistan, the unofficial activities of mahallas now included the spring festival *Navro'z*, "Memorial Day" (formerly Victory Day) (May 9), "Child Protection Day" (June 1) and "International Women's Day" (March 8); and many of these events are organized at the mahalla by the office of the mahalla committee and many children participate in them.[37] 2003 was declared as the "Year of the Mahalla" by the order of president and various traditional competitions were organized to mark this occasion.[38]

At this time, collaborative activities between mahallas and schools were encouraged by the government policy. For example, A school, a school in the Mirzo Ulugbek district, invited the mahalla's representative to the Constitution Memorial Day on December 8 to give a lecture on the theme of "Ideology – an unified national flag and society" in the lesson of the "Idea of National Independence".[39] Moreover, the mahallas' representatives participated in the school events during the "Foundation of National Independence' week".

Under Soviet Union rule, the existence and function of mahallas were almost ignored, but after independence of the state was gained, they were re-born as the base on which to build a new nation, and they were believed to play an important role in children's education. Cultural and educational activities conducted by the former Soviet Union government, such as the ones at the *Pioneer*s Palace, were shifted to the mahallas and other NGOs;[40] and instead of following the ideology of the former Soviet Union, the "Idea of National Independence" is now taught to children by mahallas.

Recently, the ties between schools, family and the mahalla are actively, and strongly, promoted,[41] and the mahallas support, and become involved in, school education more often. Thus, how do children acquire sociability and cultural succession within mahallas?

2. Children's Rites of Passage and Islam

In this Section, I will discuss children's rites of passage and the involvement of Islam and the mahalla.

Rituals conducted at each milestone in life, such as births/naming/entrance into a school/coming of age/employment/weddings/death, take on a different role and meaning based on country, ethnicity or regional area. At each ritual, a change in the position or status of the person who undergoes the ritual is apparent. The meanings of the rituals are very diverse in every country, ethnicity, area and religion; however, rituals concerning turning points of life are conducted under similar conditions in every society. The rite of passage is conducted in a spatial passage by transfer from a space to another space according to the growth process of humans and marriage etc., and the changing of lifestyle, and the shift from religious groups or secular groups to other groups. Furthermore, in the rite of passage, it is clearly displayed what kind of position or standpoint the object person shifted; which role he/she got.

For example, at the cradle ceremony at the birth of a baby is recognized by the surrounding people to be a part of their society. At the celebration of circumcision, a boy becomes a Muslim man through the act of this ceremony. At a wedding ceremony, man and woman building a family is announced to those around them, and is confirmed legally. In *kelin salom*, conducted after a wedding ceremony, the woman gets a marriage transfer to her new place of residence is showed impressive. At a funeral, the people acknowledge the person's transition from the living to the dead, and through all of these traditional rituals a strong Islamic background is demonstrated.

In Uzbekistan, these rites and rituals are an important opportunity for establishing personal connections. Exchanging presents, sharing food together and supporting each other at these rituals creates the basis of forming social networks. For example, the Uzbeks have formed a reciprocal arrangement of exchanging presents with their extended family and neighbors within their mahallas.[42] The following is a discussion about children's socialization and the cultural succession that occurs at mahallas, with first-hand examples witnessed at *ramazan hayit*, a *kelin salom* and at a *qo'rbon hayit*.

The *kelin salom* ceremony is the greeting of a bride, and from the morning after her wedding female relatives on the groom's side get together to inspect the new bride who has joined their mahalla. At the ritual, also called the "Tour to inspect the bride", the bride is required to wear a veil, bow three times and give a welcome speech. After three bows, the bride offers tea and sweets and entertains the guests. Today more families celebrate *kelin salom* either on the day after the wedding or on a religious day such as a *ramazan hayit* or *qo'rbon hayit*.[43]

In this Chapter, I will review children's socialization and cultural succession through the observation of the *sunnat to'y*, the circumcision, the celebration of *ramazan* by a family in Tashkent as well as at a *kelin salom* ceremony at *ramazan* or a *ramazan hayit*.

(1) The Circumcision Ceremony

Most of rites of passage and traditional festivals are base on the religion in which the ethnic group believes. Uzbekistan is consists of over 156 ethnic groups and the customs surrounding children are very diverse. From the moment they are born, children in Uzbekistan experience various rites of passage and traditional festivals as they grow up. Most of these rituals are based on Islam.

For example, the circumcision of Muslim boys living in mahallas is celebrated on a large-scale comparable to wedding ceremonies. Before and after a circumcision, relatives and neighbors are invited to a banquet and the whole mahalla is required to participate. Mahalla residents also support by preparing for the banquet, helping clean and receiving guests.[44]

In Uzbekistan, the *sunnat to'y* conducted by the head of the house after a circumcision (*sunnat*) is as important as the ceremony of a wedding (*to'yi*). Circumcisions are conducted on boys in most Muslim houses and these days the best age for one is said to be 3, 5 or 7.[45] For religious reasons, women cannot enter a room where *sunnat to'y* is being conducted; therefore the author analyzed video recorded about *sunnat to'y*.

At the house that the author observed, the extended family and the residents of the mahalla were first invited to the house and served with tea, sweets and fruits. After a while, a *Murrah* (an Islamic clergyman) and an *Imam* went into the room where the circumcision was to be conducted and explained the procedure to the father. Women were not allowed to enter the room.

A few minutes later, a boy of three who was receiving the circumcision that day was carried into the room. The boy, who had no idea what was going to happen to him, was put on the bed without anything on his lower body. His legs were crossed and his hands were held down at the top of his head. While the father and male relatives were watching, the *Murrah* started a prayer and after the area was sterilized, the circumcision was conducted. At the same time, the boy started crying hysterically with pain. All the adults in attendance were holding the other children down so that they would not stand up or romp around. They were trying to calm the child down. After the circumcision, an Uzbek hat called a *Doppi* was placed on the site with a towel on top of it. The relatives handed money to the still crying boy. The boy took the money, but did not stop crying. While crying, he kept receiving and throwing the money and/or staring at them. The father and the relatives were all smiling and telling him things such as "Oh, you can now buy a bicycle with the money that everyone has given to you", and tried to calm him down.[46]

A post-circumcision celebration is held after the boy's incision has healed. Although the size of the celebration varies depending on the financial situation and social status of each family, since circumcisions were officially endorsed at the end of the 1980s they have been getting more luxurious. The day before the celebration, the extended family and the residents in the mahalla gather to have a meeting about cooking, the preparation of the place, and how to respond to visitors. A professional emcee or singers are invited to perform and the guests spend their time eating, drinking and dancing. These celebrations require a large sum of money, but normally the money and presents that the host receives covers the cost, and even leaves some profit.[47]

For rites of passage such as the above mentioned circumcisions, there is of course, no initiative or self-motivation because the recipients are too young. Most boys do not remember the event or only remember the pain. The childhood rites of passage such as circumcisions and the cradle ceremony are rituals performed by adults for children and the active engagement of children at these rituals hardly ever occurs.

As such, boys grow up by undergoing a circumcision, a naming ceremony, an after-birth ceremony and many other rituals to become adults in their own rights. However, rituals such as the naming ceremony and *beshik toʻy* (a cradle ceremony), and circumcisions are performed by the parents, relatives and people in the community to wish for healthy growth and a happy life for the children. As mentioned previously, these rituals also act to maintain the social status within an area and are, therefore, "rituals dictated from above and given by adults".

Boys learn the religious meaning and procedure of circumcisions as they grow up to be adults through participating in the rituals of their brothers, or the sons of their relatives and neighbors, rather than through the participation in their own circumcisions and these are "rituals dictated from above and given by adults". Typically in Uzbekistan, circumcisions on girls are not common, so the acquisition of this religious tradition for girls is by learning about it from their brothers or boys living in the same mahalla.

(2) Rites of Passage of Children and the Mahallas

For a large-scale celebration such as the above mentioned circumcisions, the co-operation and support from the residents of the mahalla is essential. The family and relatives of the boy to be circumcised can not undertake the whole organizing of this celebration by themselves; as this includes inviting a *Murrah* and an *Imam* from the same mahalla to visit, preparing and cleaning up afterwards, and cooking a large amount of *plov* (see footnote #52 in Chapter 2) to be served on the morning of the celebration. Therefore, before and after a celebration, the mahalla committee organizes some meetings between the residents of the mahalla and the family to discuss the preparation.

Thus, the children are socialized in the ways of relating to other people and the rules and customs of their mahalla by directly watching the residents helping each other. The mahallas are the place for children to become, through these rites of passage, socialized in order to continue to live in society as well as acquire their religious traditions.

Sumida, M. indicates the importance of the local community for children's development and character formation as bellow.

Family is a destined group which children cannot choose, however children cannot chose their local community neither. Parents decide the residential area the residence for their work place, etc. They may consider the residence for children's education, but it is the parent's intention, and there is no children's contention for the selection of resident area. Local Community also destined area for children. Children's way of life and chances in life are different depending on fostering in a city or farm area, traditional area or unsettled area, and consequently children's thinking are fundamentally limited and different.[48]

From Sumida's indication, children's growth and character formation in Uzbekistan are influenced by which mahalla child was born, what kind of relationship is established between mahalla residents, and how the mahalla committee and mahalla residents contact children.

However, the role of the mahalla committee is not just in supporting its residents. The committee also helps families who cannot afford to have a ceremony, and for this purpose it also limits the number of people who can hold a lavish feast. This is so that all the families can have a similar degree of celebration.[49] Moreover, the local government gives instruction on how to conduct a celebration by convening the representatives of the mahallas and supporting them. Subsequently, the mahalla's representatives take back these instructions to their own mahallas and inform their residents.

So, how should we view the actions of the mahalla committees and local governments? From one point of view, mahalla committees and the local government support families in mahalla, especially young families who haven't conducted rituals. However, after carefully reviewing the religious and educational/cultural policies of the current government, we get the impression that the Uzbekistan government is trying to control the Islamic rituals such as circumcisions through the supervision of the mahallas. On the other hand it is also important to note, that by encouraging these rites and rituals in order to restore "religion as culture", the government is trying to break away from the old system of the Soviet Union and raise cultural awareness in the people.

On the face of it, the restoration of the traditional culture with Islam at its center is the goal of the intervention of the mahallas and government in the children's rites of passage. However, behind this context we can see the government's intentions to prevent the uprising of any anti-government religious groups and the establishment of restoration of religious ritual as symbol of ethnic culture and national identity. In the context of identity politics, mahalla is "supporter" for ritual and "intervener" at the same time.

3. Becoming Socialized through Ceremonies and Rituals Conducted at Mahallas

In this Section, I will discuss how socialization occurs through ceremonies and rituals held at mahallas through the examples of *kelin salom* at *ramazan*, and the mahalla's role as a "supporter" and "intervener".

Here, I will review children's socialization and cultural succession using examples of the ceremonies of *kelin salom* at a *ramazan hayit* and a *qo'rbon hayit* at an urban mahalla (Yunusabad district of Tashkent City), and at a rural mahalla (Kibray district of Tashkent region).

(1) Weddings and Funerals and the Mahallas

Unlike rituals such as the naming ceremony and circumcision which are conducted when the child is very young, other religious rituals such as weddings, funerals, *hayit* and *ramazan* are good opportunities for children to become socialized, and learn traditional customs and Islam voluntarily and independently.

The mahalla committee and residents provide support, funds, equipment (chairs, desks, tableware and cooking utensils) and facilities at rituals such as weddings. At the marriage ceremony conducted at either the bride or groom's family home before the wedding reception, many residents play an important role in welcoming guests from outside of the mahalla, preparing food and organizing the ceremony.

On the other hand, funerals are organized by the elders of the mahalla and the cost is also paid through the elders. Many men carry the body together to the burial site and the full participation of the mahalla's residents is necessary. As described later, at *hayit*, a religious service is conducted to honor the memory of the people who died in that year and to pray for them; and the support of the residents from each mahalla is essential in this case also.

Through participating in these rituals at their mahallas, children learn not only about their religious and traditional customs, but also about the appropriate rules and customs in society and how to relate to other children and adults.

The process of learning the social rules and values of our own community and culture is called socialization, and the social structure, religious traditions, traditional culture and the natural environment have an enormous impact on the socialization process. In the communities of Uzbekistan, the socialization process of children relies greatly on the religious traditions of their own culture. In addition, the social and cultural factors of a mahalla, which is at the center of the social structure, can affect the socialization process of children and influence the way children are reared.

(2) *Ramazan* and the Mahallas — through the Fieldwork with a Family in Tashkent City

The ninth month in the Islamic calendar[50] is the month of fasting called *Ramazan* (Ramadan), and various customs can be seen during that time. The author visited a family with a son in Year 10 of upper secondary school and a son in Year 5 of lower secondary school when *ramazan* was just about to finish and *ramazan hayit* was soon to commence.

The lady-of-the-house, who had invited the author, was Mrs. A (assumed name) who is in her 30s, lives in Tashkent and works in the mornings as a clerk at a university. The family consisted of four people, the father, the mother (Mrs. A), and the two boys mentioned above. They live in a 9-story apartment building in the old part of Tashkent city. Their apartment used to be two separate ones, but is being renovated into one and has many rooms. Half of the renovations were complete, and the other half were still underway. The furniture and electrical appliances looked expensive and they had a large car, so the family must be quite wealthy by Uzbekistan standards. They use Uzbek within the family, but the father, mother and oldest son seemed to use different languages depending on the visitors.

Mrs. A is a type of person – called "Russian Uzbek" – who smokes cigarettes, normally banned during *ramazan*, without showing any signs of remorse. According to her, *ramazan* does not mean that she is not allowed to smoke, but rather it is the time that "she does not need to hide her smoking because her husband goes to pray at the mosque every night and is not at home to check on her". Even though her family is strict in disciplining their children, and fasting during the day is strictly followed. During *ramazan*, all of the family, including the children, faithfully fasted without even drinking water. "It is easier when *ramazan* falls in winter because the days are shorter and not too hot. When it falls in summer, it is hard. The days are longer and you feel like drinking water because of the heat. You know, we are not allowed to drink water during *ramazan*" said Mrs. A describing the hardships of *ramazan*.

During *ramazan* Mrs. A and the family got up at 4am, had breakfast and prayed, then had nothing to eat or drink until sun set. When the author visited them, there was tea, fruit, water, *nisholda* (a starch-syrup like sweet made from egg whites and sugar) and bread called *Nan* on the table, but no one was eating any of it. They were all quietly waiting until the sun set.

After 6 pm, the father started a short prayer and the boys listened to him quietly. After the prayer, they all sipped water, then started to eat some fruit or something natural. That was followed by tea and *nan* with *nisholda*. Then the mother brought in *plov*. When the food that they usually ate came to the table, the tension of *ramazan* eased and they all enjoyed their dinner.

At around 8 pm, the father went to the mosque in the mahalla for night-long prayers. Some children also go to the mosque and their youngest son received phone calls from his friends, and some even came to the doorstep to ask him out. Although her son wanted to go to the mosque, his mother said "He is too young" and did not let him go. The son looked sad about the fact that he was the only one who could not go to the mosque.[51]

In this way, children learn about their religion and culture based on Islam by praying and fasting together with their parents everyday during *ramazan*. Every morning and evening, listening to parents' pray, children learn about the Koran and learn what they are allowed to eat as the first thing after fasting and the reason why they have such customs with their parents acting as role models. Although the sons at this family did not go, some boys get together at the mosque to watch the religious rituals and learn Islam, as well as learn how to relate to people, and the rules and customs that govern children's and adults' society within the mahalla.

The mosque specifically provides an important opportunity for children to learn about the Islamic principles regarding gender roles and different ethnic groups, since it is the place where only men go to pray, and it is also the place where different Central Asian ethnicities who believe in the same religion assemble; although these public rituals only became possible after independence. Therefore, the practice of *ramazan* at the mahalla is not only a place to acquire the religious and traditional customs, but is also a place full of opportunities for children's socialization.

The following is a discussion about the *kelin salom* at an after-*ramazan* celebration, *ramazan hayit*, and a *qo'rbon hayit*.

Photo 6 *Nisholda* is sold at a bazaar during *ramazan*.
(Photo is taken by the author in September 2008).

Photo 7 The number of children who go to mosque has been increasing in Uzbekistan after independence.
(Photo is taken by the author in July 2008).

(3) Religious Rituals and the Mahallas – through the Observation of *kelin salom* at 2 *hayi*ts

A few days after my visit at *ramazan*, a post-*ramazan* celebration of *ramazan hayit* was held. The family where I observed a *ramazan hayit* was a family of 5: the father, the mother, a son and two daughters, who live in an apartment on the fifth floor of a block in the Yunusabad district of Tashkent City. The mother, Mrs. B (assumed name), who invited the author to her place, is an experienced professor at a university, she is in her late-40s, and teaches Russian and Uzbek languages.[52]

As I mentioned before, *kelin salom* is quite often held at a *ramazan hayit,* and a newly married couple in Mrs. B's mahalla was having a *kelin salom* ceremony at their house. Excluding her oldest son who said that "Old men do not go to *kelin salom*", Mrs. B, her younger daughter and I, that is all the females present, visited the house for the *kelin salom* ceremony. When we entered the room where the bride was sitting, she was wearing a veil with gold decorations and was welcoming the guests by bowing. She had to bow three times per each guest and was even bowing to small children. After that, the bride served tea or juice and offered sweets. On the table there were a large cake with a doll of a bride wearing a wedding dress on top and some fruit.

As the guests came in, the bride repeated the bowing. There was a mother with two baby girls and two young boys. Whenever an old woman came in, everyone in the room stood up and addressed the woman, and the two boys went up to the woman and greeted her. Every time a new guest came in, a short prayer, to which the boys were listening to quietly with their hands put together in front of their chests, was repeated in front of the children. During a conversation after a prayer, an old lady was telling the boys "Say 'Thank you' when someone gives you a drink or passes sweets to you".

The *kelin salom* ceremony not only happens at *ramazan hayit.* At the Islamic feast of sacrifice of *qo'rbon hayit*[53], many newly married couples celebrate *kelin salom.* At the house that the author visited with a teacher who teaches at an academic lyceum, the bride of their son had married in autumn and was holding a *kelin salom* ceremony.[54]

After a while, six children of elementary school age - four girls and two boys - of their neighbours visited the bride. Wearing a white lacy veil, the bride bowed three times to the children. They were quietly watching the bride without moving. After the three bows, the bride served tea to the children. They quietly received the tea and drunk it together with some sweets.

Among the people sitting there, the most senior lady in her 20s led the conversation and asked the children questions such as "Which grade are you in?", "How are your mother and father?" The children answered each question slowly. During that time, the bride kept pouring tea for the children if they ran out of drink. When the conversation finished, the oldest lady chanted a prayer and the guests all left.

Upon returning to the teacher's house, the two-year old girl who had been there with us toddled towards a lace curtain, put it on her head and mimicked what the bride had been doing at *kelin salom.* When her grandmother and mother said "Well done! A good bride. *Kelin salom*! *Kelin salom*!", the girl started bowing. Therefore, *kelin salom,*

Photo 8 *Kelin salom* ceremony is repeated systematically in front of children.
Veiled bride bowed three times to the children.
(Photo is taken by the author in December 2007).

Photo 9 The girl used curtains instead of a veil and copied the bride of *kelin salom*.
Kelin salom also has an effect on the child as a process of being socialized.
(Photo is taken by the author in December 2007).

which had been repeated in front of the children, had had an obvious impact on the two-year-old in the form of an initial socialization process.[55]

Observing the relationship between the bride, the children, and the female guests at *kelin salom*, there is a similarity to the example of praying at mosques. The bride and female guests had the responsibility to be experienced role models to convey their religious and traditional customs to the children who participated in *kelin salom*, and the children were the active recipients. Also, this is the time to restore religious rituals which had been restricted under Soviet Union rule, and to consolidate the collective consciousness "we-feeling" of Central Asian ethnicities such as the Uzbeks who believe in Islam by looking at the prayers at mosque during *ramazan* and *kelin salom* at the two *hayits*.

Meanwhile, the government is trying to control the Islamic faith at mahallas by appointing *Murrah*s at the administrative level. Currently, in order to work as a *Murrah* in a mahalla, they are required to attend a training course and gain a certificate of completion. Also, mahalla representatives have an obligation to contact the district administration department regularly about their own mahallas and participate in meetings, therefore it can be seen that the state, through these district administrative departments, can have control over each mahalla.[56] In 1998, the presidential order for a "Ban on lavish weddings and celebrations" was enacted and various restrictions were applied to people's religious rites and rituals.

At the same time as these policies, there are now more families giving money to the newly married to buy a refrigerator, other electrical appliances or take a honeymoon trip instead of paying for a *kelin salom* ceremony, and more young couples prefer it that way. "Gorgeous *hayit* food only lasts a day, but a refrigerator lasts and is more useful for a long time" being the main reason. Also, there are more modern Uzbek families who serve food for *kelin salom* on individual plates in a European style instead of spreading it out on the table.[57]

The above mentioned Mrs. B, who invited the author to the *ramazan hayit*, says that "Traditional culture is important, but some young people today do not think that way. Times always change. My older daughter prefers food for a *kelin salom* ceremony at a *hayit* over getting a refrigerator because it only happens once in a lifetime". Therefore, due to the government's cultural and religious policies and the modernization of people's lives, the religious rituals in Uzbekistan are changing.

Conclusion

From observing children's behaviors at rituals in mahallas in present day Uzbekistan, it became clear that they are learning the rules and values based on the religion of Islam through these religious rituals regarding gender, ethnicity, age and the time in which we live. Religious rituals such as prayers in a mosque during *ramazan*, at *kelin salom* at each *hayit*, were conducted not only by the family and their relatives, but also with all the residents in the mahalla. Therefore, children experience socialization and cultural succession both actively and passively by learning the rules and values of the society they live in.

In contrast however, it can also be said that learning by children in such ceremonies is bound by social restrictions such as gender, ethnicity, age, and the post-Soviet era, and all are rooted in Islam. At rituals at a mosque or *kelin salom*, people are expected to play their roles as determined by their gender, ethnicity, or age and Muslims now live in an era in which the restoration of religious rituals has become possible, unlike during the time of Soviet Union rule. These various rituals are often seen as religious folk traditions.

The intention of the government to promote the cultural growth of its citizens can be seen in the current policies on culture, religion and education.

Mahalla may be seen as a "supporter" of these rituals in the lives as children. For example, if a family is too poor to finance a circumcision or a wedding themselves, the government will offer financial assistance to the family and use representatives within the mahalla to teach the family how to conduct a circumcision.

On the other hand, the mahalla can be seen as being an "intervener" who reflects the government's intentions. For example, a family who is planning on having a lavish party may receive instructions on its size and budget to ensure that no prominent parties are held within a mahalla. This can be seen as the mahalla "intervening" in religious rituals and the children's socializing process and cultural succession through these rituals. The same thing can be said of the state's management of *Mullahs* and mahallas, and the introduction of religious rituals into school education.

In the background, we can get a glimpse of the government's policies towards citizen development which are based on Islam and their intention to unite the nation. The government is aiming to suppress the rise in radical religions such as Islamic fundamentalism by allowing religions of a moderate nature, by uniting all Central Asian ethnicities to continue to build a state. In this sense, Islam in present day

Uzbekistan is a religion which is "traditional in form but state-led in content", by which the reproduction of the collective consciousness of people of Uzbekisan is encouraged. In this way these complicated issues in relation to the nation and rituals, and the nation and religions can be embraced.

In this Chapter, the main focus has been on rituals and the traditional customs based on Islam. However, the multi-ethnic state Uzbekistan has many non-Islamic traditions and rituals, and together with these customs and rituals, including the spring festival called *Navro'z* and the custom of *yolka* (*ёлка*, Christmas tree), a new-year event started after the time of the Soviet Union rule, are considered to have an impact on children's socialization and cultural succession. It is important to look at all these customs, together with the nation's policies, and address further research towards the issue of children's life, socialization and cultural succession in mahallas in Uzbekistan.

Notes

[1] Timur Dadabaev, *Mahalla no Jitsuzo: Chuou Ajia Shakai no Dentou to Henyou (Mahalla)*, University of Tokyo Press, 2006, p.99.
[2] Toko Fujimoto, "Kazakhstan/Kodomo no seichou girei ni miru Islam (Kazakhstan/Islam through Rite for Children's Growth)", *Ajiken World Trends*, No.85, 2002, p.18.
[3] Timur Dadabaev, *op. cit.*, 2006, p.29.
[4] Massicard, Elise, Trevisani, Tommaso, "The Uzbek Mahalla", *Central Asia: Aspects of Transition*, edited by Tom Everett-Heath, 2003, London, p.206.
[5] Timur Dadabaev, *op. cit.*, 2006, p.9, 232, 242.
[6] Information from interview with representative of A mahalla (March 10, 2007).
[7] Timur Dadabaev, *op. cit.*, 2006, p.125., Information from interview with the chair of women's committee of G mahalla (April 15, 2006) and interview with the former representative of A mahalla (April 26, 2006).
[8] Timur Dadabaev, *op. cit.*, 2006, p.103.
[9] Hisao Komatsu, "Mahalla", Hisao Komatsu, Hiroshi Umemura, Tomohiko Uyama, Chika Obiya, Toru Horikawa, eds., *Chuou Yurashia wo Shiru Jiten (Cyclopedia of Central Eurasia)*, Heibon-sha, Japan, 2005, p.484. For details, see Coudouel, Aline, Marnie, Sheila, Micklewright, John, "Targeting Social Assistance in a Transition Economy: The Mahallas in Uzbekistan", Occasional Papers Economic and Social Policy Series EPS63, UNICEF, 1998.
[10] Timur Dadabaev, *op. cit.*, 2006, pp.49-50. Sukhareva, O.A., *Bukhara XIX-nachalo XXv*, Moskva: Nauka, 1966, s.325-326.
[11] The origin and the formation process of mahalla have various opinions and theories. A study regarding Uighur children's development indicates "Residence area of kin expanded and became a mahalla" (Rizwan Ablimit, "Uighur no kodomo no hattatsu ni okeru mahalla (chiiki kyoudoutai) no yakuwari (The Role of the *Mahalla* in the Development of Uighur Children)", The Japanese Society of Life Needs Experience Learning, *Seikatsu Taiken Gakushu Kenkyu (The Journal of Life Needs Experience Learning)*, Vol.1, 2001, p.40), other research argues "Thick irrigation canal ramified small canal, and house called *uy* gathered and formed a mahalla (Yasushi Sanada, "Toshi・Nouson・Yuboku (City, Village, Nomadism)", Tsugutaka

Sato eds., *Kouza Islam 3 Islam ·Shakai no Shisutemu (Lectures on Islam 3 Islam and Social System)*, Chikuma Shobo, 1986, pp.116-117).

[12] *Madrasa* are traditional education facilities in Islam which existed in the 20th century in Northeast Iran. *Madrasa* is property of the *Waqf* (donation system of Islam for benevolence) which consist of only private property, and has the character of a private school. Firstly, students learn the alphabet of Arabic language, after mastering the Arabic language, they start learning ethics. Finally, they aim to learn *Fiqh* (Islamic law, i.e. *sharia*). Hisao Komatsu, Hiroshi Umemura, Tomohiko Uyama, Chika Obiya, Toru Horikawa, eds., *op. cit.* 2005, p.479, 483.

[13] Bendrikov, K.E., *Ocherki po istorii narodnogo obrazovaniya v Turkestane (1865-1924gg.)*, Moskva: Akademiya Pedagogicheskih Nauk RSFSR, 1960, s.27-60. Also, see Shoshana Keller, "Going to School in Uzbekistan", Jeff Sahadeo, Russell Zanca eds., *Everyday Life in Central Asia: Past and Present*, Indiana University Press, 2007, pp.250-254.

[14] Tam zhe, 1960, s.28.

[15] Muminov, I.M. i dr, *Istoriya Samarkanda*, Tom pervyi, Tashkent: Fan, 1969, s.293.

[16] Bendrikov, K.E., *op. cit.*, 1960, s.41.

[17] Tam zhe, 1960, s.41-42.

[18] Muminov, I.M. i dr, *op. cit.*, 1969, s.290.

[19] Bendrikov, K.E., *op. cit.*, 1960, s.61.

[20] Tam zhe, 1960, s.69-70.

[21] Timur Dadabaev, "Chuou ajia shokoku no gendaika ni okeru dentouteki chiiki shakai no arikata to yakuwari — Uzbekistan no 'mahalla' wo chushin ni (The Ideal Existence and Roles of the Traditional Local Community in the Modernization of Central Asian Countries: Focusing on 'mahalla' of Uzbekistan)", *Toyo Bunka Kenkyusho Kiyou (The Memoirs of the Institute for Advanced Studies on Asia)*, Vol.146, 2004, pp.257-258.

[22] Timur Dadabaev, same as above, 2004, p.259.

[23] Agitator means those who are activists and instigators, and they broaden communism and Soviet ideology people.

[24] Muminov, I.M. i dr, *op. cit.*, 1969, s.292.

[25] Tam zhe, 1969, s.227.

[26] Tam zhe, 1969, s.295.

[27] Tomiak, J.J., *Soviet no Gakkou (Schools of Soviet)*, Meiji Tosho, 1976, p.98.

[28] Tomiak, J.J., *op. cit.*, 1976, pp.98-99.

[29] Shiro Murayama, *Natsuyasumi Seikatsu Gakkou —Pioneer Kyanpu no 1 Kagetsu (Summer Vacation Living School-One Month in Pioneer Camp)*, Minshusha, 1979, p.152.

[30] Tomiak, J.J., *op. cit.*, 1976, p.100.

[31] Tomiak, J.J., *op. cit.*, 1976, p.101. For example, there were 3,148 in the Pioneer Palace, Pioneer House and Pupil's House, 348 in the Children engineer station and 272 in the children natural scientist station in 1960. After that, the number of these facilities increased as 3,781 in the Pioneer Place, Pioneer House and Pupil's House, 553 in the Children engineer station and 327 in the children natural scientist station in 1969. Tomiak, J.J., *op. cit.*, 1976, p.101.

[32] Shiro Murayama, *op. cit.*, 1979, p.152.

[33] Shiro Murayama, *op. cit.*, 1979, p.154.

[34] Timur Dadabaev, *op. cit.*, 2006, p.69. Instead of a traditional wedding, young people wear a suit and wedding dress, sit next to each other, and conduct the wedding ceremony.

[35] For instance, the poster for candidate of president and the canvassing of voting the Election of the President of the Republic of Uzbekistan, which was held on December 23, 2007, were wrote in the Cyrillic alphabet.

[36] Kostetsukii, V. A., *Azbuka etiki 4 klass*, Tashkent: Natsional'noe obshchestvo filosofov

Uzbekistana, 2007, s.87., Kostetsukii, V. A., Mametova, G. U., Mal'kumova, L. A., Sergeeva, H.I., *Chuvstvo rodiny 6 klass*, Tashkent: Yangiyul polygraph service, 2007, s.51-52.

[37] Information obtained through interview with a representative and former representative of A mahalla (April 26, 2006, March 10, 2007, May 4, 2007), Information obtained through interview with the adviser of the women's committee of G mahalla (April 15, 2006), and with former representative of O mahalla (June 7, 2007), JICA Senior Volunteer (March 19, 2007).

[38] O'zbekiston Mahalla xayryya jamg'armasi, *Mahalla*, Toshkent, 2003, b.200-236.

[39] Internal materials of A school in Mirzo Ulugbek district, Tashkent City. Information obtained through interview with a vice-principal of A school (Mach 10, 2006).

[40] For example, courses and international conferences for fostering ethics, spirituality, traditional culture, patriotism, citizen awareness of youth organized by various youth organization and NGOs in current Uzbekistan. Information obtained through interview with the head of "Spirituality and Education (*Ma'naviyat va Marifat*)" Tashkent department, (December 13, 2007), interview with the director of international relations and public affairs division of *Kamolot* (January 7, 2008), interview with the director of the Independent Institute for Monitoring the Formation of a Civil Society in Uzbekistan (February 20, 2008). In addition, a member of an assembly of the legislation side mentioned a method for the fostering of public spirit, traditional culture, patriotism of children and youth; 1) enriched ethic subject in school education; 2) promotion of participation of children and youth in traditional festival. Information obtained through interview with a Senator who belonged in committee of Senator for issue of science, education, culture, sports (February 19, 2008).

[41] O'zbekiston Respublikasi xalq Ta'limi Vazirligi, Yo'ldoshev, H. Q., *Barkamol avlodni tarbiyalashda oila, mahalla, maktab hamkorligi kontseptsiyasi*, Toshkent, 2004, b.7.

[42] According to Hiwatari, a private mutual aid which not concerned with kin relationships, territory of mahalla residents to be meaningful for residents. Masato Hiwatari, *Kanshu Keizai to Shijou ·Kaihatsu—Uzbekistan no Kyoudoutai ni Miru Kinou to Kouzou (The Customary Economy and Economic Development: The Community-based Structure of a Mahalla in Uzbekistan)*, University of Tokyo Press, 2008, p.125.

[43] Information obtained through participatory observation at a family of Yunusabad district (October 13, 2007), participatory observation at a family of U mahalla, Kibray district, Tashkent region (December 19, 2007).

[44] Timur Dadabaev, *op. cit.*, 2006, p.99.

[45] Hisao Komatsu, Hiroshi Umemura, Tomohiko Uyama, Chika Obiya, Toru Horikawa, eds., *op. cit.*, 2005, p.268.

[46] Information obtained through a video which recorded *sunnat to'y* at a family in Tashkent City (November 22, 2007 watched).

[47] Hisao Komatsu, Hiroshi Umemura, Tomohiko Uyama, Chika Obiya, Toru Horikawa, eds., *op. cit.*, 2005, p.268.

[48] Masaki Sumida eds., *Kodomo to Chiiki Shakai (Children and Local Community)*, Gakubunsha, 2010, p.5.

[49] Information obtained through interviews with staff of the local government of Yunusabad district, Tashkent City (December 11, 2007). According to interview, the local government supported 7 poor family's *sunnat to'y* in the district in 2007. In addition, economical and human support for wedding ceremony are conducted.

[50] Basically, the month of *ramazan* is shifted every year, and *ramazan* was conducted in October in 2007 when the author observed.

[51] Information obtained through participatory observation at a family of S mahalla in Shaykhontohr district (October 8, 2007).

[52] Information obtained through participatory observation at a family in Yunusabad district (October 13, 2007). Participation in kelin salom as foreigner was very welcomed by family of

Uzbekistan, furthermore, it was very important opportunities for grasp of feature of *kelin salom*. In addition, author could meaningful compare with ritual time and family's conversation after rituals.

[53] *Hayit (iid)* is Islamic two big festivals. A festival of *Eid ul-Fitr* (in Uzbekistan *ramazan Hayit*) after ramadan is celebrated in the Islamic world during 1st to 3rd of Shawwal month. Oher festival *Eid ul-Adha* (in Uzbekistan *qo'rbon hayit*) is conducted for four days during 10-13 of *Dhu al-Hijjah* month of pilgrimage month. The 10th day is last day of pilgrimage of Mecca, and each family slaughter sacrifice for festival in Islamic world. During festival, people wear their best clothes and go out, visit kin, each other, and celebrate each other. Nihon Islam Kyokai , *Islam Jiten (Encyclopedia of Islam)*, Heibonsha, 1982, pp.98-99.

[54] Information obtained through participatory observation at *kelin salom* in U mahalla in Kibray district, Tashkent region (December 19, 2007).

[55] Basically, socialization divided into that first socialization up to learn language, and second socialization after learning language. First socialization as a basic socialization step is to listen, read and write a language which is used in the society. First socialization indicates the lower grades of elementary school, from around 6-8 years.

[56] Iwane Takahashi, *Uzbekistan Minzoku ·Rekishi ·Kokka (Uzbekistan Nation ·History ·State)*, Soudosha, 2005, p.148.

[57] Information obtained through participatory observation of a Family in the Yunusabad district (October 13, 2007).

Chapter 4

Mahalla in School Education

Uzbekistan, which consists of various ethnicities, cultures, and religions, has been tackling the issue of "how to get out of the Soviet Union and proceed with national integration, forming a new nation and maintaining it" since their independence after the dissolution of the Soviet Union. It became their priority to put the system of the new nation into its course, eliminate the worries and dissatisfaction of the citizens during the system change, and enhance the centripetal force of the nation. In the education reform, they had the formation of national identity of "Uzbekistan citizen" through Uzbek language and ethnic culture in 4-5-3 school system with common curriculum throughout the nation and rapid promotion of next generation fostering represented in "National Programme for Personnel Training (NPPT)".[1]

In the present, however, they are starting to have various issues with "national construction from above" such as problems of the suppressed ethnic cultures and identities of people other than Uzbek, regional differences and a lack of the human resource development in upper secondary and higher education institutions.

In this situation, mahalla, which is the traditional local community in Uzbekistan, was implemented in the school education. Mahalla is a "traditional space" where ritual and traditional culture exists, "fundamental space for national integration" centering on the core of the home town, as well as a "space for mutual help" where neighbors help each other and do community work. So, the government is focusing on those functions. History and traditional culture of mahalla is restored and abstract love for the hometown is mature in mahalla. Mutual assistance is done beyond the wall of ethnicity and it can assist socially vulnerable people, such as poor families and senior citizens, leading the nation toward integration. Also, it allows them to appeal the modernism in the new system after independence such as the mahalla committee and social security system in the traditional mutual help in mahalla. Therefore, Ministry of Public Education recently established the ministerial ordinance concept "Cooperation among families, mahalla, and school in the mature generation's development" and promoting cooperation among each organization.[2]

In Chapter 4, I will clarify the following after discussing the actual situation of the implementation of mahalla in school education based on the affairs of Uzbekistan.
1) What the background and purposes of implementing mahalla in school education are.

2) How mahalla is treated in school education. 3) How the function of being the "space for mutual assistance" of mahalla is related to national integration.

Previously, the focus was on the educational aspect of mahalla, the elements of informal education such as rites of passage, religious events, and interactions between different age groups. For example, Ablimit researches on mahalla in Xinjiang Uyghur Autonomous Region, China pointed out that mahalla provides a place to play for children and children relate to others through playing and develop sociability such as skills in human relations. Also for the relationship between mahalla and schools, it was mentioned that they digest and practice the knowledge they learned in school at mahalla and that the educational function and school education have a relationship of mutual supplementation.[3]

However, these are from the point of view of mahalla; for what purpose mahalla is implemented in the school education and how they are treated. In other words, the position of mahalla in the education policy of the nation has not been discussed thus far.

Analysis of mahalla in school education discussed in this chapter is not only for suggesting the new aspects of mahalla, but also allows the discussion of modern issues that show how the multi-ethnicity of Uzbekistan and the locality of Central Asia is reflected on the public education in the nation.

1. School System of Uzbekistan and Educational Reform after the Independence

In Section 1, I will focus on the educational reform that is promoted as one of the important issues in the current Uzbekistan.

(1) Switching from Old 11-year Education to 12-year Compulsory Education

The educational reforms taken right after independence in 1991 were the establishment of a new curriculum, development and implementation of textbooks, revision of educational methods, and the implementation of a certification and authentication system for educational institutions. Right after independence, the Law of Education (Law of the Republic of Uzbekistan "On Education" July, 1992)[4] was established, giving a legal foundation for the promotion of these educational reforms. Here, they aimed for the construction of a new school educational system through the reforms mentioned above.

They also aimed at the establishment of new educational institutions such as "kindergarten-school complex" where pre-school educational facilities are attached to elementary and general secondary educational schools as well as "Gymnasiums" and "Lyceums", which are elementary and general secondary educational schools that provide special education for the gifted.[5] Also for higher education institutions, such as universities, they revised the old Soviet system that they only receive diploma instead of a degree at the graduation. They moved to a system where internationally recognized degrees, such as the bachelor's degree, are given.

However, educational reform at the time of independence was going along with the educational policy of *Perestroika* promoted by the Soviet government toward the end of 80s. It was not too different from educational reform done by other newly independent nations.[6]

The educational system at the time of independence was that compulsory education included elementary and lower secondary education. However, children who started school at 6 years old attended compulsory education for 9 years where as children who start school at 7, which was more common, attended compulsory education for 8 years. So, the duration of compulsory education was not consistent.

This issue of entry at 6 years old was pointed out around the end of the Soviet period and an example of this issue was reported as follows.

In 1986 and 87, facilities that started entry at 6 years old were not sufficiently prepared, so only one third of the children at that age started school. According to the report by Shcherbakov, among the new first graders who started, 35.5% and 26% of 6-year-olds learned at school and 10% learned at pre-school education facilities. For this problem, the regional difference was quite significant and it was especially delayed in Uzbekistan, Tajikistan, Turkmenistan in Central Asia, Armenia and Azerbaijan along the Black sea and the Caspian Sea. Improvement of the educational conditions, mainly improving the facilities and equipment, were in demand. The improvement of pre-school education was also an issue along with the entrance of 6-year-olds. A "Kindergarten education and motivation program" was composed recently by the Uzbekistan Academy of Sciences, Scientific-Research Institute of Pedagogical Sciences in order to improve the educational content and method. Based on this, they are planning to focus on the creativity of the children as well as aiming for a balanced education starting this year. At the same time, they have a plan to increase the facility and by 1990, facilities for 4.4 million students will be finished.[7]

As it was mentioned, the problem of 6 years old entrance is yet to be solved after going through the Soviet period, the dissolution of Soviet Union, and independence.

And this issue is creating not only the difference in academic abilities among children, but also regional difference in education between the urban and rural areas.

For example, regardless of the fact that it is a compulsory education, there is a large difference for the duration education in urban and rural areas. In urban areas, it is standard to have integrated education of 10 to 11 years from elementary, secondary, and general education, but in rural areas, it was only 3 to 4 years of elementary education or lower secondary education which totaled 8 to 9 years.[8]

In order to solve the problem that was mentioned above at the time of independence, a new education law, which was revised from the education law established in 1992, was established in September 1997. This law determined that they use 12 years of compulsory education consisting of 9 years of elementary and lower secondary education in addition to the 3 years of upper secondary education.

For the pre-school education, it is following a program for preparing students for school effectively, as well as offering spiritual and ethical education. Pre-school education generally starts from 3 to 6 years old either at home or in kindergarten. The government policy that aims to promote the cooperation of family, education facility, and local community promotes a kindergarten network which is based on families and programs that connect kindergarten and general secondary education smoothly, such as "From kindergarten to school", are also expanding nationwide.

Furthermore, 250,000 children every year learn at the special center, prep group in kindergarten, and weekend schools, and many youth organizations, NGOs, and NPOs are active in teaching children foreign language, music, art, and computer skills.[9]

Elementary education is the first grade through fourth grade, starting at either 6 or 7 years old. The lower secondary education starts at 10 to 11 years old and is from 5th grade to 9th grade. As it was mentioned earlier, the upper secondary education, which is 3 years, was implemented when the education law was revised in 1997, so a 12 year compulsory education system was established by law.

In this new system, 4 years of elementary education and 5 years of the lower secondary education is common curriculum, but 3 years of the upper secondary education is divided into academic lyceum, which is a course for students who wish to go to university, and professional college courses.

About 10% of the students choose academic lyceums and they are set up as an attached facility to a comprehensive university where students learn specialized subjects. For example, in the academic lyceum called the Yunusabad Lyceum, attached to Tashkent State Institute of Oriental Studies, has an international relations department, international economics department, and literature department. Students learn math and biology in the first and second years, but after the third year, they emphasize more on language such as Japanese, Korean, and Arabic, which is the main reason for entering the institute.[10]

On the other hand, professional college, where 90% of students go, mainly focuses on training for workers in the actual production. Vocational technical schools and secondary specialized schools are planned to move into professional college.

As it shows, policy that was "making a single-track from secondary education to higher education by integrating the upper secondary education to higher education (connecting high school and college/university)" allows students to receive specialized education of their choice from early on, but also limits their opportunities to learn a wide variety of areas that they may be interested in.

The completion goal for 12 years compulsory education was postponed from 2005 to 2009. According to the then manager of the Tashkent department of Public Education, Tashkent was at the last stage of the transition from a 11 year compulsory education to a 12 year compulsory education, and there are 43 schools in the city with students who received 11 years of compulsory education in the old school system. There was no 10th grader in the old system, and it is transitioning to elementary education (1st to 4th grade), lower secondary education (5th to 9th grade), and the upper secondary education (10th to 12th grade). Tashkent was planning on making the transition to the new school system with from 2007 to 2008.[11] However, in some local areas, the transition to the new system after the revision of the education law in 1997 from the system they used at the time of independence was still continuing.

Higher education usually starts at 18 to 19 years old, and they are divided into two levels; bachelor's and master's. Bachelor's (*bakalavr*) is the first stage of the higher education which continues for over 4 years, and is given when they graduate higher education and specialized education. Master's is a specialized higher education for master's program (*magistratura*) that is based on the master's degree. The degree is given after the national examination and a research report. Doctorate candidates (*aspirantura*) must do a maximum of 3 years of research. Furthermore, in order to receive a doctorate (*doktorantura*), they have to do 3 more years of research.

Higher education of Uzbekistan consists of a total of 75 institutions, 19 universities and 37 institutes, 2 academy, 11 branches of uzbek HEIs and 6 branches of foreign universities.[12] Close to 200,000 students learned and 18,500 teachers worked in the higher education institutions in 2003.[13]

What is the educational principle of the government that makes such rapid educational reform? *Idea of Nation Independence* mainly edited from the writing of

President Karimov has items on education and training, and it mentions 5 challenges in the future.[14]

> 1) Social evaluation of the citizen for the foundation of general learning is done by establishing an effective method and procedure of an independent nation to every citizen's consciousness.
> 2) Continuous activities of character formation in children and students for the ideology and principles of the independent nation is communicated in the basis of "National Programme for Personnel Training" (NPPT).
> 3) The ideology, contents and real nature of independence is deeply reflected in the learning program, textbooks, and teaching materials.
> 4) Demand of ideology education from the people must be brought up to the modern standard in schools, academic lyceums, professional colleges, institutes, and universities.
> 5) Knowledge in the educational field can be broadened regarding the issue of ideology.

In the five challenges mentioned above, the word "ideology" was repeated multiple times. It means that there is a strong emphasis that education, the framework of the character formation of children and youth, must have the ideology of national independence. In other words, they are getting out of the Soviet and old basis for the educational system, and expanding to a new education principle and system. However, when we look at what the ideology of the independent nation is, it shows that the definition of ideology itself is not strictly indicated in the educational principles; the educational principle of the nation is very vague and is not clearly stated.

Currently, countries in Central Asia such as Uzbekistan, Kazakhstan, and Kyrgyz are conducting educational reform while staying away from the education model of the old Soviet Union, but their national budget is getting worse as the economic situation declined after independence. As it got worse, the budget for the education has been decreasing and the quality and quantity of education is getting low.

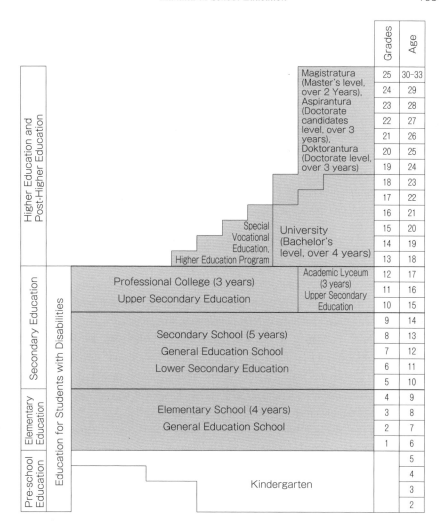

Figure 4　System of Education in Uzbekistan

Source: *Ta'lim taraqqieti 2 maxsus son*, Toshkent: Sharq, 1999, *O'rta maxsus, kac'-hunar ta'limining umumta'lim fanlari davlat ta'lim standartlari va o'quv dasturlari*, Toshkent: Sharq, 2001, Tukhliev, Nurislom, Krementsova, Alla, eds., *The Republic of UZBEKISTAN*, Tashkent, 2003, Japan International Cooperation Agency (JICA), *Central Asia (Uzbekistan, Kazakhstan, Kyrgyz) Report of Research Group on Aid, Present Data Analysis*, Part II Uzbekistan, Chapter 9 Education, 2001, p.55.

(2) Educational Reform with the "National Programme for Personnel Training (NPPT)"

After independence in 1991, their economy was slowly changed to a market economy mainly by President Karimov instead of rapid marketing and democratization in Uzbekistan. During this process, they aimed for the human resources training which corresponds to the national construction and market economy after independence. Because of this, they aimed to train elites, such as government officials and executives of corporations. These elites are required to share in the awareness of the nation and citizens as well as have their own specialized knowledge.

The background of training the elites who will be in charge of the future of the government is an unexpected aftershock of independence after the dissolution of the Soviet Union. During the Soviet period, the people who had a large portion of the governmental power in the Uzbek Soviet Socialist Republic (Uzbek SSR) were Russians who were dispatched from the Soviet central government. Most of the foreign affairs, legislations, and foreign related economies were ruled by the central government in Moscow. In the level of Uzbekistan government, how loyally they could respond to the directions and orders from the central government was emphasized.

Since such a governmental system was established in Uzbekistan, all those national functions mentioned above must be done by the Uzbekistan government after independence. It was the same for educational administration such as legislation for educational policy. Because of such drastic social changes, it was an urgent matter to train elites that would be in charge of the governmental situation.

However, it was not just the training of a few elites that Uzbekistan had to do. They also had to train the general population who support them and actually work in the field. So, the academic lyceums had the function of training the elites and the professional colleges were expected to train the general population.

Also, the reason for implementing "National Programme for Personnel Training" (NPPT) was not only to train political elite and citizen training. After independence, Uzbekistan was phasing into market economy from the planned economy during the Soviet period. In this situation, they were required to train people with knowledge of the market economy and market, language ability to negotiate with foreign countries, and knowledge of technology such as high-tech device and computer for corresponding with internet. These are some of the reasons for the national program.

The then Minister of the Public Education, Ministry of Public Education of the Republic of Uzbekistan mentioned how the education should be for children during such a reform period.

Education for children must be a free compulsory education, and the national education standard and program must correspond to the development of the students. The relationship with the students must be sincere and it must be guaranteed that education is provided by experienced educators. In classrooms, it is necessary to have an interactive teaching method between students and teachers. It is also essential to have services that correspond to the need of everyone. I know there is regional difference in education because I have lived in rural areas due to my father's job as well as Tashkent. However, there are universities in those areas and people can study. Now, universities in rural areas are developed so there are people who get their bachelor's degrees in those universities and then learn the master's and doctorate in Tashkent. It is true that in the urban areas such as Tashkent have various facilities and are convenient, but instead, children in rural areas seem to be more motivated and spiritually strong.[15]

The minister mentioned the regional difference in education, but it is more severe than how he mentioned it. For example, during the harvesting season of cotton, children in rural areas are used as helpers in the field and schools are closed during that period so they can pick cotton. Furthermore, children are forced to stay overnight to pick cotton when they are in the lower years of their secondary education. During the framing season in spring, children are treated as valuable labor force and have them help farming. Children in Tashkent study for 9 months from September 2nd to May 25th the following year, whereas children in rural area are picking cotton and farming most of that time.[16]

Also, the rate of students in the academic lyceums and professional colleges mentioned before is quite different in urban and rural areas. In summary, about 10% of the students in the upper secondary education in Uzbekistan attend academic lyceum and the rest of the 90% attend the professional college to train human resources that work in the actual job scenes. Although we have to consider the population difference in urban are and rural area, it is general that most of the students go to a professional college in rural area compared to those of Tashkent.

For example, the number of academic lyceums and professional colleges is significantly different in regions. Professional colleges are located throughout Uzbekistan but academic lyceums, which is a university advancement course, is only located in 1 to 3 schools of rural cities other than Tashkent. Samarkand, which is the second biggest city in Uzbekistan, has 25 professional colleges but only 2 academic lyceums. Compared to Samarkand, there are 25 professional colleges and 18 academic lyceums in the capital Tashkent.[17] The regional difference is significant not only in the number of schools, but also in staff, materials, and educational budget.

Relating to the regional difference in education, this impressive answer came back from the librarian in a city library in rural area when I asked if there is master's and doctorate programs in the university in this town: "Master's and doctorate program? It isn't necessary. Bachelor's is enough".[18]

In present Uzbekistan, the regional difference in education mentioned above is becoming a big hindrance in various scenes, such as job opportunities and limited access to higher education. In order to solve the problem of regional differences in education, not only school education, but also cooperation between family education and social education as well as the cooperation among school, families, and local society is required to supplement what is lacking in school. Instead of the fixed conception of education where "education is done in school", they need to emphasize a more fluid educational role where families and local communities other than schools and tackle the problems that are common in all three. In other words, the transition to cooperation between school and society as well as a unified system are necessary and desired.

2. The Political and Social Background of Implementing Mahalla in School Education: "From a Strong State to a Strong Civil Society", Mahalla as a Social Foundation

In Section 2, I will discuss political and social background for implementing mahalla, mainly, the government policy that emphasizes on mahalla.

It is common between the Soviet period and the present after independence that the Soviet and Uzbekistan governments used mahalla to form "Soviet citizens" or "Uzbekistan citizens". However, what is clearly different between the Soviet period and the present is whether they deny the traditional part of mahalla. During the Soviet period, the government's view was that the traditional culture and the education provided there was behind the times, even though they used the mahalla system.[19] The Soviet government promoted the integration of the nation and formation of "Soviet citizens" by denying the traditional aspects and pre-modern parts of mahalla and emphasizing the modern and advanced national system of the Soviet Union.

On the other hand, the Uzbekistan government after independence emphasizes the traditional functions of mahalla as being part of forming "Uzbekistan citizens" by ethnic culture and national integration policy. Furthermore, we cannot forget that they are putting forward new governmental functions that are mentioned in the following.

First, in order to get out of the Soviet system, they separated the Soviet and Russian culture from the culture of Central Asian ethnicities, mainly Turkic and Persian. Why do they focus on cultures that are common in the ethnicities of Central Asia instead of culture unique to Uzbek people? It is because, until the national delimitation in Central Asia in 1924[20], the ethnic consciousnesses between the ethnicities were not so clear, and even now, various ethnicities are living in a mix. Also, Karakalpakstan, which is in Uzbekistan, has a different ethnicity. Because of these complicated issues, they cannot emphasize solely on the culture and values of the Uzbek people.[21]

Next, after making the ethnicities of Central Asia and Uzbek people vague, they diffused the governmental framework of the newly independent nation to the country and integrated the citizens. Mahalla is a local community that exists in Muslim societies, not only in Uzbekistan, and it has been pointed out that they exist in Tajikistan, which is a neighboring nation. They first bunched the ethnicities of Central Asia, many of which are Muslim, with the common core value of mahalla. Next, they would diffuse the policy for the citizens through mahalla committee and Fund "Mahalla". Mahalla was an excellent vehicle for getting out of the Soviet system, integrating the ethnicities of Central Asia in Uzbekistan, and expanding the new national system under the name of "restoration of ethnical culture".

In the background of implementing mahalla in school education, there was an intent to diffuse the traditional aspects of mahalla and political aspects after independence mentioned above to students.

3. Mahalla's Image in School Education and Principles

In Section 3, I will analyze what kind of mahalla images and principles are shown in school education using the concept related to the "National Standard of Uzbekistan".

(1) The National Standard of Uzbekistan: A National System of Continuing Education Standard of Uzbekistan

Here, I will first discuss the position of mahalla in the "National Standard of Uzbekistan", the national system of continuing education standards of Uzbekistan (hereinafter referred as the national standard) that was established by the Ministry of Higher and Secondary Specialized Education for academic lyceums and professional colleges, which are the upper secondary education. In the subject of "Foundation of

Spirituality", mahalla is taught to the students as "spirituality of the environment of mahalla and family; foundation of the national development". In the national standard, mahalla is described as the following.

> Residential formation that integrates the residents is basically similar to the labor union. To be specific, *Aul* (village) for livestock farmer, *Qishloq* (village) for farmers, *Shahar* (town) for handicraftsmen, and mahalla are the examples. This is historically unique to Uzbekistan, and it is influencing the residential formation and concept of the citizenry. Mahalla has solidarity through the interaction of people, and it is the same for the eastern spirit. It is most emphasized to follow the community and *oqsoqol* (elder). The common saying "Mahalla is a father and mother", "For one child, 7 mahallas will be the father and mother" shows the true nature of mahalla. Because of independence, a wonderful solidarity of leading and managing residents by mahalla is functioning.[22]

In the national standard, eastern aspects of mahalla are emphasized, and this "eastern spirit" is considered to have the same meaning as culture and identities that are common in the ethnicities of Central Asia mentioned before. Emphasizing the same aspects is linked to the removal of the soviet system and the solidarity of the Central Asian ethnicities, and also enhancing national awareness of "the Uzbekistan nation as a member of Central Asia".

This point is seen in the textbook as well as the national standard. In the textbook for the upper secondary education, it mentioned the part of national standard that says "Mahalla has solidarity through the interaction of people, and it is the same for the eastern spirit. It is most emphasized to follow the community and *oqsoqol* ".[23]

Furthermore, it is characteristic that the policy of enhancing the governmental function of mahalla after independence is indicated directly in the national standard. As the core of mahalla in the country, the government established Fund "Mahalla" by order of the president, but the national standard mentions the Fund "Mahalla" as well. Textbooks also deal with Fund "Mahalla", and the history textbook mentions the activity of Fund "Mahalla".[24]

Based on these, the following three points can be considered as the view of mahalla from the government in the national standard. 1) Mahalla as a "traditional space" that has eastern aspects which are common in the ethnicities of Central Asia linking to the cultural restoration of Uzbekistan. 2) Mahalla as a "basic space for citizen integration" that was given a new governmental function which makes it become the foundation of the independent nation. 3) Mahalla as a "space for mutual assistance" shown in the two common sayings "Mahalla is a father and mother" and "For one child, 7 mahallas will be the father and mother", which has the meaning that "Children of mahalla will be raised by the whole mahalla". Based on the mahalla view mentioned above, the government formalized mahalla as the end unit of the governmental system with the related law and mahalla committee from the traditional mahalla that had neighboring relationship and activities, and implemented them in school education.

(2) Concept of "Cooperation Among Families, Mahalla, and School in the Mature Generation's Development"

For what purpose is mahalla implemented in the current school education and how are they treated? The concept of "Cooperation among families, mahalla, and school in the mature generation's development", the purpose of the implementation is mentioned that "the basic purpose of the concept is to complete the activity of national ideology education for the citizens. In the concept, it mentions the necessity to indicate the challenges for families, mahalla, and schools, enhancing the cooperative activities among families, mahalla, and school for the education for students, and to establish the system to do so".[25]

"National ideology education" mentioned here indicates ethics education and ideology classes such as "the idea of national independence". Also, the goal of mahalla is indicated as "to reflect the socio-economical view from the nation to school in order to nurture strong students and children".[26] It means that mahalla is viewed to have a supplemental role to formal schooling, such as teaching children about the nation of Uzbekistan and development of attitude as citizens. Therefore, it was implemented to school education as a channel to diffuse the policies for education and social security. It was expressed vividly in the official report on the school events in the year of 2005 to 2006 in "families, mahalla, school" for A school, which is an integrated school of elementary, lower secondary, and upper secondary education located in Mirzo Ulugbek district.

For the monthly open school, we invited representatives of the mahalla committee and educational organization. The class leader had the activities to discuss the problem of mahalla, school, and families. We conducted a joint research of minors and the market in the district relating to theft by minors without notice. In three mahallas, sporting events were held on "Fighting AIDS day", December 1st. As a support activity, winter clothes were donated to poor families. On "the day to recognize people with

> disabilities", December 3rd, students went to people with disabilities, and gave presents and assistance. Students participated in *hashar* (mutual assistance) in mahalla located in the school district. In class, on "Constitution day", December 8th, the representative of the mahalla committee was invited.[27]

It shows various events are held with mahalla and strength of influence of mahalla personnel. In order to diffuse the policy, mahalla was implemented to school education as a channel that has the reality of being the children's living area.

4. The Actual Situation and Significance of Implementation of Mahalla in School Education

In Section 4, I will analyze the actual situation and significance of implementation of mahalla in school education based on participatory observation in class and school events. As a summary, I will clarify what issues are still left in the implementation of mahalla in school and its advantages.

Photo 10 A school in Mirzo Ulugbek district in Tashkent, a research subject. (Photo was taken by the author in March 2006)

As pre-research, I visited mahallas in two cities and conducted interviews with mahalla committee members on educational activities in mahalla and cooperation with schools. At U mahalla located in the center of Tashkent, I participated in making *Sumalak* for the traditional festival of *Navro'z*, to be mentioned later, and found out how citizens participate and work with the mahalla committee as well as the residents' attitude of mahalla via interviews and participatory observation. Also at Z mahalla located in Angren, Tashkent Region, I visited the office of the mahalla committee and interviewed the representative of mahalla about the daily work of mahalla and how the residents are, as well as the cooperation situation with schools. Based on the interview, it became clear that level of residents' participation in events held by mahalla and cooperative activities with the school have to deal with the ethnical element. The results of these interviews are the opinions and impressions of the mahalla representative, executives of mahalla committee, and residents who are actively participating in the events, so this cannot directly reflect the public opinion of mahalla and image of what people expect in the educational role of mahalla. However, it gave a large index in constructing a hypothesis for this research and selecting the mahalla and school. Based on the pre-research mentioned above, the following hypothesis and research topics were brought up.

(1) It is natural to teach the traditional culture of the Uzbek people in schools that are taught in the Uzbek language, but would it cause some type of contradiction when teaching Uzbek culture in schools that are taught in other language? For example, schools taught in Russian, which is the second most common after the Uzbek language, how are they teaching the Uzbek culture such as mahalla?
(2) Are the cooperative activities of mahalla and school influenced by ethnic factors to some degree? In a mahalla that has both Russian and Uzbek schools, is there a difference in cooperation between them?

For these two points, I will conduct research on how they select schools that use language other than the Uzbek language in Tashkent, how mahalla is treated in those schools, and how they conduct cooperative activities between mahalla and school.

In current Uzbekistan, it is determined by law that school is taught in one of seven languages. According to the Ministry of Public Education details on the seven languages are indicated in Table 3.

The numerical value shows that the majority, 90%, of schools use the Uzbek language. However, in order to illustrate the hypothesis (1) and the research topic, I selected the Russian schools, which are the next largest number of schools following the Uzbek language schools. Also, to discuss the hypothesis (2) and the research topic, I selected a mahalla that is located in the school district of both Russian and Uzbek language schools. Among the schools and mahallas that satisfy the conditions mentioned above, Russian schools (herein after referred as A schools), A mahalla, and G mahalla in Mirzo Ulugbek district in Tashkent were selected for research and analysis was done based on the results.

Table 3 Language used in class for general secondary school

Uzbek language	8,867 schools (90%)
Russian language	739 schools (7.6%)
Kazakh language	505 schools (5.1%)
Karakalpak language	383 schools (3.9%)
Tajik language	267 schools (2.7%)
Kyrgyz language	62 schools (0.6%)
Turkmen language	50 schools (0.5%)
Total	9,765 schools

Source: Ministry of Public Education material (the year of 2007 to 2008)

Table 4 Implementation system of mahalla in Uzbekistan school education

Stage of education	Applicable subject
Elementary education (4 years)	Field of study: Ethics Study subject: Moral lesson
Lower secondary education (5 years)	Field of study: Ethics Study subject: Moral lesson, Homeland Consciousness, Idea of National Independence and Foundation of Spirituality
Upper secondary education (2/3 years)	Field of study: General education Study subject: History of Uzbekistan, Foundation of Spirituality

Source: *Ta'lim taraqqieti 2 maxsus son*, Toshkent: Sharq, 1999, b.10-13., *O'rta maxsus, kac'-hunar ta'limining umumta'lim fanlari davlat ta'lim standartlari va o'quv dasturlari*, Toshkent: Sharq, 2001, b.20-22.

This is a residential area reconstructed after a large earthquake in 1966, and little over 1,000 students are enrolled in A school. It is an integrated school with 11 years of elementary, lower secondary, and upper secondary education inherited from the ol Soviet school education system. It was mentioned earlier that schools in Uzbekistan are in transition from an 11 year system to a 12 year system, and this school was still in the process of transitioning to 12 years. The lessons are taught in Russian, but students in this school are from various ethnic backgrounds such as Russian, Uzbek, Korean, Tajik, and Tatar.[28] This school was selected as the research subject because it is considered to be the best environment to analyze how mahalla is taught to Uzbek people and other ethnicities without attaching too much importance to Uzbek people and Muslim culture. Also, it was an important factor that this school is in contract with three mahallas, G mahalla, B mahalla, and A mahalla on educational activities, sports, cultural activities, school events, and responding to students who display problem behaviors.[29]

(1) **Mahalla in Classes**

Here, I will clarify how they treat mahalla in classes based mainly on textbooks for history and "Foundation of Spirituality", the national standard, reports written by students after the lesson, internal materials for school, and interviews with members of the mahalla committee and teachers.

Table 5 Hours of instruction by subject of general education in academic lyceums and professional colleges

Subject	Total time/ year	Academic Lyceum			Professional College		
Grade		1st year	2nd year	3rd year	1st year	2nd year	3rd year
Speech Culture and Language	80			80		40	40
Native Language and Literature	120	120			80	40	
Foreign Languages	160	80	80		80	40	40
Russian (Uzbek)	120	80	40		80	40	
History	160	80	80		80	60	20

Individuals and Society	40			40			40
Math	200	120	80		80	60	60
Information	120	80	40		80	40	
Physics	160	100	60		80	80	
Astronomy	40			40			40
Chemistry	80	80			80		
Biology	80	80			80		
Economy and Geography	40	40			40		
Enlisting Preparation	140		60	80		70	70
P.E. (Physical Education)	160	80	40	40	80	40	40
Information Technology	40			40		20	20
Foundation of the State and Laws	80		80				80
Foundation of Spirituality	40	40			40		
Family Psychology	40			40			40
Art	40	40			40		
Total	1,940	1,160	420	360	920	530	490

Source: Composed by the author based on *O'rta maxsus, Kac'hunar* ta'*limining umnmta'lim fanlari devlat ta'lim standartlari va o'quv dasturlari,* Toshken: Sharq, 2001, b.20-22. Also, total time for the 1st and 2nd year in an academic lyceum is different than the material, but the author calculated based on the number indicated in the original document.

Table 6 List of themes for "Foundation of Spirituality" class in upper secondary education

Theme	Time	
	(Lessons) Theory/Practice	Total
1. Introduction "Foundation of Spirituality", concept, and structure	2/1	3
2. Spirituality-Development of humanism, spiritual heritage, value, their forms and mutual relationship	2/2	4
3. Religion and spirituality, spiritual completion and problem of people for the studies in Islam and Sufism	2/2	4
4. Political life of the society, ideology and spirituality	2/1	3
5. Spirituality and economy, their mutual relationship, maintenance of social life development	2/2	4
6. Spirituality and education, selection of knowledge and special art-the human condition	2/1	3
7. Love for humanity, Patriotism and peace-basic index of individual spirituality	2/2	4
8. Nature, humanity and spirituality	2/1	3
9. Environment of mahalla and spirituality of the family-foundation of national development	2/1	3
10. External and internal spirituality in the individual and mutual relationship	2/1	3
11. Ceremony-reflection of spirituality of the nation and individuals	2/1	3
12. Conclusion, duty of the individual citizens in a nation that is gaining independence	2/1	3
Total:	24/12 [*sic*]	40

Source: Composed by the author based on *O'rta maxsus, Kac'hunar ta'limining umnmta'lim fanlari devlat ta'lim standartlari va o'quv dasturlari*, Toshken: Sharq, 2001, b.212. Also, the total time for (lessons) theory/practice is inconsistent, but it indicates the original document of the national standard that was issued by the Ministry of Higher and Secondary Specialized Education.

As it was indicated in Table 4, mahalla was defined as "it is necessary to support families who do not have sufficient living in the new social security system after independence"[30] in Uzbekistan history, and taught as such to students. Mahalla is under the guidance of the local government and benefits have been given through mahalla to socially vulnerable people since 1994 and children since 1997. They also teach such governmental aspects of mahalla in Uzbekistan history. Also, mahalla is taught in "the principles of the independent nation and the foundation of ethics". This subject is taught once a week in 7th, 8th, and 9th grade in the lower secondary education so, over the three years, a total of 102 classes are given as a national standard.[31] In academic lyceum and professional college, they have 40 classes on "foundation of spirituality" over the three years. As it is indicated in Table 6, three classes about mahalla are given.

In the textbook, there was an assignment "what is the factor that can improve the environment of mahalla?" What does the expression mahalla and neighbors are the foundation of national development mean, and comment on the saying "for one child, 7 mahallas will be the father and mother".[32] Especially in 2003, the "Year of the Mahalla", students learned the meaning of the existence of mahalla in the "Idea of National Independence". After the class, students were assigned to write a report and wrote about the characteristics of their mahallas and what they are proud of. The following was extracted from the report[33] that was evaluated highly by the teacher, saved and then publicized.

Student's assignment report in "Idea of national independence" class
1) "Mahalla-the first school of democracy" Report by a student in 7th grade B class

It was declared that 2003 is the "Year of the Mahalla". Mahalla is the origin of ethics and education. Mahalla has a large educational function and it is from the tradition of ethnicity from a long time ago. Wise advice from the elder, rich experiences of old people, good harmony of neighbors by the resident conscience brings and settles a feeling of appreciation. Family harmony means a lot in the relationship of the residents and mahalla activists and the women's committee has a large influence over the education of youth.

In the constitution of our country, it clearly declares our rule of democracy in the nation under the proclamation of human rights and social justice. The basic law called fundamental law was declared in order to construct a democratic constitutional state and a civil society. Mahalla plays a large role in forming a strong civil society. Therefore, the declaration of the "Year of the Mahalla" has a great significance. President Islam Karimov mentioned that "we know that the role and significance of mahalla is improving daily in the operation of individual, family, nation, and society, solidarity of people, strengthening the rights and expansion of the self-governing system".

In order to maintain the peace and stabilize the ethnicities, we are required to devote to our duty as ourselves, residents, and wider society.

2) "My mahalla" Report by a student in 8th grade G class

From the conference with the representative of Fund "Mahalla" and the elder conference in Tashkent.

Mahalla started the spiritual education and enlightenment activities. President Islam Karimov declared that 2003 is the "Year of the Mahalla". Nurturing the respect for culture of the home country, which educates the love for their country, history, tradition, knowledge of their rights, and duty, which are not only nurtured in school, but also among children and among people who live in mahalla.

I live in G mahalla. Our mahalla is a very friendly mahalla. We live in the Mirzo Ulugbek district and this district is the most beautiful district in Tashkent. The representative of the mahalla's women's committee provides supports in solving problems, education for the youth, and mannerisms. Today, mahalla has a large role in constructing a residential society. While overcoming various issues after independence, the significance of mahalla is becoming larger.

In those reports, mahalla as a "traditional space", "basic space for citizen integration" and "space for mutual help" mentioned earlier is expressed in "the tradition of ethnicity from a long time ago" and the president's quote "solidarity of people" and "devoting to our duty as ourselves, residents, and wider society".

Not only the textbook, but students' reports are also written in a way that follows the national standard. Mahalla is treated in class as a foundation of mahalla emphasis policy which is symbolized in the historical and traditional aspects, the aspect as a governmental institution that promote the citizen integration after independence, and the aspect of mutual help in a social security system and mahalla committees after independence.

Students are composing reports based on newspaper articles, the internet, the declaration of the "Year of the Mahalla" by the president, and stories of government members and people in mahalla. The second report especially links to the declaration, the policy of national institution, Fund "Mahalla", and activities of the women's committee of the mahalla. Having an assignment to relate their classes with the mahalla they live in will help them incorporate a stronger image of mahalla that the government declares. In addition, in the "Idea of national independence", representative from A mahalla was invited and gave a lecture with the theme of "Ideology-integrated national flag and society" and participated in the class.[34]

(2) Mahalla in School Event: Event Related to the Spring Festival "*Navro'z*"

At A school, school and mahalla hold many school events based on the contracts with each mahalla. Here, I will clarify how mahalla is treated in the event for the spring festival, "*Navro'z*"[35], held at the same school via field research. The author was invited to this event as a guest and conducted a participatory observation.

First, before *Navro'z*, KVN^{36} event was held. *KVN* is a popular joke competition in the old Soviet area. When I went through the entrance with a large banner saying "Hello *Navro'z*!" and got to the cafeteria/hall, the *KVN* event had already started. It was not jokes, but representatives of 7 classes from the 7th grade were singing, reciting poems, performing traditional and dance and a short play to compete for score.

The theme of poems and short play were "*Navro'z* in mahalla" and they often use the expression "my mahalla" and "our mahalla". Tradition of *Navro'z* and mahalla are directly connected and its history, and customs were explained in detail. In a short play from one class, four male students played a scene where mahalla residents were talking and cutting carrots for using in the *plov* that is served in a wedding. In a wedding, a few hundred guests arrive, so it was necessary to help one another and mutual help among the residents has been done traditionally. Plays displaying mahalla as a "space for mutual help" were performed in the student's short play.

A few days after the *KVN* event, *Navro'z* event for A school was held. The event started at 8 o'clock in the morning on the patio, and there were little over 200 participants including students, teachers, parents, and mahalla residents. Similar to the *KVN* event, they had the recitation of poems and performance of traditional dance. In the event hall, artworks that are made with cloth and traditional food made by students were displayed.

In the afternoon, a competition is held every year that parents and mahalla residents also participate in. In the competition, performance from mahalla residents, traditional dance ensembles, introduction of customs, tradition, rituals of the Uzbek people, recitation of poems by the students, "Father, mother, and me –Sports family", family competitive games where families from each mahalla play against one another, recitation of poem relating to "*Sumalak*"[37], commendation of wall newspaper composed by the students with the theme of "prospering mahalla" and "hello *Navro'z*". Most of

Photo 11 Picture display on *Navro'z*. In the center, it says "Hello *Navro'z*!". There is a picture of making *Sumalak* in mahalla.
(Photo is taken by the author in March 2006).

Photo 12 Short play by four male students performing the scene of cutting carrots.
(Photo is taken by the author in March 2006).

Photo 13 Students from various ethnicities wearing native Uzbek costumes and reciting a poem. (Photo is taken by the author in March 2006).

the program is played between 3 mahallas, A mahalla, B mahalla, and G mahalla, and students and parents representing their mahalla will compete for with performance, recitation of poems, family competitions, and wall newspaper. This also creates competition among mahallas.[38] In the school, there are pictures with the theme of *Navro'z*, people making *Sumalak* in mahalla, and native costumes, and I saw many of pictures that they drew of mahalla.

At the school event of *Navro'z*, traditional aspects of mahalla such as short plays, traditional foods, and traditional dance by the students and aspects of mutual assistance in traditional rituals were emphasized. This event was an opportunity to realize that the traditional culture and mutual help of the residents still exists in the mahalla they live in and to enhance their knowledge and fondness toward mahalla. Students nurture love for their home town and the knowledge of mahalla and traditional culture through the process of preparing for their poem recitations and short plays. Also, by competing with other mahallas in various areas, they can feel this more realistically. The interactions with the mahalla committee and guests are also believed to promote the governmental aspects of mahalla, which was only in the classrooms.

Since there were students from various ethnic backgrounds such as Russian, Korea, Tatar, Tajik, and Armenia, mahalla education in school is taught to all students of all ethnic backgrounds. For hypothesis and research topic (1) "It is natural to teach the traditional culture of Uzbek people in schools that are taught in the Uzbek language, but would it cause some type of contradiction when teaching Uzbek culture in schools that are taught in other languages? For example, schools taught in Russian, which are the second most common after the Uzbek language, how are they teaching the Uzbek culture such as mahalla?" since a Russian female student was conducting the event wearing an Uzbek native costume, and students from various ethnic backgrounds were performing a dance wearing Uzbek native costume, students were enjoying the event regardless of their ethnicity and there were no contradictions.

From this fact, it can be said that mahalla in school education is considered to be a place for traditional culture and to nurture the fondness of their own mahalla, a governmental foundation that supports the nation after independence, and a place for traditional mutual help from a long time ago and to promote mutual help in the new government system after independence. Mahalla as a "traditional space", "basic space for citizen integration" and "space for mutual help" is prominent in school education.

Takao Sakamoto mentions the following about the relationship between nation and ethnicity.

Photo 14 Display of traditional food and tools related to *Navro'z* prepared by the students. Barley sprouts; an ingredient for *Sumalak* is decorated as well.
(Photo is taken by the author in March 2006)

Photo 15 Dance performance by the students during the celebration event of *Navro'z* with guests from mahalla. Female students are wearing the Uzbek native costume. (Photo is taken by the author in March 2006)

Since the nation is formed on the specific land, the citizens are usually from a few ethnicities that are on that land. Then, the concept of universal human rights beyond ethnicities is supported by the nation, but the specific method of the national system and national identities are based on the ethnicity which is the majority in the area, so the problem of ethnic minorities occurs.[39]

In order to avoid theses ethnic collisions as much as possible, they focus on "humanity, eastern civilization and ethnicity of Central Asia, enhancement of spiritual knowledge created by the Uzbek people, ideas that revive the great home country, Islamic culture and ethical knowledge"[40] taught in "foundation of spirituality". By teaching an ethnic mentality based on the religion and humanity and traditional culture beyond the boundaries of ethnicity and nation, students nurture their humanity, form a national identity, and lastly, they can promote national integration. Mahalla is an excellent material that has various elements such as history of the ethnicity, tradition, religion, humanity for mutual help, and is an end system of the government for the current nation. It is clarified by the quote from the history textbook "A system like mahalla is to concord the human model and ethnic mentality".[41]

Especially, mahalla as a "space for mutual help" is emphasized in various aspects such as helping each other in rituals, social security that is implemented by mahalla committee, ethnic mentality and humanity. Mahalla, as a "space for mutual help", can reach the Uzbek people and other ethnicities as "a space for traditional mutual help in the nation of Uzbekistan" and "a space for mutual help beyond the walls of ethnicities". This aspect of mahalla is important for a government in promoting the mutual help of residents, aiding socially vulnerable people, and promoting national integration at the same time. So, they implemented mahalla in school education.

(3) "Cooperation Between Schools and Society and Unification" in Uzbekistan
1) Slimming of school and the policy for cooperation between schools and society

Theory of the slimming of school and the policy for cooperation between school and society is used often when discussing the policy for cooperation between schools and society. "Cooperation between schools and society" is a concept that means "the concept of schools and the local community (it sometimes indicates social education related departments) will work together to support children and students, the utilization of local material and human resources, and promoting the children's participation in local events and local activities".[42] However, the slimming of school means "to eliminate the school supremacy and return some of the job that was beyond the responsibility of the school back to the local community and families, and raise children under their responsibility".[43]

Reconsidering the original educational role of school and home, and local community and working together to raise children is important in promoting the "cooperation between school and society" and "the slimming of school". In other words, the area that relied on school education is given back to the educational power of the families and local community. The recovering, activating, and development of the educational power of families and homes are required.

However, if the education power of families and the local community seems insufficient, the slimming of school should be avoided since, when it is promoted, families and communities receive the burden. First, they have to look at the situation and determine whether they should enhance the education power of families and local community or improve the education power by the slimming of the schools.

Then what kind of policy for cooperation between school and society is implemented in the current Uzbekistan?

The concept of "Cooperation among families, mahalla, and school in the mature generation's development" aiming for the cooperation between schools, mahalla, and families mentioned earlier indicates the purpose for the implementation as: "a basic purpose of the concept is to complete the activity of national ideology education for citizens. The concept suggests challenges for families, mahallas, and school, and creates the system to enhance the cooperation among them for the education of students".[44]

Here, "national ideology education" means ethical and ideological education such as "the idea of national independence" in school education. A challenge for mahalla, they indicate that they have to sufficiently reflect the social and economic views of the nation to school in order to nurture strong children and students.[45] In other words, mahalla is positioned as having a supplementary role to school when teaching students about the nation and building their character as citizens.

On the other hand, A school located in the Mirzo Ulugbek district reports in their official report for the school event for the year of 2005 to 2006 on "families, mahalla, and school" that they had a sprout of "school and society integration" where they are not only the supplementary role of the school, but also share part of each other's function and tackle issues in the cooperation with two or three parties. From this, mahalla is not just invited to class and events at school, but students and teachers are participating in the mutual help and mahalla events. The cooperation activities between school and society that are based on the concept of promoting the cooperation of families, mahalla, and schools, were actually developed into unification activities of school and society in various scenes.

Based on these, it can be understood that cooperative activities between school and mahalla for students are a place for traditional culture where they can nurture their love for their mahalla, the governmental foundation that supports the nation after independence, and forms of mutual help from traditional aspects as well as the new governmental system after independence.

On the other hand, from the viewpoint of mahalla residents, *Navro'z* event at school is a place of self-expression via various forms of performance, and is a place for enhancing their love for their home town and their mahalla via interaction among residents through competition among families and mahallas. These activities mentioned above are usually done in their mahalla, but having these events in a wider public venue, i.e. the school, has a greater effect and diversity. This also showed the unified activities between school and society, such as a shared function for promoting the students' love for their home town and residents as well as learning their tradition and tackling the same project together, such as holding a *Navro'z* event.

However, there were at least some "differences in awareness among mahallas" in these cooperation and unification activities between school and society. This leads to the hypothesis (2) and research topic "Are the cooperative activities of mahalla and school influenced by ethnic factors to some degree? In a mahalla that has both Russian and Uzbek schools, is there a difference in cooperation between them?" As I mentioned earlier, A school has contracts with three mahallas but their enthusiasm for cooperating with school is different among mahalla. For example, the representative of G mahalla says that "We have nothing to do with A school. We have a great connection with B school where they teach in the Uzbek language". On the other hand, the representative of A mahalla emphasized the strong connection with A school.[46] Even when the school initiates a project for mahalla, it may not go forward, depending on the awareness of the mahalla. It is necessary to consider the ways which allow schools to cooperate with various mahallas, instead of only getting the support from certain mahallas.

Conclusion

Based on these facts mentioned above, mahalla is implemented in the school education as a "traditional space", "fundamental space for national integration" and "space for mutual help" through textbooks, classes, and school events. For the background, there was a government plan to get out of the Soviet system, integrate the ethnicities of Central Asia in Uzbekistan, and expand the new national system. The implementation of mahalla had the goal of diffusing the traditional and governmental sides of mahalla after independence and to materialize the government's plan. In reality, mahalla is treated as a place for traditional culture and nurturing their love for their mahalla, foundation for a government system that supports the nation after independence, and a place that promotes mutual help from traditional aspects as well as the new governmental system after independence. Especially, mahalla as "a space for mutual help" is emphasized in the ethnic mentality and humanity. This aspect of mahalla allows the promotion of other ethnicities than Uzbek and is emphasized by the government to promote the community life of the residents, assistance to socially vulnerable people, and national integration. So, they implemented it in school education. However, there were various problems during the implementation stage.

The first one is the "difference in awareness among mahallas". A school has contracts with three mahallas, but there were differences in enthusiasm for participating in cooperative projects among the mahallas. This fact was significant in G mahalla, who emphasized their stronger connection with B school, which teaches in Uzbek language, rather than A school, which teaches in Russian.

The second one is the difference in the view of mahalla depending on the ethnicity.

Slavic and Korean people were not mentioned in this book in detail. In the previous research, less than 20% of the people in Slavic populations support mahalla.[47] However, education on mahalla is implemented in all ethnicities, including Russian, but the implementation of mahalla in school education may be forced upon other ethnicities. Mahalla is a tradition a vehicle for molding "Uzbekistan citizens" and a nurturing device for love of one's home town. It is also an end unit of the government system and a place of mutual help, but it could warp the relationship between Uzbek people and other ethnicities.

The third one is the problem of "the loss of the uniqueness of cooperative activities". Content of the class and reports written by students are based on the mahalla view that was implemented in the government's mahalla emphasis policy. Schools are also doing projects that suite the mahalla policy of the local educational department and Ministry of Public Education.[48] Therefore, if the schools and mahalla cooperate more, mahalla would promote activities that suit the needs of the school and government. Or possibly, mahalla activities could be standardized throughout the nation, thus losing the uniqueness of the cooperative activities.

This chapter also discussed the policy, and the actual situation, of cooperation between schools and society in current Uzbekistan through the concept of "cooperation among families, mahalla, and school in the mature generation's development" and school events.

As it is seen in the assignment that as required from the mahalla in the concept "to reflect the socio-economical view from the nation to school in order to nurture strong students and children", the system of "cooperation between school and society" was emphasized such that a mahalla must have a unique educational function on top of supporting the educational activities at school. In other words, a one-sided cooperative activity in public education that was managed by the government was imagined by the education administration.

However, in the actual cooperative activities, they had activities on "unification of school and society" where mahalla not only had a supplementary role to the school system, but also shared educational functions such as the self-expression and learning of students and residents and to host cooperative projects and events.

In this situation, there is a slight difference between the image of the education administration and the actual activities of school and local society relating to "cooperation between schools and society" and "unification of school and society". In the future, when the Uzbekistan government promotes the policy of "cooperation among schools, families, and mahalla", they need to grasp the situation and make a policy of school and society cooperation and unification which is already sprouting. The implementation of mahalla in school education was started recently, and has been experiencing problems. However, implementation in schools that are located all over the nation does not bear only problems, but also has the potential for evening out the difference in human resource training in urban and rural areas. In the future, it is necessary to compare the differences in the implementation of mahalla in multiple localities across the nation and discuss the issues.

Notes

[1] Kuniko Mizutani, "Uzbekistan—Koukou reberu no kyoiku kaikaku wo chushin ni—Datsu roshia no tame no jinzai ikusei (Focusing on the Educational Reform at the High School Level —Human Resource Development for Moving Away from Russia)", *Science of humanity Bensei*, Vol.36, Benseishuppan, 2001, p.44.

[2] O'zbekiston Mahalla xayryya jamg'armasi, *Mahalla*, Toshkent, 2003, b.333.

[3] Rizwan Ablimit, "Uighur no kodomo no hattatsu ni okeru mahalla (chiiki kyoudoutai) no yakuwari (The Role of the *Mahalla* in the Development of Uighur Children)", The Japanese Society of Life Needs Experience Learning, *Seikatsu Taiken Gakushu Kenkyu (The Journal of Life Needs Experience Learning)*, Vol.1, 2001, pp.39-47. Other works, Bendrikov, K.E., *Ocherki po istorii narodnogo obrazovaniya v Turkestane (1865-1924gg.)*, Moskva: Akademiya Pedagogicheskikh Nauk RSFSR, 1960, s.27-28. also argued on impact of religious courtesies in family and life in society children.

[4] Kabinet Ministrov Respubliki Uzbekistan Gosudarstvennyi Tsentr Testirovaniya, Zakon Respubliki Uzbekistan "Ob obrazovanii", 1992. http://www.test.uz/index.php?exid=3&PHPSESSID=73c42e8456e1a19bc685e34496bcc188. (December 20, 2004 browsed).

[5] Yukiko Sawano, "'Shimin shakai heno ikou wo unagasu shougai gakushu taikei no kouchiku —Uzbekistan kyouwakoku no kyoiku kaikaku (Constructing the Lifelong System that Promotes the Transition to a 'Citizen Society'—Educational Reform in the Republic of Uzbekistan)", *Roshia・Yurashia Keizai Chousa Shiryou (Vestnik ėkonomiki ĖKS-SSSR, Russian-Eurasian economy)*, No.798, 1998, p.2.

[6] Yukiko Sawano, *op. cit.*, 1998, pp.2-3. Regarding criticism of Soviet education and educational reform during *Perestroika*, for details see Shiro Murayama, Shinichi Tokoro eds., *Perestroika to Kyoiku(Perestroika and Education)*, Otsukishoten, 1991. This book examines educational reform in the *Perestroika* period through renewal of textbook of history and "Code of laws on students' rights".

[7] Satoshi Kawanobe, *Kakunenshi/Soren Sengo kyoiku no tenkai (Annual History/Soviet Union: Development of post war education*, MTsyutupan, 1991, p.246.

[8] Japan International Cooperation Agency (JICA), *Central Asia (Uzbekistan, Kazakhstan, Kyrgyz) Report of Research Group on Aid, Present Data Analysis*, Part II Uzbekistan, Chapter 9 Education, 2001, p.56. http://www.jica.go.jp/activities/report/country/2002_02_02.html. (November 15, 2004 browsed).

[9] Tukhliev, Nurislom, Krementsova, Alla, eds., *The Republic of UZBEKISTAN*, Tashkent, 2003, pp.258-264.

[10] Information obtained through Interview with a principal of Yunusabad Lyceum attached to

Tashkent State Institute of Oriental Studies (August 13, 2004).

[11] Information obtained through Interview with the then manager of Tashkent department of Public Education (August 23, 2004), the then manager of Tashkent department of Public Education (December 13, 2007).

[12] Ministry of Higher and Secondary Specialized Education Site, http://www.edu.uz/en/tashkent_list/higher-education-institutions/ (February 26, 2015 browsed).

[13] Tukhliev, Nurislom, Krementsova, Alla, eds., *op. cit.*, 2003, pp.258-264.

[14] *Ideya natsional'noi nezavisimosti: osnovnye ponyatiya i printsipy*, Tashkent: O'zbekiston, 2003, s.61-62.

[15] Information obtained through Interview with Mr. Gairat Shoumarov, former minister of Ministry of Public Education (August 19, 2008).

[16] For example, children who live in a town of rural area are roped in to sow seeds of farm products in spring season and harvest in autumn. Especially, picking cotton is rigor. In the season, middle grades of general education school to university students stay overnight at farm and pick cotton (Field work in Gulistan City, Syrdarya Region, September, 2008). Recently, Government of Uzbekistan decided to abolish child labor of cotton picking with increasing pressure from foreign countries and boycott of Uzbekistan's cotton by foreign large companies.

[17] Statistics 2001-2002 of *Atlas 8 klass*, Tashkent, 2003, s.29. The newest data of number of academic lyceum and professional college, refer to http://centr.markaz.uz/test/joomla/ru/o-tsentre/professionalnye-kolledzhi (July 30, 2014 browsed).

[18] Information obtained through Interview with librarian in a rural city (September 9, 2008).

[19] Dadabaev, T. pointed out a word "Mahalla-bred" means children who grow up in area impacted by mahalla, and the word also includes nuance of negative and pre-modern. Timur Dadabaev, *Mahalla no Jitsuzo: Chuou Ajia Shakai no Dentou to Henyou (Mahalla)*, University of Tokyo Press, 2006, pp.70-71.

[20] National delimitation in Central Asia is territory division which based on ethnicities in 1924. Administrative division founded on ethnic theory of Soviet would introduce into the national delimitation, and the Soviet Government tried to obstruct political unification plan like uniting of Central Asian people and Turk Soviet Republic. The National delimitation became the archetype of ethnic group and state in Central Asian countries, however, due to mark off a boundary with mixed ethnicity, many complicated issue are contained. Hisao Komatsu, Hiroshi Umemura, Tomohiko Uyama, Chika Obiya, Toru Horikawa, eds., *Chuou Yurashia wo Shiru Jiten (Cyclopedia of Central Eurasia)*, Heibon-sha, Japan, 2005, p.486.

[21] Seki also indicated relevant point in her works. For details, see Keiko Seki, "Uzbekistan ni okeru minzoku・shukyou・kyoiku — Ningen keisei no shiten kara no kosatsu (Ethnicity, Religion, and Education in Uzbekistan — a discussion from the perspective of character formation)", *Roshia・Yurashia Keizai Chousa Shiryou (Vestnik ėkonomiki ĖKS-SSSR, Russian-Eurasian economy)*, No.812, 2000, pp.12-27. In addition, not only literature of Uzbek people, but also common epic "*Alpamysh*" of Kazakh and Karakalpak people is published in textbook "Native language and literature" of the upper secondary education. Rafiyev, A., G'ulomova, N., *Ona tili va adabiyot*, Toshkent: Sharq, 2007, b.113. Regarding Karakalpakstan, see Hisao Komatsu, Hiroshi Umemura, Tomohiko Uyama, Chika Obiya, Toru Horikawa, eds., *op. cit.*, 2005, p.141, p.145.

[22] *O'rta maxsus, kac'-hunar ta'limining umumta'lim fanlari davlat ta'lim standartlari va o'quv dasturlari*, Toshkent: Sharq, 2001, b.220.

[23] Nosirxo'jayev, S. H., *Ma'naviyat asoslari*, Toshkent: Sharq, 2005, b.192.

[24] Dzhuraev, N., Faizullaev, T., *Istoriya Uzbekistana II*, Tashkent: Sharq, 2002, s.117-120.
[25] O'zbekiston Respublikasi xalq Ta'limi Vazirligi, Yo'ldoshev, H. Q., *Barkamol avlodni tarbiyalashda oila, mahalla, maktab hamkorligi kontseptsiyasi*, Toshkent, 2004, b.7. Ministry of Public Education bring up slogan every year, and slogan 2005-2006 was "Promotion of cooperation between family, mahalla and school".
[26] O'zbekiston Respublikasi xalq Ta'limi Vazirligi, Yo'ldoshev, H. Q., same as above, 2004, b.11.
[27] Internal materials of A school in Mirzo Ulugbek district, Tashkent City.
[28] Internal materials of A school in Mirzo Ulugbek district, Tashkent City.
[29] Internal materials (Contract between mahallas) of A school in Mirzo Ulugbek district, Tashkent City.
[30] Dzhuraev, N., Faizullaev, T., *op. cit.*, 2002, s.117-120.
[31] *Ta'lim taraqqieti 2 maxsus son*, Toshkent: Sharq, 1999, b.12. The subject "Idea of national independence and foundation of spirituality" is included in a field of ethics in the lower secondary education, and it taught student with moral lesson and "Homeland consciousness". On the other hand, subject "Foundation of spirituality" in the upper secondary education is included in general education, and taught with history, mathematics, physics.
[32] Nosirxo'jayev, S. H., *op. cit.*, 2005, b.204-205.
[33] Internal materials (Students' report on the "Year of the Mahalla") of A school in Mirzo Ulugbek district, Tashkent City.
[34] Information obtained through Interview with a representative of A mahalla (April, 26, 2006).
[35] *Navro'z* is also national holiday in Kazakhstan, Kyrgyz, Tajikistan and Turkmenistan. Hisao Komatsu, Hiroshi Umemura, Tomohiko Uyama, Chika Obiya, Toru Horikawa, eds., *op. cit.*, 2005, p.208. Regarding the custom, refer to Karabaev, U., *Etnokul'tura*, Tashkent: Sharq, 2005, s.40.
[36] KVN (in Russian *КВН*) is an abbreviation for *Клуб Весёлых и Находчивых*. Its means club of the funny and inventive. In Russia and former Soviet countries, a variety of KVN TV program are produced by TV companies.
[37] *Sumalak* is traditional food in Uzbekistan concerning *Navro'z*. It is the ancient Turkish tribes who lived in Central Asia, is a favorite dish of the people of Central Asia during the holiday of *Navro'z*. In the season of *Navro'z*, people such as classmate of school, residents of mahalla, kin etc. gather at home or space of mahalla, and make *Sumalak*. People muddle that *Sumalak* do not burn all night. In the interval of making *Smalak* in mahalla, people eat *plov*, converse with residents, dancing and they share the joy of spring comes.
[38] Information obtained through Interview with vice-principal of A school (March 10, 2006), "Plan for '*Navro'z*' national holiday event trough cooperation with A mahalla, B mahalla and G mahalla", participatory observation in *Navro'z* school event (March 20, 2006).
[39] Takao Sakamoto, "Kokumin to minzoku (Nation and ethnicities)", *Readings Nihon no Kyoiku to Shakai (Education and Society of Japan)*, No.5, *Aikokushin to Kyoiku (Patriotism and Education)*, Nihon Tosho Center, 2007, p.177. (Takao Sakamoto, *Kokkagaku no Susume (Encouragement of Political Sciences)*, Chikuma Shobo, 2001, Chapter 3).
[40] *O'rta maxsus, kac'-hunar ta'limining umumta'lim fanlari davlat ta'lim standartlari va o'quv dasturlari*, Toshkent: Sharq, 2001, b.207-208. Addtionaly, "*Navro'z*" also teach students as one of the teaching materials. Qarshiboyev, M., Nishonova, S., Musurmonova, O., *Milliy istiqlol g'oyasi va ma'naviyat asoslari 8-sinf*, Toshkent: Ma'naviyat, 2003, b.101-110.
[41] Dzhuraev, N., Faizullaev, T., *op. cit.*, 2002, s.118.
[42] Takashi Sasanuma, "Shogai gakushu shakai ni okeru gakkou kyoiku no arikata wo meguru ichi shiron: Gakusha renkei·yugou no rironteki kousatu wo kirikuchi ni shite (A Prospect of the School Education in the Lifelong Learning Society: A Theoretical Attempts at the Fusion of School and Social Education)", Center for Education and Research of Lifelong Learning,

Utsunomiya University, *Annual Reports of Lifelong Learning*, 1999, p.124. Furthermore, Tsuneo Yamamoto highlighted and defined "cooperation" and "fusion" as "usual cooperation is to coordinate school education and social education from one's own standpoint, and there are no points common to each other. (snip) On the other hand, fusion creates activities as school education and also social education, or to recognize either activity as common activities". Tsuneo Yamamoto, "Fusion of School and Society", *Weekly Educational Public Opinion*, No.489, 1996, p.36.

[43] Takashi Sasanuma, *op. cit.*, 1999, p.125.

[44] O'zbekiston Respublikasi xalq Ta'limi Vazirligi, Yo'ldoshev, H. Q., *op. cit.*, 2004, b.7.

[45] O'zbekiston Respublikasi xalq Ta'limi Vazirligi, Yo'ldoshev, H. Q., *op. cit.*, 2004, b.11.

[46] Information obtained through Interview with representative of G mahalla (March 16, 2006), Interview with representative of A mahalla (April 26, 2006). In addition, only a visitors of A mahalla participated in A school's graduation ceremony and extended congratulations to students (Participatory observation at the graduate ceremony of A school, May 25, 2006).

[47] Timur Dadabaev, *op. cit.*, 2006, pp.188-189.

[48] Department of Public Education, Mirzo Ulugbek district, "Plan for teachers' educational and ethics activities in cooperation of family, mahalla, school and social organizations by 2003 the 'Year of the Mahalla'", Internal materials (Plan of events in the "Year of the Mahalla" by A school, Mirzo Ulugbek district) of A school in Mirzo Ulugbek district, Tashkent City.

Chapter 5

Raising "Citizen" Awareness in Uzbekistan through a Combined Effort between Mahallas and Schools

Since the Republic of Uzbekistan gained its independence in 1991 following the collapse of the USSR, people began to search for the answers to questions raised in conjunction with educational reform such as: "What is the state of Uzbekistan?", "Who is the nation of Uzbekistan?" After losing the concept of "USSR" and "the Soviets" to define the state and people as a whole, a new framework to replace the previous one is needed.

General concepts of citizenship have been defined as "the right of members in a society under a welfare state system—a civic right or a civil right",[1] "the right which people have automatically at birth by being a member of a welfare state which guarantees their right to live a basic level of life; in other words, the fundamental right that people are entitled to if they are citizens of the state",[2] "concepts were derived from political concepts, such as the concept of a 'nation's people' (= 'citizen'), and the makeup of a modern society as a community formed into a 'nation (= 'nation state')'",[3] and "legal and political concepts about the rights and obligations of the people who have been recognized as members of the state, built after the establishment of modern society".[4] Most of these definitions are based on Marshall, T.H.'s concept of citizenship: "the status of people who are recognized as formal members of a state which is a political community and are given the equal rights and obligations".[5] The common key concepts in these definitions are "state", "national system", "nation state" and "nation's people". On the basis of the concept or definition of citizenship, concepts such as "state", "nation's people" and "nation state" existed a priori.

However after the end of the Cold War, globalization has occurred with the rapid movement of people, goods and money, whereby people from different ethnicities and nationalities now live together in one state as its "citizens" and the concepts of "nationhood" and the "nation's people" have begun to crumble. The comparability of a "nation's people to equal citizens" or "state to equal nation state" may not be established any longer, and the time has come to face and address the issues of what citizenship is and how it should be defined in a modern context. Therefore, discussion and education about issues of citizenship are required so that citizenship is not just a right given by the state, but that it can also be seen as a quality to be used proactively to fulfil the obligations and responsibilities as belonging to a state as well as a society.

For example, in the United Kingdom, Anthony Giddens, the mentor of the Theoretical policies of Tony Blair's government which started in 1997, hammered out a new democratic socialism movement called "The Third Way" to replace Margaret Thatcher's New Liberalism/Neo-conservatism. In this "Third Way", which means "a new way to transcend the impasses that both neo-liberalism and conventional social democracy are currently facing", is a program of "'equality as inclusion' depicted by 'fostering an active civil society' through 'community renewal', 'respect of citizenship' and 'guaranteed involvement in public space'"[6] which is said to embody his theory. Encouraged by this, The Advisory Group on Citizenship, chaired by Barnard Crick, was established in 1998 and, the "Education for citizenship and the teaching of democracy in schools: Final report of the Advisory Group on Citizenship" (The Crick Report)[7] was presented to the government. In relation to this report, in 1999, "Citizenship" was included in the National Curriculum and became an individual and compulsory subject.[8] At this time there was heated debate about the concept of citizenship and its education not only in the UK, but in other countries around the world as well.

Amid such efforts, new definitions of citizenship were being formulated in Japan. One of these is the "right of individuals to express themselves as individuals within a diverse society, while being afforded protection by themselves, the right to self-fulfilment and the right to take part in areas of decision-making, as well as contributing to the betterment of society".[9]

In Japan, a 9-year compulsory education curriculum from elementary and junior high schools was implemented as pioneering experiment in the Shinagawa Ward of Tokyo in 2006. At all grades, "Shiminka" (Citizen Study), which set a high value on students' autonomy and is a subject which combines ethics, special activities and a comprehensive learning period, was included in order to determine a future direction in all areas of the Shinagawa Ward. The "Shiminka" is an original subject of the Shinagawa Ward, appointed as special ward for educational reform by the Cabinet Office of Japan, and textbooks are also created by educational board of Shinagawa Ward. In the beginning of the "Shiminka" Guide of Instruction, the depreciation of citizenship education was indicated by the educational board as "it is important that students learn citizenship to conduct their roles as social members".[10] As such, citizenship is considered as a new movement towards a mature civil society, and as the ability to participate within society voluntarily and action for concrete social participation.[11]

Such efforts in the areas of citizenship education and the promotion of the social awareness of "citizenship" began to be implemented not only in Europe and Japan, but also in the Central Asian country of Uzbekistan. In the background, there are factors such as (1) a need to develop a population that has an awareness of the issues in regards being a "nation's people" and "state" in order to promote an independent state which is different to the system of the former Soviet Union and (2) in Uzbekistan, however, with the Karakalpak Republic in the middle of the country, the framework of a state is rather vague because it is a multi-ethnic country where the equality of "one state, one ethnicity" does not apply, and therefore, a more holistic framework which includes all the ethnicities is required. There are also major issues surrounding a sense of "belonging" for the many different ethnic groups which were divided by (artificial) borders during the time of Soviet Union rule. With this history it has become important to raise the social awareness of "citizenship" as being part of a civil society and to foster a new national focus and public awareness in Uzbekistan.

In Chapter 5, I will first examine the social and political background of Uzbekistan to address why fostering an awareness in its "citizens" is currently important; then I will discuss how this issue of citizenship has been placed in the educational policies of the state as well as how they have been addressed within school education. Secondly, I wish to highlight the mahallas as a place to learn about the quality of "citizenship" and also as a place to foster a social awareness of "citizenship" in collaboration with schools. Lastly, the future possibilities offered by these collaborations between citizens, schools and local communities in order to foster greater social awareness will be explored.

As the research method, I used local school textbooks, the National Standard of Uzbekistan (hereinafter referred as the national standard) set by the Ministry of Public Education and the Ministry of Higher and Secondary Specialized Education, an analysis of laws, interviews with relevant people from the mahalla committee, and school as well as students.[12]

1. Fostering "Citizen" Awareness in Young People after the Independence of Uzbekistan

Behind the introduction of citizenship education in the UK, there were concerns about young people's indifference toward politics, decreasing voter turnout at elections, localities not functioning as communities, and the lack of opportunity for citizens to participate in local-level activities.[13]

In this section, I will discuss how "citizenship" was instituted in the education policy of Uzbekistan after gaining independence. Considering the social situation of Uzbekistan, I will explain why fostering a social awareness of "citizenship" is currently required in the country. Moreover, issues of how it is placed in to educational policies of the state and how it is dealt with in the school education will be reviewed.

(1) The "Citizens" of Uzbekistan after Independence

On August 29, 2002, President Islam Karimov made a speech before the Independence Day of September 1 at *Olii Majlis* (Congress), titled "Basic policy for the democratization of Uzbekistan and forming the foundations for a civil society". In this speech, he described the concept of "From a strong state to a strong civil society", the slogan recently promoted by the Uzbekistan government to emphasize the roles and issues of non-governmental agencies. He also mentioned mahalla as being "in the center of our thoughts, and that there should be development of mahalla as a facility for problem-solving and enabling citizens' autonomy".[14]

As embodied in this speech, although the legal and administrative development of non-government organizations and mahallas are specified, the entire change needs to involve not only government organizations, but also non-government organizations in present day Uzbekistan in order to shift various functions in the project of building a new state after independence. Such strategies will have a double or triple effect by complementing the current government's reputation and in understanding the entire state including both urban and farming areas at the micro and local level of community, as well as by enabling to appeal the "autonomy of citizens", "residents' empowerment" and the "democratization" of all citizens in the state and in the world. Because of this social and political background, a strong civil society as well as a "strong citizenry" that supports it is essential nowadays. Regarding this fostering of "citizenship", President Karimov spoke as follows:

> The most important thing in forming the basis of a civil society is to constantly develop growth in education, and in the minds of individuals. It is result of constant government ordinance and foundation, base of social development, establishing a consistent system of rules, the people can gain the following three things: spirit, morality and education. These three factors are the values that we have always respected.[15]

Basically, in order to foster "citizenship" or for our nation's people to become "citizens" by themselves, he insisted that a sense of spirituality, morality and education would be essential. Looking at school education, the President's speech alluded to the issue that children were required to gain the three principles of becoming "citizens" through school subjects such as "Courtesy", "Homeland Consciousness", "Foundation of Spirituality", "Foundation of the State and Laws" and "Individuals and Society". Naturally, in school education in present day

Uzbekistan, "Homeland Consciousness" and "Foundation of Spirituality" are included as individual subjects and are compulsory from the first year of elementary school through to the 12th year of upper secondary school. In addition, behind this development there are issues of to do with human resource development in the nation's process of a transitional economy, as well as the above mentioned social and political factors.

In Uzbekistan, while adhering to the moderate reform line and authoritarian system of President Karimov, only a "mild market-oriented economic reform" has been implemented rather than one of a rapid increase in marketization or democratization. In the process, human resource development has been sought in response to nation-building and the market economy after independence. Under the Soviet Union's rule, the top positions, such as executive officers of business, state organizations, academic and research institutions, were taken by Russians. After independence, those officials returned to Russia, leaving a serious shortage of human resources in management and specialized professions. In addition, Uzbeks are now required to conduct diplomacy, security, development of legal systems and administrative reform on their own, and therefore personnel for these projects are also needed.[16]

For these reasons, the training civil servants and professionals in business who are the basis of new nation-building is the present goal in Uzbekistan, and these professionals will be required to have a national focus and public awareness on top of their specialized knowledge.[17] Not just personnel are required in these professional groups, but also the training of the general public will be needed to carry out the actual work on sites to support these experts. The development of personnel with a consciousness of their home country and an awareness of nation people is therefore ideal. Government advances to foster "Strong citizens" like in President's address.

(2) The Positioning of "Citizens" in Educational Policy

One of the representative examples is the "National Programme for Personnel Training (NPPT)" announced in October, 1997. The educational reform that has been taking place in the country after independence is a transformation from the educational system of the former Soviet Union to a new system of a new country. Due to the amendment of the Education Law in 1997, with its 4-5-3 grade system, a total of 12 years of education is free and compulsory. The upper secondary level is divided into two groups: academic lyceum, where 10% of the total students who wish to go to universities go, and professional colleges where 90% of students go; and the purpose of academic lyceum is to learn specialized subjects and that of professional colleges is to gain professional skills. In other words, while the training of professionals who will lead the country in the future is being implemented, the training of the general public who will support these experts is also being implemented at professional colleges. Both courses have the common goal of developing personnel with a national focus and awareness of nation people and in the development of a social awareness about "citizenship".

From the description about the contents of school subjects and textbooks defined by the national standards, it can be understood that the development of citizenship awareness is to be done in four aspects: (1) "citizens" who have political ability and the administrative, political and legal knowledge necessary for building a new state, (2) "citizens" who have a love of their nation and hometown, (3) "citizens" who support the restoration of ethnicity, languages and traditional customs, and (4) "citizens" who are part of a multi-ethnic and multi-cultural state, within Central Asia and the international community (Table 7).

C.L Hahn described that there are four essential components to effective citizenship education in democracies: "to acquire knowledge from carefully planned instruction", "debate about public issues and make decisions", "engage in civic action" and "develop a positive identification with local, national, regional and global communities".[18] Although it is not easy without to apply these components of western democracies that Hahn exemplified without modification to current Uzbekistan,due to the different historical backgrounds and current situation the secomponents are compatible with the four aspects of "citizens" mentioned in the preceding paragraph. Specifically in relation to local communities, where the traditional local communities called mahallas are included in classroom lessons about Ethic and History; as well as collaborative activities between schools and mahallas that are now being implemented in Uzbekistan.

In what follows, these four aspects to be implemented in school education will be explored using textbooks and the national standards, especially through the point of students' political cultivation with (1) "citizens" who have a political ability in regard to political participation such as elections as well as administrative, political and legal knowledge.

Table 7 Fostering a social awareness of "citizenship" in school education

4 aspects for fostering "citizens"	School Subjects	Textbooks
(1) "citizens" who have political ability and the administrative, political and legal knowledge necessary for building a new state	Elementary Level: "Courtesy" Lower Secondary Level: "Foundation of the State and Laws" Upper Secondary Level: "Foundation of the State and Laws", "Individuals and Society"	Elementary Level: "The Alphabet of National Constitution", "Courtesy" Lower Secondary Level: "Trip to the World of National Constitution" Upper Secondary Level: "Foundation of the State and Laws", "Laws"
(2) "citizens" who have a love of their nation and hometown	Elementary Level: "Courtesy" Lower Secondary Level: "Courtesy" "Homeland Consciousness", "Idea of National Independence and Foundation of Spirituality" Upper Secondary Level: "Foundation of Spirituality"	Elementary Level: "Courtesy" Lower Secondary Level: "Homeland Consciousness", "Idea of National Independence and Foundation of Spirituality", "History of Uzbekistan" Upper Secondary Level: "Foundation of Spirituality", "History of Uzbekistan"
(3) "citizens" who support the restoration of ethnicity, languages and traditional customs	Elementary, Lower/Upper Secondary Levels: "Native language and Literature", "Music Culture", "Uzbek Language", "History of Uzbekistan"	Elementary, Lower/Upper Secondary Levels: "Native language and Literature", "Music Culture", "Uzbek Language", "History of Uzbekistan"
(4) "citizens" who are part of a multi-ethnic and multi-cultural state, within Central Asia and the international community	Elementary Level: "Courtesy" Lower Secondary Level: "Foreign Languages", "Literature", "World History" Upper Secondary Level: "Foreign Languages", "Literature", "World History", "Individuals and Society"	Elementary Level: "Courtesy", "The Alphabet of National Constitution" Lower Secondary Level: "Foreign Languages", "Literature", "World History" Upper Secondary Level : "Foreign Languages", "Literature", "World History"

Source: The author created this table with the reference of Oʻzbekiston Respublikasi Xalq Taʻlimi Vazirligi., *Taʼlim taraqqieti 2 maxsus son*, Toshkent: Sharq, 1999, b.10-13., *Oʻrta maxsus, kacʼ-hunar taʼlimining umumtaʼlim fanlari davlat taʼlim standartlari va oʻquv dasturlari*, Toshkent: Sharq, 2001. Due to textbooks and the contents of classes, there are some subjects that appear more than twice.

2. Fostering the Social Awareness of "Citizenship" in School Education in Uzbekistan

In this chapter, I will discuss the issue of fostering the social awareness of "citizenship" in the educational policy of Uzbekistan. In particular, I will analyze the "National Programme for Personnel Training (NPPT)" and the "National Standard", school textbooks of "Foundation of Spirituality", "The Alphabet of National Constitution" and "Courtesy".

1. Fostering Social Awareness of "Citizenship" in the "National Standard of Uzbekistan"

Table 7 shows the class contents incorporating the four aspects in subjects taught at elementary, lower/upper secondary levels. For (1), the contents are mainly about the state laws, the election system, and human rights that the state army is taught; for (2), the contents are about the state and society and patriotism are included; for (3), the contents aim to recognize old traditions through art such as literature and music as well as language in order to develop personnel; and for (4), the contents are aimed to communicate with people other than Uzbeks and to learn history and other languages to increase their knowledge and skills to live in a unified state together, as well as boosting an awareness as a member of Central Asia.[19]

2. "Citizens" Awareness as Seen in Textbooks of "Foundation of Spirituality", "The Alphabet of the National Constitution" and "Courtesy"

Usually the class's contents are planned in a mutually complementary manner between subjects and textbooks. For example, the textbook called "The Alphabet of the National Constitution" of the 2nd year of the elementary level contains material not only about the constitution, but also an explanation about the national emblem, president and election by coloring in the emblem and flag and a doing a puzzle with the names of the national symbols.

Below is the description about the constitution and the election in the 2nd year "The Alphabet of the National Constitution" textbook.

> 3. Constitution – Base Law of the State
> December 8, 1992 is one of the most important dates for our state. It was the day when the "National Constitution of the Republic of Uzbekistan", the base law of the state, was enacted. It is the most important law to describe the rights and obligations of all the people living in Uzbekistan.
>
> 5. Voting
> The headperson of the Republic of Uzbekistan is President Islam Karimov. He was elected to become our president in 1992 by the people of the entire state.
>
> Election
> We have Hamida and Kostya here and we have to choose one of them as our class leader. Who would like Hamida to be the leader? Please put your hands up. Then, who would like Kostya to be the leader? Whoever receives the most votes gets to be chosen as the class leader. Such an activity is called voting.
> The president of our government is elected in the same way. The majority of the residents of the Republic of Uzbekistan voted for President Karimov.[20]

This textbook first mentioned that Mr. Islam Karimov was elected for the president and shows an example of how to select a class representative. By explaining about voting and illustrating a more accessible example, it also explains about the presidential elections of the state. In the textbook there is a photo of children raising their hands voting and a photo of President Karimov.

On the other hand, other themes such as "Our homeland—Uzbekistan", "This is who we are!", "Our official language—Uzbek", "Citizens of the Republic of Uzbekistan", "Learning is light", "You are different from your friends", "Live healthy!" and "the military strength of the Republic of Uzbekistan" are included in conjunction with each article of the constitution distributed throughout the textbooks in order to teach the contents of (1), (2), (3) and (4) in Table 7. Also, it is designed so that children can consider the contents of these textbooks on their own as their learning levels increase. It should be worthwhile to note that the theme of "citizens of the Republic of Uzbekistan" in Year 2 and "citizens of the state" in Year 3 changes to "I am a citizen of the Republic of Uzbekistan" in Year 4.[21] Here are the mechanisms that students apply for their own life the concept of "citizen" in class.

In language subjects including Uzbek, English and Russian, themes such as the traditional spring festival of "*Navro'z*", "constitution", "national flag", "national emblem", "national holidays", "our homeland—Uzbekistan" and the "spirit of citizens/public" are included; and human resource development as a citizen and member of society in Uzbekistan is aimed for at the same time as acquiring the new language skills of each language.[22]

As such, school is a suitable place to learn new knowledge and from the past experience of others systematically. However, in order for students to acquire the knowledge and skills about the new constitution and elections after independence, it is also important to provide some opportunities to learn knowledge and skills proactively, voluntarily and positively in response to the changes occurring in society at present through other places and people rather than just at schools in order to lead to opportunities to participate in society. In present day Uzbekistan, local communities called mahallas are implementing their own activities and collaborative activities with schools for the purpose of developing human resources with a social awareness of "citizenship".

3. Fostering a Social Awareness of "Citizenship" by Mahallas

As for the individual activities of mahallas in Uzbekistan after the independence, there have been various events at each of the mahalla's grounds and at the mahalla committee's office on the day of the spring festival *"Navro'z"*, "Memorial Day" (previously "Victory Day"), "Child Protection Day" and "International Women's Day". They also organize courses in computing, hair dressing and baking for unemployed young people and women to gain professional skills.[23] In the new constitution enacted in 1992, there was a high regard for mahallas and in the law of the Republic of Uzbekistan "On Education", there is an article for "Assigning full powers to *hokimiyat* (local government) in the division of education (Article 27)".[24] Also, 2003 was declared as the "Year of the Mahalla" by the order of president and competitions of traditional sports and various events were organized.

More recently, due to the government policy, the collaborative activities between mahallas and schools are encouraged. At A school in the Mirzo Ulugbek district, as stated below in the public report of the school, mahalla's representatives were invited to the school on Constitution Memorial Day on December 8 and they were also invited to give a lecture on the theme of "Ideology – an unified national flag and society" in the class of the "Idea of National Independence".[25] Moreover, the mahallas' representatives participated in the school events during the "Foundation of National Independence" week.

Jan Kerkhofs outlined the ways in which schools and local communities could be connected through student activities such as "meeting members of the local council", "visiting rest homes to perform a concert with the school choir, forming a theatre group for young children with disabilities, organizing exhibitions of photos/film/art, creating a school magazine or becoming its editor".[26]

Through these collaborative activities between schools and mahallas in Uzbekistan, students reviewed local mahallas and created a record, called "Passport", of each mahalla (including population, address of the office, list of the representatives, list of the facilities such as a mosque and a museum within the Mahalla and history of the Mahalla), and wrote a report after interviewing the relevant people of the mahallas, visited people with disabilities and gave them some presents, published wall newspapers and wrote essays about their mahallas.

The following is a discussion on the importance of collaboration between schools and local communities in fostering a social awareness of "citizenship".

In this section, I will review the issue of fostering social awareness of "citizenship" through an example of collaborative activities between a mahalla and a school which took place at the school event on "Memorial Day". Lastly, the significance of the collaborative activities between mahallas and schools in relation to fostering a social awareness of "citizenship" will be looked at.

(1) Collaboration between a Mahalla and a School at the School Event of "Memorial Day"

Aristotle Kallis points out that "the strength of national identity occurs through pride and a strong feeling of achievement and because of the ethnocentrism of history education, it was normal to focus on the significant contributions of each nation when teaching about World War II", and therefore, the commonality between textbooks in Europe is that they describe only their country's participation in allied military operations.[27] Textbooks in Uzbekistan are no exception. The contents of these textbooks show how much the people of Uzbekistan contributed to the wars and how much sacrifice was made to defend the USSR. Along these lines, school events related to World War II are held every year.

At the above mentioned school ceremony of "Memorial Day" of World War II at A school, approximately ten guests were invited from the mahalla which had a strong connection with the school. Some guests were wearing military uniforms with many medals on their chests and some were wearing traditional Uzbek hats on their heads.

At first, a student read a war-themed poem aloud and a traditional Uzbek dance followed. Some women were in tears listening to the girl's poem which told people how sad and horrible war was. Other students were watching the scene solemnly.

As representatives of the guests, a former serviceman and woman who conducted various supporting activities during war time made a speech to tell the students about their experiences. Both of them insisted "how hard they tried to protect their country", "how they were fighting on the front lines" and "how they survived with little food and how they overcame that problem".

After the talks by the two guests, another dance by student representatives started and towards the end of the music all the guests from the mahalla joined them to make a large circle around the dancers. At the end of the event, students gave flowers and presents to the other war veterans. Groups of students visited these people at home to hand them presents directly, and listened to more stories of war experiences and carried out interviews with other war veterans.

In this event, war veterans were considered to be "people who contributed in the protection of the homeland" and students learned about what it was like at that time. The important thing here is that these "people who contributed in the protection of the homeland" came from their mahalla. After the event of the "Memorial Day", one student said to me:

"That is Mr. xx who was at the event. Do you remember him? He owns a café and you can always see him there. He lives in G mahalla".

Students, therefore, learn that people who protected their country may live nearby and that by listening to these people, students can acquire knowledge about their own mahalla. By taking flowers and presents to the houses of elderly people, they also learn their roles and responsibilities as a member of their mahalla to support and respect old people. Students also realize that the place to practice this is in their own mahalla.

Moreover, during World War II, Uzbekistan was a part of the USSR and the two guest speakers used the phrase "during the time of rule by the Soviet Union" very often to refer to that time. Through their talks, students touched on the history of the USSR, which they did not really know. They learned about what happened in their own country at that time and how people who live in the same mahalla as them lived through that time. In this context, the mahalla can play a role in connecting students and war veterans.[28]

This school event on "Memorial Day" is considered to be the one which would lead to (2) "'citizens' who have a love of their nation and hometown" as mentioned in Table 7, and their mahalla has worked here in a way to add reality to that love. A state is such a virtual reality for its people that they do not feel it closely in their everyday life, so in order for them to feel a love of their nation and hometown, they need people who they feel close to. Therefore, mahalla was placed in the center of the place to foster a social awareness of "citizenship" as an existence between the state and its people together with schools.

H. Arendt determined the characteristics of the modern age as creating a "social realm"[29] as a result of destroying the division between the public and private realms. The division between public mahallas and the traditional private territorial network in

Uzbekistan is also becoming blurred by legal and administrative developments. Whether mahalla can be a "social realm" will need to be addressed by further research. In regards to fostering a social awareness of "citizenship" mahallas, at least, have a role in the activities of school education, and within mahallas they can cover both the public and private realms.

As mentioned above, the significance of using schools and local communities in order to foster a social awareness of "citizenship" in Uzbekistan will be shown through the following four points.

Firstly, students can learn political ability and political and legal knowledge in a place that is close to their residence. This enables them to understand what they learn at school by making it more relevant. Reports made from interviews with relevant people from the local mahalla seem to mirror the outcome of the combined effort to connect state organizations and the mahalla committee, and is just one example. Secondly, it can be shown that they can use local human resources other than school teachers for fostering a social awareness of "citizenship". Activities such as inviting representatives of the local mahalla for a talk in the class about the "Idea of National Independence" are some other examples. Thirdly, students can learn the contents taught in the classrooms more widely. After independence, when the emphasis of history is not placed on the USSR rule, but on the time of the Timur Empire, talks from war veterans are valuable opportunities for students to learn about the history of USSR rule. Lastly, mahallas are the place to implement what students have learned in schools and mahallas and, through that, students will become aware of themselves as members of that area and of society. Providing winter clothes for needy families, providing support and presents to people with disabilities, and participating in the *Hashar* (mutual aid) activities of the mahalla in their school zone and supporting old people on the "Memorial Day" are excellent examples.

(2) Activities within mahallas and a fostering social awareness of "citizenship"

The mahallas in Uzbekistan are the places for children to learn, and the mahalla committee is an important player, supporting them in many different aspects.

For example, at the new-year's spring festival of *"Navro'z"* in Uzbekistan, *Sumalak* is cooked for the mahalla and a celebration is organized for local people. For any celebration, many people in the area of the mahalla, from children to adults, participate, but the preparation of tea and setting sweets and drinks on the tables are the children's jobs. When old people of the mahalla come, children serve them tea and this continues quietly even while singing and dancing are performed behind them. Children start eating sweets and drinking tea only after the majority of the residents have left.

Photo 16 A woman from the local mahalla giving a speech at the school event on "Memorial Day". (Photo was taken by the author in May 2006)

Such celebrations within their mahallas teach children the awareness of being members of the mahallas and the responsibility and confidence that comes with it, because the celebration cannot move smoothly without them. This is a way to make the children realize that they are a part of the society around the mahalla and that they are respected members who make up that society. It is not difficult to see that the awareness of their residence in the "mahalla" created through participating in such events will lead to a social awareness of "citizenship".

Mahallas are considered as a "traditional space" for the succession of traditional customs and local culture and a "place for mutual cooperation" to exist through mutual support between the residents; but it is important to note that after independence, they are also places to encourage a public awareness and national focus by being a "basic space to integrate people".

While, at the same time, fostering a social awareness of "citizenship" as a member of the local community, mahallas are places to restore mahalla's history and traditional customs, encourage the love of homeland and to implement co-operative activities beyond ethnicity within the mahalla. These activities will lead not only to saving families from poverty, including old people and other vulnerable groups, but also to the integration of all people. In addition to fostering a social awareness of "citizenship", to be called "the citizens of Uzbekistan" not just by their own ethnicities, will reduce the feeling of "otherness" and the sense of alienation while also enabling the introduction of a new identity for all "citizens" as people of the state. In this way, the government can promote the integration of a multi-ethnic state. In present day Uzbekistan, "citizen" means the same as "people of the state", and therefore, this can be seen as a government new strategy for the integration of the state and its people.[30]

Conclusion

In this chapter, I described how Uzbekistan positioned a social awareness of "citizenship" in the state's education policy, and how it was dealt with in school education. This allowed the involvement of the local community, called a mahalla, to have collaborative activities with schools; these efforts were reviewed.

In school education in Uzbekistan, various subjects are established to foster awareness of being a "citizen" and to develop it from there, and there is collaboration between the mahalla and schools in school events such as "Memorial Day" and children's activities at the mahalla. The mahalla is, in its own sense, a place for children to learn and mahalla committee is an important participant that supports children in different ways.

However, in present day Uzbekistan, fostering a social awareness of "citizenship" tends to be equated with public awareness and a national focus as envisaged by the government, and the curriculum and teaching methods may be standardized on a national scale. Therefore, fostering a social awareness of "citizenship" only from a government's initiative may only result in the awareness that the government wishes its people to have.

Amid such movements, apart from schools, mahallas and children's homes, a new actor has joined in to foster a social awareness of "citizens", this being the many youth organizations and NGOs that have started to gain attention recently in Uzbekistan. With their own philosophies, these groups are working to nurture young people to support a civil society through volunteer work in cleaning and hospital visits in the city of Tashkent.[31] Together, with the existing government-led initiatives, broader efforts from various groups to foster the awareness of "citizens" are expected in relation to youth organizations and NGOs.

Fostering an awareness in the "citizens" of Uzbekistan may also lead to the possibility of a developing co-operation within the Central Asian region. Recently, the Japanese government has implemented support activities for Uzbekistan, Kazakhstan, Kyrgyz and Tajikistan individually through ODAs, and they are considering about supporting not only individual countries, but also targeting the region of Central Asia as a whole. This is so that countries in Central Asia may co-operate on common issues in areas such as education, infrastructure development and market-oriented economic reform; and if this kind of support is to be implemented, each country will be required to have a more national focus and public awareness as well as an awareness of what it means to be "citizens" of Central Asia and the greater international community.

The importance of the awareness of the meaning of "citizens" in Uzbekistan will be further increased. More research is needed in the future in order to clarify the actual outcomes and issues of these efforts to raise social awareness of "citizenship" by the mahalla, the youth organizations, and NGOs that I could not deal with in this chapter in detail.

Notes

[1] Shigeo Kodama, "Citizenship kyoiku no igi to kadai (Significance and challenges of citizenship education)", Zaidanhojin Akarui Senkyo Suishin Kyokai, *Watashitachi no Hiroba*, Vol.291, 2006, p.4.

[2] Shigeo Kodama, *op. cit.*, 2006, p.4. Kodama also referred to Marshall's citizenship concept, and clarified changes of citizenship concept that "citizenship of civic right developed civic right like individual freedom in 18th century to social right in the revel of social state in 20th century trough political right such as suffrage and participation in politics in 19th century". Shigeo Kodama, *Citizenship no Kyoiku Shisou (Educational Thought of Citizenship)*, Hakutaku-sha, 2003, p.12.

[3] Junko Ono, "Chiiki shakai wo katsuyou shita shiminteki shishitsu・citizenship wo hagukumu tame no kyoiku kaikaku: chiiki no kakaeru shomondai he kakawaru koto no kyoiku teki igi (Educational reform for development citizenship in a local community: The importance of the challenge of teaching local issues)", *St. Andrew's University Bulletin of the Research Institute*, Vol.31, No.2, 2005, p.100.

[4] Kazuhiko Fuwa, *Seijin Kyoiku to Shimin Shakai—Koudouteki Citizenship no Kanousei (Relationship between Adult Education and Citizenship)*, Aoki shoten, 2002, p.13.

[5] Kazuhiko Fuwa, *op. cit.*, 2002, p.14. Marshall, T. H. mentioned components of citizenship as "civil, political and social rights and obligations" together with concept of citizenship. Kazuhiko Fuwa, *op. cit.*, 2002, p.14.

[6] Shigeo Kodama, *op. cit.*, 2003, p.14. Anthony Giddens, *Daisan no Michi—Kouritsu to Kousei no Aratana Doumei (The Third Way: The Renewal of Social Democracy)*, Nihon Keizai Shinbun Sha, 1999.

[7] The Advisory Group on Citizenship, *Education for Citizenship and the teaching of democracy in schools: Final report of the Advisory Group on Citizenship*, September 22, 1998.

[8] Jiro Hasumi, "Eikoku no citizenship kyoiku—Keii・Genjo・Kadai— (Citizenship education in England: past, present, and future)", *Seiji-Kenyu*, No.55, Seiji-Kenkyukai (Institute for Political Science), Kyushu University, 2008, p.68.

[9] Ministry of Economy, Trade and Industry, *Report of Study Group on Citizenship Education and People's Activities in Economic Society*, March 2006, p.20.

[10] Educational Board of Shinagawa Ward, Creation of *"Shiminka"* Curriculum section, Set of unified elementary and Jr. High school education *Guide of Instruction of "Shiminka"*, Kyoiku Shuppan, 2006, p.1.

[11] The Society for Citizenship eds., *Citizenship no Kyoikugaku (Pedagogy for Citizenship)*, Koyoshobo, 2006, p.1. Regarding Textbook of "Shiminka" of Shinagawa Ward, Harada points out that wards such as "Politics", "Democracy" and "Parliament" are not indicated in textbook even once, and political dispute and relevant political activities are not existed in the same unit neither. Harada also highlighted that lack of political implication in "Shiminka" is exactly "political implication" of "Shiminka", and it would be related to a critical defect of citizenship

education in Shinagawa Ward. Shiori Harada, "Shinagawa ku 'Shiminka' kyokasho no seijigaku teki bunseki (A political analysis on textbook of 'Shiminka' of Shinagawa Ward)", *Gakusei Hosei Ronshu*, No.4, Kyushu Daigaku Hosei Gakkai, 2010, pp.116-117.

[12] This Chapter is consisted of results of relevant materials, materials of international conference and field work which conducted at Schools, mahallas, Fund "Mahalla" and relevant institutions in Uzbekistan by author from September 28, 2006 until September 27, 2007.

[13] "Tokushu Shiminsei Kyoiku wo Kangaeru (Special Issue Considering about Citizenship Education)", Zaidanhojin Akarui Senkyo Suishin Kyokai, *Watashitachi no Hiroba*, Vol.291, 2006, p.4.

[14] Karimov, I. A., *Izbrannyi name put'-Eto put' demokraticheskogo razvitiya i sotrudnichestva s progressivanym mirom*, Tom 11, Tashkent: Uzbekistan, 2003, s.24, s.26.

[15] Tam zhe, Karimov, 2003, s.28-29.

[16] Kuniko Mizutani, "Uzbekistan—Koukou reberu no kyoiku kaikaku wo chushin ni—Datsu roshia no tame no jinzai ikusei (Uzbekistan: Focusing on the Educational Reform at the High School Level—Human Resource Development for Moving Away from Russia)", *Science of humanity Bensei*, Vol.36, Bensei Shuppan, 2001, p.43.

[17] Seki pointed out that "ethnic-lingualization of educational reform is very useful to exclude Russian people who were former majority and have not learned Uzbek language from elite class". Keiko Seki, *Taminzoku Shakai wo Ikiru—Tenkanki Roshia no Ningen Keisei—(Living in Multi-Ethnic Society—Character Formation in the Transition Period of Russia)*, Shindokushosha, 2002, p.246.

[18] Hahn, C., "Kakkoku ni okeru 'seijiteki ni naru' to iu koto (Becoming political in different countries)" in Roland-Lévy, R. and Ross, A., eds., *Oushu Tougou to Citizenship Kyoiku—Atarashii Seiji Gakushu no Kokoromi (Political Learning and Citizenship in Europe)*, Akashi Shoten, 2006, p.126. (Original: Stoke on Trent: Trentham Press, 2003, p.78.)

[19] In the subject "Individuals and Society" at the upper secondary education revel, "opinion about human and society of philosopher in Central Asia" is taught at class. *O'rta maxsus, kac'-hunar ta'limining umumta'lim fanlari davlat ta'lim standartlari va o'quv dasturlari*, Toshkent: Sharq, 2001, b.153.

[20] Kostetsukii, V., Chobrova, T., *Azbuka Konstitutsii 2 klass*, Tashkent: Sharq, 2004, s.12-13.

[21] Tam zhe, Kostetsukii, V., Chobrova, T., 2004, s.12-13., Kostetsukii, V., Chobrova, T., *Azbuka Konstitutsii 3 klass*, Tashkent: Sharq, 2006, s.13., Kostetsukii, V., Chobrova, T., *Azbuka Konstitutsii 4 klass*, Tashkent: Sharq, 2006, s.7.

[22] Tolipova, R., Is'hoqova, M., Ikromova, N., *O'zbek Tili ta'lim boshqa tillarda olib boriladigan maktablarning 2-sinfi uchun darslik*, Toshkent: O'zbekiston, 2007, b.25, 27, 41, 46, 59, 61-65, 71., Talipova, R., Salikhova, M., Tsuvilina, E., Niyazova, Z., Nurmukhamedov, T., *Russkii yazyk 2 klass*, Tashkent: O'zbekiston, 2006, s.40-41, 46, 54-55, 56-59., Dzhuraev, L., Khan S., Kamalova, L., Hoshimov, U., Ganiyeva, H., Ziryanova, R., Ernazarova, S., Tursnova, T., *Fly High English 5*, Tashkent: O'qituvchi, 2007, pp.45, 73, 117, 124, 133-135., Dzhuraeva, Z. R., Kucharov, T. U., *Russkii yazyk kollej*, Tashkent: Sharq, 2007.

[23] Information obtained through Interview with the former representative of A mahalla (April 26, 2006, March 10, 2007, May 4, 2007), Interview with the advisor of the women's committee of G mahalla (April 15, 2006), Interview with the former representative of O mahalla (June 7, 2007), Interview with a JICA senior volunteer (March 19, 2007).

[24] *Barkamol ablod-O'zbekiston taraqqiyotining poydevori, sharq nashrie-matbaa konsternining bosh tahririyati*, Toshkent, 1997, b.28.

[25] Internal materials of A school in Mirzo Ulugbek district, Tashkent City. Information obtained through Interview with vice-principal of A school (March 10, 2006).

[26] Jan Kerkkhofs, "Yoroppa no kachi to seiji kyoiku (European values and political education)", Roland-Lévy, R. and Ross, A., eds., *op. cit.*, 2006, p.258.

[27] Alistteres, A., Karis., "Rekishi kyoiku ni okeru jiminzoku chushin shugi no jojutsu to 'yoroppa' no jigen (Description of ethnocentrism in education of history and 'European dimension')",

Roland-Lévy, R. and Ross, A., eds., *op. cit.*, 2006, p.107.

[28] Information obtained through participatory observation at A school (May 7, 2006, School event was held on May 7 because of "Memorial Day" May 9 was National holiday, and school was not opened.). Information obtained through Interview with former representative of A mahalla (March 10, 2006), Interview with vice-principal of A school (March 10, 2006), Interview with student of B class of A school.

[29] Ardendt, H., *Ningen no Joken (The Human Condition)*, Chikuma Gakugei Bunko, 1994, pp.43-131. (Original: The University of Chicago Press, 1958, p.48.).

[30] Asuka Kawano, "Uzbekistan no gakkou ni okeru chiiki kyodoutai (mahalla) no kyoiku: Seihu no mahalla seisaku tono kanren de (Community education in Uzbekistan in relation to the mahalla policy)", The Japan Comparative Education Society, *Comparative Education*, 2007, pp.166-182.

[31] In international conference, *Kamolot*, Independent Institute for Monitoring of the Formation of Civil Society, "Voce of future" and NGO "NANNOUz" reported their contents of activities. Mezhdunarodnaya konferentsiya, "Rol' molodezhi v grazhdanskogo obshchestva", 27 Sentyabrya 2007, Tashkent.

Chapter 6

Youth Education through the Cooperative Activities of Institutions: Examples from Mahalla, NGOs, and International Organizations

It is discussed in various places that the basic assignments of youth education are 1) independence of the youth themselves and 2) participation in the society. "Independence" is sometimes confused with economic independence, but here it is in a different dimension. Independence means to be mentally independent and to become a member of a society. Independence, and participation, within a society, and the education to promote them is considered to be an important element for the growth of young people.

In other words, young people relate themselves with society by using their own judgment, expressing their opinions, and cooperating with other members of the society in various issues. They also develop their unique ability and incorporate new abilities into their own role in the community. And through experiencing these processes, they acquire their certain independence. When that happens, awareness related to living in the world such as having an awareness of being a "citizen" and social awareness are necessary.

Etsuko Yaguchi defines youth as "the period between childhood and adulthood consisting of multiple transitions, and this period has its own meaning at the same time".[1] The environment surrounding the youth of Uzbekistan is changing drastically due to the birth of an independent nation, Uzbekistan, from the dissolved Soviet Union, along with the change in education system which has accompanied it. Because of these, mental and social fluctuations are seen in various scenes in the youth of Uzbekistan in the present.

After independence in 1991, questions of "what is Uzbekistan?" and "who are we, Uzbekistanis?" arose in citizens along with the reform of the educational system in Uzbekistan. Previously, Uzbekistan was a part of the Soviet Union, so they needed to eliminate the idea of the being a Soviet citizen from the people living there and create a new concept.

Previously, citizenship was "created mainly by political concepts, and it means to be a member of a nation (=citizen) that is formed as a community of that nation (= citizen nation) in modern society".[2] However, the concepts of nation and citizens have been shaken due to the globalization of the society after *Perestroika*.

The construction of an independent nation is ongoing in the current Uzbekistan, and the development of a new generation that has the awareness of being a "citizen" and having national awareness is necessary. However, since Uzbekistan is a multi-ethnic culture, the framework of "one nation=one ethnicity" does not exist, so they are required to construct new foundation.

In this social and national situation, Uzbekistan requires the development of the awareness as "citizen" of Central Asia as well as their own national awareness. This is because they are required to integrate the ethnicities in Central Asia that live in the country and national construction in cooperation with four other nations in Central Asia (Kazakhstan, Kyrgyz, Tajikistan, and Turkmenistan). Because of this, the school education in current Uzbekistan, students study themes such as "Central Asia is our common home" and the "Uzbek people are Central Asians".[3] The policy to enhance the awareness of being a "citizen" that accompanies the awareness of also being a "Central Asian" is promoted strongly.[4]

On the other hand, various forms of assistance from international organizations such as UNDP, UNICEF, and UNESCO and foreign organizations such as Ebert Memorial Fund from Germany, NDI (National Democratic Institute) from the US, SOS Children's Villages from Austria, JICA from Japan, and KOICA from Korea were developed after the independence of Uzbekistan. The support for Uzbekistan from these institutions includes technology, the formation of a civil society and promoting the social participation of the youth.

Within these circumstances in Uzbekistan, what kind of role do mahallas, youth organizations, and international organizations play in the youth education of Uzbekistan? And what is the significance in cooperation among institutions in youth education?

In this chapter, I will discuss how mahallas, youth organizations, and international organizations have activities for youth education and significance of their cooperation.

1. Position of NGOs and Youth Organizations in Uzbekistan and Their Activities

In Section 1, I will position NGOs and youth organizations in Uzbekistan and their activities and discuss the activities of "*Kamolot*" by the Central Council for Youth Social Activities, and "Voice of the Future" by Youth Initiative Center. I will also focus especially on the National Association of Nongovernmental and Nonprofit Organizations of Uzbekistan (NANNOUz).

Here, I will first give a general view of how youth education is developed in the education policy of Uzbekistan.

The education law (Law of the Republic of Uzbekistan "On Education") was revised in September 1997, and the reform of educational system is still continuing now. This new law determined that the compulsory education is a 4-5-3 system (total of 12 years) and education for the new generation is done in the process of the construction of the nation and market economy.

Furthermore, the "National Programme for Personnel Training (NPPT)", which is a national program for developing a new generation, was selected in October of the same year. This program focuses on the upper secondary education which students are divided into academic lyceums and professional colleges where the academic lyceum provides special subjects and the goal of the professional colleges is to teach occupational techniques.

As of February 2008, a lower committee related to education is still under discussion and the proposal for this revision is to develop a "National Programme for Personnel Training (NPPT)" and enhance support for people with disabilities.[5]

There are various definitions for the youth in current Uzbekistan, but many of the institutions who conducted interviews defined the youth as being from the upper secondary education (high school level in Japan) to 30 years old. For example, the youth organization "*Kamolot*" defines youth as people from 14 to 30 years old.[6]

According to the Ministry of Public Education, about 40% of the population is under 19 years old and about 64% of the total population is under 30 years old.[7] Because of this, upper secondary education and higher education, which are the foundation of the youth education, and youth education places other than schools are required to have rapid development. In the following, I will examine the organizations that support the youth education other than schools such as "*Kamolot*" by the Central Council for Youth Social Activities, "Voice of the Future" by Youth Initiative Center, and the National Association of Nongovernmental and Nonprofit Organizations of Uzbekistan (NANNOUz), along with their organizational form and activities.

(1) NGOs and Youth Organizations in Uzbekistan and Their Trend
1. Youth Organization "*Kamolot*"

"*Kamolot*" is a nationwide youth organization in the Republic of Uzbekistan Central Council for Youth Social Activities and was organized in August 2001 by the order of the president. These organizations have unique activities based on programs that emphasize critical issues in the lives of young people such as the unification of young people in Uzbekistan, the construction of free and developed nation, and ensuring the rights and requests of young people. Among those, they especially emphasize the environment, health, and nurturing of patriotism.

There are 17,000 branch offices of *Kamolot* throughout the nation, and they are located in the buildings of universities, academic lyceums, and professional colleges. They also publish five papers for their newsletters such as "Turkistan", and "The Youth of Uzbekistan."

In addition, they organized a children's organization in the Republic "*Kamalak*" and have activities. *Kamalak* integrates over 4 million children in the nation who are from 5 or 6 years old to under 14 years old, and they have activities that enhances the children's patriotism who are in charge of the future and improve the historical knowledge in the area where they live.[8]

The system and activities of *Kamolot* and *Kamalak* give an impression that they are extremely similar to *Oktyabryata, Pioneers,* and *Komsomol* (refer to Chapter 3, page 75 to 77), but it has been pointed out that *Kamolot* continues to use the old building of the headquarters of the Republic *Komsomol* after independence and has activities that meet the demand of the time era such as promoting the "democracy" led by the government.[9] Either way, the fact that the youth organizations are positioned under the strong guidance system of the president or the government was the same during the Soviet period as it is after independence, and those organizations are greatly influencing youth education.

2. Youth Initiative Center "The Voice of the Future"

The youth initiative center, "The Voice of the Future", is a youth organization founded in March, 2006. They explain the significance of their activities as "allowing the youth to be self-dependent and demonstrate their abilities". This center has "clubs of their interest" and organizes various activities conducted by the activists in the center.

The framework of "The Voice of the Future" is various youth project and young people. They actually have various projects hosted by the center with over 2,000 youth leaders where they can try exerting their own principles and creativity.

Also, the center is active in promoting the project on "youth and social issues" and they plan and implement training, seminars, and meetings to improve the knowledge level of the youth while expanding their vision.

Furthermore, this center cooperate with other youth organizations such as *Kamolot* mentioned earlier and promote cooperation with other project in the center and try to prevent the vertical split of the organization. This center has also had cooperative relationship with "International House Tashkent", which is an academic lyceum that provides lessons mainly in English, and multiple universities in Tashkent.[10]

3. Citizen Association "National Association of Nongovernmental and Nonprofit Organizations of Uzbekistan"

Citizen Association "National Association of Nongovernmental and Nonprofit Organizations of Uzbekistan" explained their value and the challenges of their activities as the following.

The most important activity of NANNOUz is to ensure the value of democracy, rights, freedom, and the importance of social legislation. In order words, it is to protect the citizens of our nation. Therefore, NANNOUz should provide overall support in the liberation, modernization, and national reform in all areas of the democratization of the society and social life as a whole.

I will take a look at the specific activities of this association in the following. Other than that, the Republic Ethics Education and Popularization Center "Spirituality and Education (*Ma'naviyat va Ma'rifat*)" also cooperates with local government, mahalla, universities, academic lyceums, professional colleges, and various NGOs and have activities, lectures, events, and meetings with themes including "Constitution of Uzbekistan", "Duty and Rights of Citizens", "What is Uzbekistan Citizen", "Political Party", "Presidential Election" and "Traditional Culture of Uzbekistan".[11]

(2) Example of NANNOUz Cooperating with Other Institutions

Currently, NANNOUz cooperate with various organizations such as "*Karate* League", "Association of All Clinical Doctors", the tourism development center *Zierat*, and teachers' associations. To join NANNOUz they must be a volunteer organization. Once they are approved as a member of NANNOUz, they become a non-national not for profit organization. If an organization wishes to join, they first have to agree to the rules of NANNOUz, then, they are registered within the Republic of Uzbekistan and follow the regulations and pay the joining fee. The groups that have joined have headquarters not just in Tashkent, but also in various regions of Uzbekistan such as Samarkand and Karakalpakstan.

As it shows, NANNOUz and their member organizations have a strong network through activities based on following the rules and duties determined by NANNOUz and ensuring, and using, their rights as a member. NANNOUz benefits by understanding the regional situation of Uzbekistan and the integration and management of member organizations, while the member organizations can request support and direction from the national organization structure of NANNOUz as well as the organizational stability received from a group on a national scale; both parties benefit.

One of the examples of their activities is on May 9th "Memorial Day", which is a holiday that is celebrated every year in Uzbekistan. On May 11th, 2007, an event related to NANNOUz's social and human project was held at Gafur Gulom Memorial culture and relief park. This event was held for military members, orphans, evacuees, and other citizens. NANNOUz has many events planned and held related to holidays in Uzbekistan other than "Memorial Day".

Furthermore, 2007 was determined to be the "Year of Social Security" by the president's order, so non-national and not for profit institutions had events related to solving the problem of social security as well as the governmental institution.[12]

Also, this association participated in the international roundtable held by the youth organization *Kamolot* mentioned earlier, and exchanged opinions. At the international roundtable held in February 2008 on "the significance of getting ahead in the youth policy of Uzbekistan in the formation of a civil society" a few students who were hosting a youth club in a university requested the following.

"We need support from three areas in order to do club activities. First is the support of the facilities. It is necessary to improve the hardware, such as tools and infrastructure, in order to promote the activity of clubs. The second one is the support in the methods of having activities. We want some coaching in order to have better activities. The third one is support in information. We would like to know about the activities of other institutions and have access to examples. We would like to have the opportunity to know those kinds of information".

For those requests, participants of the roundtable from NANNOUz responded that it is possible to provide support from those three aspects and that they would like to exchange opinions and support them in the future.[13]

This organization also cooperates with international organizations and has various activities. On June 7th, 2007, a spiritual enlightenment seminar "the improvement of the representative of non-national and not for profit organizations and education skills of teachers" was held by NANNOUz and UNICEF. The protection of children, boys and girls, is a permanent issue, so the nation puts emphasis on it. For this problem, international regulation represented by the Convention on the Rights of the Child was used in the law making of Uzbekistan. They are also currently trying to revise the court system in relation to minors.

The change of social and legal foundations in the present suggests the necessity and challenges in specialized education for lawyers, judges, prosecutors, representative of social groups, and other professionals. As shown in the example of the spiritual enlightenment seminar mentioned before, NANNOUz gives instructions to aim for improving the education skills of specialists who are active in educating legal disputes subjecting minors via a partnership with the nation and national institutions. This spiritual enlightenment was not hosted by UNICEF, but held by a NANNOUz project which was supported by UNICEF, so it was especially emphasized that specialists from the country and abroad participated in the training.

Other agreements on cooperation related to the issues of human resource training from 2005 to 2009 were the enhancements of the cooperation between Uzbekistan's government and UNICEF.[14]

UNAIDS (the Joint United Nations Programme on HIV/AIDS) also has activities to diffuse knowledge about HIV/AIDS for young people in cooperation with NGOs and NPOs both in and outside of Uzbekistan. UNAIDS' activities are done in cooperation with the Women's Committees of the Republic of Uzbekistan and NGOs.[15]

As it shows, the current support activities of international organization not only support the social infrastructure and improvements of the school environment, but they also reach the area of qualitative principle support, such as supporting young people and specialists who support them. The characteristic in recent years has been that these support activities of international organizations do not stop at the government, but also reach youth organizations, NGOs, and NPOs.

The cooperation of institutions in youth education makes it easier to do their activities all over Uzbekistan and allows local areas and small organizations to communicate their requests. Also, by having large scale organizations such as *Kamolot* and NANNOUz and small scale organizations and local organizations will deepen the interaction among small scale organizations and local organizations. Because of this, the increase of opportunities to receive various forms of support and participate in the activities can be expected. On the other hand, if the network become too strong or vertical division become too much, there is a danger that the originality of each organization may become too weak. As a result, the organization may be standardized in the nation and support that corresponds to both the local environment and the needs of young people may be overlooked.

2. Cooperative Activities of Each Institutions and Mahalla

Next, I will examine examples of the cooperative activities between each institution and mahalla.

(1) Youth Education in Mahalla

The social and structural changes of mahalla today are causing various changes to society, education, etc. In this situation, what kind of role does mahalla have for youth education? Also, how do mahalla committees have activities?

Mahalla has been in the nation for a long time and has been traditionally dealing with the protection of moral and historical tradition as well as social activities. After independence, mahalla as a residents' self-governing institution was required to act as the new foundation for the nation. Therefore, after 1992, the resolution of many issues for local government was commissioned to mahalla, and the Law of the Republic of Uzbekistan "on residents' self-governing institutions" was revised on April 14th, 1999. Mahalla's political and legal foundation was enhanced, and position as an end institution for the government was established legally and politically.

During the Soviet period, mahalla committees kept track of the exact number of children who were in school and supervised those children by visiting their schools. After the independence of Uzbekistan, the position of mahalla committees has been expanding because of the establishment of the Law of the Republic of Uzbekistan "On residents' self-governing institutions".

Currently, some mahallas provide education such as computer, cooking, and sewing courses for young people who do not have a job, and provide educational opportunities for the local residents. Also, due to the national policy, the cooperation between mahalla and schools is becoming closer.[16] For example, representatives of mahalla are invited to the event for the Constitution day on December 8th and classes on "Idea of National Independence" and give lectures to the class.

Also in one mahalla, the representative of mahalla and the mahalla committee invited university professors and poets to have lectures in mahalla for youth education. Another mahalla owns sports facilities and equipment for residents and promote sports to young people at the direction of mahalla representative. The objective of such mahalla activities is to have young people focus on academics and sports and prevent them from engaging in deviant behavior.[17]

(2) Cooperative Activities of International NGO "SOS Children's Village" and Mahalla

Recently in Uzbekistan, there has been an increase in cooperative activities between mahalla, international organizations and international NGOs. "SOS Children's Village", which is an international support group from Austria, has orphanages in Tashkent and Samarkand and has their own activities.

For example, "SOS Children's Village" in Tashkent has "Schooling" and "FSP-Family Strengthening Program", and they have 14 family cottages, a kindergarten, management building, hotel, garage, and house for the director and teachers in the facility. Especially "FSP" is carried out with the cooperation of mahalla, and support from mahalla for young people who have graduated from the upper secondary education and advanced their academics or got a job is critical in choosing their educational path and ensuring their employment.[18]

Recently, cooperative activities with mahalla and international organizations or international NGOs have been increasing. There are many advantages for international organizations to have more activities in mahalla; funding, know-how of the activities, and ensuring various human resources. This is because they can expect to provide support that suites the situation of the local community by utilizing the local human resources of that community. However, a success in one mahalla does not guarantee a success in other mahallas. It is because factors such as the mahalla's local structure, ethnic structure, male to female ratio, existence of schools, and the characteristics of the mahalla representative and mahalla committee are involved in the activities of each institution and mahalla. The fact that it is difficult to generalize the success of an example in a community must be solved through the future activities of international organizations and international NGOs in mahalla.

3. Image of Local Community for Young People in Uzbekistan and the Activities of Each Institution: Based on a Survey from Multiple Universities

In Section 3, the image of the local community for young people in Uzbekistan will be described based on survey research conducted at multiple universities in Uzbekistan. In this research, a survey with closed- and open-ended questions on "research on the view of Central Asia and local community for young people" was composed and the survey was conducted at two universities in Uzbekistan using the self-recording and collection method. The purpose of this research is to clarify how much young people in

Uzbekistan participate in local community activities, how many opportunities they have to interact with other countries in Central Asia, and how they understand local communities and Central Asia. In other words, it was to clarify the young people's participation rate, their situation in the local community and their image of local community and Central Asia. However, the young people's view of Central Asia is not directly related to the main focus of this book, so the discussion of these results will be done in the future and the questions in the survey are not indicated.

Generally, open-ended questions have a lower response rate than close-ended ones, but the purpose of this research was to grasp the image of local community in free images in order to avoid the dangers of making inappropriate choices or arbitrarily guiding the answers of the respondents. So, author used a combination of open- and close-ended questions.

The research subject was co-ed national universities with multiple ethnicities in Uzbekistan, and universities that have various specialized departments and graduate school were selected. As a result, (1) Tashkent State Institute of Oriental Studies and (2) University of World Economy and Diplomacy, which have various departments in the academic departments of culture and sociology such as international relations, economics, and literature departments, were chosen.[19]

Participants included 81 students from Tashkent State Institute of Oriental Studies who are in their 1st through 4th year and are learning Japanese (18 male students and 53 female students. 10 students answered the questionnaire but did not answer the section on sex and ethnicity) and 33 students from the University of World Economy and Diplomacy who are in their 1st through 4th year and are learning Japanese (20 male and 12 female students. 1 student answered the questionnaire but did not answer the section on sex and ethnicity) and it was done from March to April in 2008.[20] The survey was done in Russian, and it was distributed after Japanese or history class, and further explanation was provided when they did not understand the meaning or content of questions in Russian. The survey was distributed and collected in class so the collection rate was 100%.

The participant details are as follows, 37 Uzbek people, 13 Russians, 6 Koreans, 5 Tatars, 2 Armenians, 3 Uighurs, 1 Azerbaijan, 3 Kazakhs, 1 Turkmen, and 10 people that did not respond from Tashkent State Institute of Oriental Studies, and 28 Uzbek people, 1 Russian, 1 Korean, 1 Tatar, 1 Kazakhs, and 1 person who did not respond from University of World Economy and Diplomacy. The total number of research subjects was 114.

As a preliminary research for the study in Uzbekistan, similar research was done from

February to March 2008 for 22 students who were learning Japanese in the second and third year at Kazakh National University in Kazakhstan and 31 students who are in their fourth year in the translation department and humanity department of Kyrgyz Turkish Manas University in Kyrgyz. Based on the collection and analysis of the question received from the students, comments and advice about the questions from students, and opinions on survey structures and question methods from the local teachers, a final questionnaire for the research in Uzbekistan was composed (page 160 to 162 in this chapter). The details of the research items are indicated in the following.

Table 8 Items on questionnaire survey

a) Question related to the respondent Age, sex, ethnicity, place of birth (city and region): At the end of the questionnaire
b) Questions related to the young people's image of local community, level of participation in the activities of local community and its content: Questions (1), (2), (4) Attitude toward contributions to society: Question (3) Attitude toward the activities of the local community: Question (5), (6) How they view their local community: Question (7), (8)

Table 9 Ethnicity and Sex of the respondents
(Unit: People. % is the ratio of total number of people)

	Uz	Ru	Ko	Ta	Ar	Ui	Az	Ka	Tu	No response	Total
M	32	2	1	0	0	1	0	1	1		38
F	33	12	6	6	2	2	1	3	0		65
Total	65 (57%)	14 (12%)	7 (6%)	6 (5%)	2 (1%)	3 (3%)	1 (1%)	4 (4%)	1 (1%)	11 (10%)	114

Source: Composed by the author based on the results of survey research in Uzbekistan.
* Uz (Uzbek), Ru (Russian), Ko (Korea), Ta (Tatar), Ar (Armenia), Ui (Uighur), Az (Azerbaijan), Ka (Kazakh), Tu (Turkmen).

In the framework of analysis for the research items indicated in Table 8, I assumed a difference in opinion based on their ethnicity and sex, but as it is indicated in Table 9, there is uneven distribution of ethnicity and sex, so I did not examine the ethnicity with small number of sample, and instead discussed the difference between Uzbek people and other ethnicities. Also for the responses without the indication of ethnicity and sex, they were only included in the number when it was necessary to understand the research result, such as detail of the sample indicated before, but are excluded from examination based on ethnicity. Also for the difference between male and female, it was not compared because the number of females was almost double the number of males and therefore difficult to examine. Furthermore, since almost all of the students who were research subjects were taking Japanese lessons, it was difficult to represent the attitude of all university students and young people of Uzbekistan. I also note that they often see and hear foreign language and domestic and international news, as well as having the opportunity to study abroad and have interaction with foreigners.

(1) The Level of Participation and Participation Situation of Local Activity for Young People

In the questionnaire, I asked the question "(1) Do you participate in the activities of your local community? If so, please indicate the specific events and activities". and "(2) If you participate in the activity of local community, how often do you participate?" in order to research the level of participation and participation situation of young people in their local community.

Survey

Цель анкеты: исследование взглядов молодёжи на Центральную Азию и общество. Ответьте на 14 вопросов, отметив один ответ из четырёх вариантов (a, b, c, d) или написав своё мниение.

The objective of this survey: Please answer the following 14 questions for the research regarding young people's view of Central Asia and local community. Please choose one answer among 4 (a, b, c, d) and circle one, or write down your thoughts and opinions.

(1) Принимаете ли Вы участие в деятельности местного сообщества жителей (местной организации жителей)? Если участвуете, напишите в каких мероприятиях (например: празднование Навруза, волонтёр, уборка и т.д).

---

a. Сейчас участвую   b. Раньше участвовал(а)   c. Буду участвовать
d. Совсем не участвую
(Конкретные мероприятия   )
(1) Do you participate in the activities of your local community? If so, please indicate the specific events and activities? (Example: *Navro'z* event, volunteer activity, cleaning, etc.
   a. I am currently participating.   b. I have participated before.
   c. I plan to participate in the future.   d. I don't participate at all.
     (Specific activities:)

(2) Если Вы участвуете в деятельности местного сообщества жителей, то как часто?
(Например: один раз в неделю, один раз в месяц, только во время конкретных мероприятий)
(2) If you participate in the activities of the local community, how often do you participate?
(Example: Once a week, once a month, only when an event is held, etc.)

(3) Обычно хотите ли Вы быть полезным обществу?
   a. Всегда   b. Иногда   c. Не задумываюсь над этим вопросом
   d. Совсем не думаю о том, чтобы быть полезным обществу
(3) Do you wish to contribute to society as a member of the society on a daily basis?
   a. Always   b. Sometimes   c. Not very often   d. Not at all.

(4) Бывает ли, чтобы Вы делали что-либо совместно с жителями своего района или города?
   a. Постоянно делаю   b. Иногда делаю   c. Делаю, но не часто
   d. Совсем ничего не делаю
(4) Do you have the opportunity to do something together with people who live in the same town or area?
   a. Often   b. Sometimes   c. Not very often.   d. Not at all.

(5) Когда представляестя возможность, хотите ли Вы сделать что либо совмстно со жителями вашего райлна?
   a. Обязательно хочу   b. Иногда хочу   c. Не особенно хочу   d. Совсем не хочу
(5) If there is an opportunity, do you want to do something together with adults in the

local community?
a. I am eager to do so.   b. I want to do it sometimes.
c. I don't want to very much.   d. I don't want to at all.

(6) Когда Вы участвуете в деятельности местного сообщества жителей, то какие преимущества (положительные стороны) Вы видите для себя и для общества?
(6) What do you think are the advantages in participating in local community activities?

(7) Какие у Вас ассоциации со словом «сообщество»(community)? (что Вы представляете себе при этом слове?) Напишите своё мнение.
(7) What is your mental image when you hear the word local community or community? Please write down your opinion freely.

(8) Что такое «сообщество» для Вас?
(8) What does local community or community mean to you?

Допишите, если у Вас по данному вопросу есть свое собственное мнение или пожелания.
If you have any opinion or request, please feel free to write them down.

Возраст(на 1 Февраля 2008г.) Age (as of Feb. 1st, 2008)	Пол 1.М 2.Ж Sex 1. Male 2. Female	Национальность Ethnicity	Место рождения Область: Город: Place of birth State: City:

Спасибо за ответы!
Thank you for your participation.

Асука Кавано,   (ТГПУ имени Низами, Университет Кюсю)
Asuka Kawano (Tashkent State Pedagogical University, Kyushu University)

During the analysis process, among the 114 total respondents, the 103 people who answered their sex and ethnicity were subject of analysis. For the question "(1) Do you participate in the activities of your local community? If so, please indicate the specific events and activities, 23 people answered a. I am currently participating, 31 people answered b. I have participated before, 15 people answered c. I plan to participate in the future, and 34 people answered d. I don't participate at all.

34 people among the 103 research subject (33% of the total analysis subjects) answered that they do not participate at all to the activities of the local community, more than the 23 people who answered that "they are currently participating" (22% of the total analysis subjects). This result exposed the low participation level of young people in the local community. Even when I consider the results without indicating ethnicity or sex (65 Uzbek people and 38 other ethnicities), 17 out of 38 people (about 45% of the people are other ethnicities) from ethnicities other than Uzbek chose "I don't participate at all" and it clarified the low level of participation in the activities of the local community. However, contrary to what was expected, 26% of Uzbek people answered that "I don't participate at all", more than the 22% who answered "I am currently participating".

Table 10 Level of participation to the activity of local community according to their ethnicities
(Unit: People. % is the ratio of total number of subject of 103 people)

Response	Uz	Ru	Ko	Ta	Ar	Ui	Az	Ka	Tu	Total
a	14	4	1	0	1	1	1	1	0	23 (22%)
b	23	1	1	4	0	0	0	1	1	31 (30%)
c	11	1	1	0	0	2	0	0	0	15 (15%)
d	17	8	4	2	1	0	0	2	0	34 (33%)

Source: Composed by the author based on the result of the research.

Based on the results indicated above, about half of the people in ethnicities other than Uzbek do not participate in the activities of their local community or, in other words, their mahalla. Moreover, about a quarter of Uzbek people also do not participate in the activity of mahalla. This shows that there is a difference in the level of local community activity participation of other ethnicities, but it also shows that when we examine it only for Uzbek people, their participation rate is not so high either.

Also relating to the question (1), for the question asked "(2) If you participate in the activities of the local community, how often do you participate?", 53 people (41 Uzbek people, 5 Russians, 1 Kazakh, 3 Koreans, 1 Tatar, 1 Turkmen, and 1 Armenian) answered "only when an event is held". Also, 9 people answered once a month (8 Uzbek people, 1 Uighur), and one person answered twice a month (1 Uzbek). Other answers were "when I have time", "at the time of *Hashar* (mutual help)", "sometimes", "once to 6 times every 3 months" with one person answering for each question. Although most of the students answered "only when an event is held", 5 students answered "I participate once a week" and they mentioned "cleaning, "*Hashar*", "volunteering", and "*Navro'z*" as the activities they participate. In addition, a few people answered the holidays and events unique to Uzbekistan such as the celebration festival for the birth of Amir Timur, celebration for international women's day, celebration of teachers' day (October 1st every year), and local meetings.

Also for the question "(4) Do you have the opportunity to do something together with people who live in the same town or area?" to clarify how often young people participate in the activities to cooperate with others, 5 people answered "a. often", 28 people answered "b. sometimes", 44 people answered "c. not very often", and 25 people answered "d. not at all". This result clarified that it is not true that young people do not participate in the activities of their local community at all, but they do not participate in them on a daily basis either. Also for the level of cooperation with the local community, Uzbek students have a slightly higher participation level when compared to other ethnicities such as Russian and Korean.

Either way, why is the participation rate of the university students low even though the Ministry of Higher and Secondary Specialized Education, local government, Fund "Mahalla", youth organization "*Kamolot*", educational institution in mahalla and mahalla committee are promoting the young people's participation in the activities of mahalla?

One of the reasons may be the change of lifestyle to being busy with their studies at the university or other activities. One of the causes is that they spend less time in the local community compared to the after school time of elementary and lower secondary education, instead they spend time in other places than mahalla such as restaurants at the university, entertainment facilities like movie theaters where many young people gather and spend their time freely. Another reason is the change in human relationships involving young people. Until they are in university (or the upper secondary education) the living area of a child is relegated to within the mahalla, where they live in proximity with family, relatives, local residents, and friends at school. In other words, when they are a child, their only human relationships are limited to within their mahalla, but as

Table 11 Level of cooperation with surrounding people
(Unit: People. % is the ratio of total number of subject of 103 people)

Response	Uz	Ru	Ko	Ta	Ar	Ui	Az	Ka	Tu	Total
a	4	0	0	0	0	1	0	0	0	5 (5%)
b	22	2	1	0	0	1	0	2	0	28 (27%)
c	29	4	4	2	1	1	1	1	1	44 (43%)
d	9	8	2	4	1	0	0	1	0	25 (24%)
Other	1	0	0	0	0	0	0	0	0	1 (1%)

Source: Composed by the author based on the results of the research.

they enter university, new lifestyles and human relationships are constructed and their sense of belonging to mahalla is less than it was when they were a child.

The students who were the subjects of this research were studying foreign language, Japanese or some other language, so they are either interested in a foreign country or wishing to study abroad. The fact that they have more opportunity to focus on other places than mahalla and Uzbekistan could be a factor in their detachment from the local community (mahalla).

This trend shows significantly in the mahalla activity participation levels. There are only a few students who participate in the activities of their mahalla periodically, so there are more students who only participate when they have an event where they can re-recognize that they were a resident of the mahalla.

Students from Kazakhstan and Kyrgyz, whose ancestors were nomads and do not have traditional local community like mahalla, responded similarly.

Among the 22 students from Kazakhstan, only 2 people are currently participating in the activities and other students either "participated before (15 people) or "do not participate at all (5 people). Also, there were no students who plan to participate in the future.

On the other hand, among the 31 students from Kyrgyz, 6 students answered "currently participating", 9 students answered "participated before", 2 students said "plan to participate in the future", and 11 students answered "not at all" being the largest number, and 3 students were unknown.

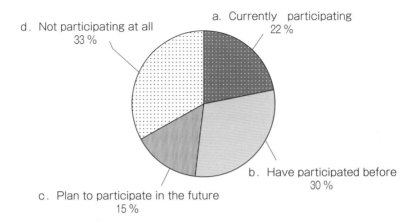

Figure 5 Young people's participation situation in their local community
Source: Composed by the author based on the result of the research.

On the other hand, the question that asked the attitude toward social contribution, "(3) Do you wish to contribute to society as a member of that society on a daily basis?" 40 students answered "a. always" and among those, Uzbek people were the most with 31 people. Also, 51 students answered "b. sometimes" and when it is limited to Uzbek people, numbers of "always" and "sometimes" were competing against each other. There were 12 students who answered "not very often" and none answered "d. not at all".

Based on these results, it was clarified that most of the Uzbek students want to make some type of contribution to the society. When analyzing the responses of students from backgrounds other than Uzbek, the responses of "a", "b", "c" are evenly distributed, but for Uzbek students, almost all of them answered "a" or "b" and only two students chose "c".

Table 12 Attitudes toward making a contribution to society
(Unit: People. % is the ratio of total number of subject of 103 people)

Response	Uz	Ru	Ko	Ta	Ar	Ui	Az	Ka	Tu	Total
a	31	1	1	1	1	3	1	1	0	40 (39%)
b	32	7	4	4	1	0	0	2	1	51 (50%)
c	2	6	2	1	0	0	0	1	0	12 (11%)
d	0	0	0	0	0	0	0	0	0	0 (0%)

Source: Composed by the author based on the results of the research.

Table 13 Attitudes toward cooperating with people in their local community (Unit: People. % is the ratio of total number of subject of 103 people)

Response	Uz	Ru	Ko	Ta	Ar	Ui	Az	Ka	Tu	Total
a	28	2	2	0	0	2	0	1	0	35 (34%)
b	24	3	2	4	0	1	1	2	1	38 (37%)
c	12	7	2	1	2	0	0	1	0	25 (24%)
d	1	2	1	1	0	0	0	0	0	5 (5%)

Source: Composed by the author based on the results of the research.

Attitude towards the activity in their local community was asked in questions (5) and (6). For question "(5) If there is an opportunity, do you want to do something together with adults in the local community?" four choices of "a. I am eager to do so", "b. I want to do it sometimes", "c. I don't want to very much", and "d. I don't want to at all" were set up. A total of 35 students answered "a. I am eager to do so", a total of 38 students answered "b. I want to do it sometimes", a total of 25 students answered "c. I don't want to very much" and a total of 5 students answered "d. I don't want to at all".

The question (5) clarified that a majority of the young people wish to do some type of activities in cooperation with people in their local community. Here, Uzbek students showed a more positive attitude toward the cooperative activities with people in their local community.

The question "(6) what do you think are the advantages in participating in local community activities?" was asked in a free-writing question so students could respond freely with their own concepts. Here, there were opinions such as "being able to learn with the surrounding people", "cooperative activities with local residents", "mutual understanding", "opinion exchange", "an increase in closeness in the local community", "understanding", "being able to be a great person" and "mutual help". This shows that young people see a certain degree of value in the activities of local community. However, it was mentioned earlier that there are only a few young people who actually participate in the activities of their local community.

The responses from university students show that even though the government and various institutions encourage young people to participate in the activities of mahalla, young people are gradually detached from mahalla because of the change in their living environment.

(2) Local Community for Young People

As detachment from mahalla is progressing, what do young people think about mahalla and local community?

In the questionnaire, questions "(7) what is your mental image when you hear the word local community or community?" and "(8) what does local community or community mean to you?" were given in order to research the young people's view of mahalla. Since the format was in free writing, there were many students who did not answer.

The responses included "group of people", "group of people in a cooperative body", "group of good people", "group of people with the same hobby", and "family". There were a few students who answered mahalla as their response but there were no answers that said group of people who live in the same area or society formed from regional bonds.

Based on the answers above, students who responded to the questions basically consider community to be a group of people who are connected. Mahalla is community that is formed from the street and structured based on the regional bonds of people who live in the same area. Of course, mahalla is structured based on the mutual relationship of the people who live there as well as the street, but based on the student's response, the structural elements of mahalla and young people's images of local community and community are gradually separating.

In the present situation, when mahalla, youth organizations, NGOs have activities for young people in mahalla, it is essential to have the activity while having a good understanding of the young people's image of local community and community.

Conclusion

In this section I examined the activities of international organizations for youth education in Uzbekistan mainly with mahalla, youth organizations, and UN organizations. As a result of this examination, the significance of their cooperative activities of those institutions is as follows.

(1) Network with Each Institution

The first point is that a strong network is made between mahalla and youth organizations. Small scaled organizations and local organizations have financial and geographic limitations. In order to overcome those problems, large scaled and nationwide organizations such as *Kamolot* and NANNOUz provide assistance and guidance to those organizations. These large scaled institutions act as mediator between small scaled organizations and local organizations.

In Uzbekistan, where various organizations were made and began their activities after independence, having guidance and support from the main organization is significant in promoting the activities of small scaled and local organizations. Also, cooperating with mahalla, where the young people actually live, allows institutions to provide support activities that are close to the young people. It has the same significance that international organizations and international NGOs also cooperate with those large scaled institutions and spread their support activities nationwide.

(2) Openness of the Activities

The second point is that activities of each institution were held through international conferences and events. As it was mentioned above, at International Roundtable held by *Kamolot*, Independent Institute for Monitoring of the Formation of Civil Society, and the Ebert Memorial Fund of Germany representatives of the student club in university requested three supports from the presenters of NANNOUz. It shows the attitude to publicize that horizontal connection such as NANNOUz, *Kamolot*, Youth Initiative Center "Voice of the Future" to the youth; the receivers of that support.

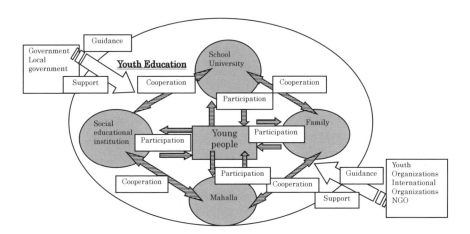

Figure 6   Correlative figures centering on young people in youth education
           Composed by the author

(3) Decrease in Unique Activity and Differences in Enthusiasm between Institutions and Young People

However, there are some issues in the activities of these institutions. For example, because of the strong network, there is a danger that the uniqueness of each institution may be lost, and there is a difference in the degree of participation depending on the organization. There is a chance that those organizations that depend on the support and guidance from the nationwide institutions and, in the process, are in danger of losing their uniqueness. Also, the difference in enthusiasm for participation in each institution may cause differences of opportunity for the youth education.

Furthermore, when the activity takes place mainly in mahalla, they need to plan the activity while considering the young people's image of local community and community on top of their needs and lifestyle.

In the future, it is important for each institution to balance the support and guidance from large scaled institutions with the uniqueness of their own institution as they develop various activities in youth education. And international organizations and international NGOs should understand the situation of Uzbekistan and project the opinions and needs of the young people who are the actual receivers of the support and have activities that people can participate in voluntarily.

This Chapter mainly dealt with the activities of large scaled institutions such as *Kamolot*, NANNOUz, and other international organization. How small scaled organizations and local institutions receive the guidance and support of the large scaled institutions mentioned above, how small scaled organizations and local organizations communicate their requests and opinions to those large scaled institutions, activities of small scaled organizations in mahalla and young people's participation situation, and how they are received will be a future assignment.

Notes

[1] Etsuko Yaguchi, "Ningenteki jiritsu to seinen kyoiku (Human Independence and Youth Education)", *Kouza Gendai Shakai Kyoiku no Riron II Gendaiteki Jinken to Shakai Kyoiku no Kachi (Lecture Theory of Modern Social Education II Modern Human Rights and Value of Social Education)*, Toyokanshuppansha, 2004, p.224.

[2] Junko Ono, "Chiiki shakai wo katsuyou shita shiminteki shishitsu・citizenship wo hagukumu tame no kyoiku kaikaku: Chiiki no kakaeru shomondai he kakawaru koto no kyoiku teki igi (Educational Reform for Development Citizenship in a Local Community: The Importance of the Challenge of Teaching Local Issues)", *St. Andrew's University Bulletin of the Research Institute*, Vol.31, No.2, 2005, p.100.

[3] *O'rta Makhsus, Kac'-Khnar Ta'limining Umumta'lim Fanlari Davrat Ta'lim Stabdartlari va*

O'quv Dasturlari, Toshkent: Sharq, 2001, b.209.

[4] In addition, under graduate students answered "My home", "My country, motherland and neighbor countries" about question "What is Central Asia is for you?" at questionnaire survey that was conducted under graduate students at Al-Farabi Kazakh National University, Kazakhstan on Februaly 29, 2008.

[5] Information obtained through Interview with a member of the committee for Issue of Science, Education, Culture and Sports of the Lower House (Februaly 12, 2008).

[6] Information obtained through Interview with the director of international relations and public affairs division of *Kamolot* (January 7, 2008).

[7] Information obtained through Interview with the former minister of public education of the Republic of Uzbekistan (August 19, 2008) and material of Ministry of Public Education.

[8] Xalqaro ilmiy-amaliy konferentsiya, *Fuqarolik jamiyatini shakllantirishda yoshlarning roli*, Toshkent, February 18, 2008.

[9] NIHU Program for Islamic Area Studies, IAS Center at University of Tokyo, Group 2, Database of "Structure Transfiguration of Politics of Middle East", "Democratization of Middle East", Masaru Suda, "Uzbekistan · Political Party", http://www.l.u-tokyo.ac.jp/~dbmedm06/me_d13n/database/uzbekistan/political_party.html (June 10, 2010 browsed).

[10] Youth Initiative Center "The Voice of the Future" Site, http://www.kelajakovozi.uz/?section=trends&subsection=pmin, http://www.kelajakovozi.uz/?section=trends&subsection=education (February 16, 2008 browsed), TSMI «Kelajak ovozi» proekty.

[11] Information obtained through Interview with a member of the staff of Yunusabad local government, Tashkent (December 11, 2007), Interview with the chief of Tashkent bureau of the Republic Ethics Education and Popularization Center "Spirituality and Education (*Ma'naviyat va Ma'rifat*)" (December 13, 2007).

[12] NANNOUz Site http://www.ngo.uz/gn204.php?Lang=ru, http://www.ngo.uz/zadachi.php?Lang=ru (February 16, 2008 browsed).

[13] Discussion at International Round Table which cosponsored by *Kamolot*, Independent Institute for Monitoring of the Formation of Civil Society, Friedrich Ebert Memorial Foundation (Germany), "Pioneering Significance of Youth Policy of Uzbekistan in Formation of Civil Society", Republican Center of *Kamolot* (February 23, 2008).

[14] NANNOUz Site http://www.ngo.uz/projects_1.php?Lang=ru (February 16, 2008 browsed).

[15] *Strategicheskaya programma protivodeistviya rasprostraneniyu VICH-infektsii v Respublike Uzbekistan na 2007-2011gg.*, Tashkent, 2007, and interview with UNAIDS, HIV/AIDS Programme Officer (March 13, 2008).

[16] O'zbekiston Respublikasi xalq Ta'limi Vazirligi., Yo'ldoshev, H.Q., Barkamol avlodni tarbiyalashda oila, mahalla, maktab hamkorligi kontseptsiyasi, Toshkent, 2004, b.7. In Uzbekistan, slogan is holded up every year. For instance, 2003 was declared by president as "Year of the Mahalla", and 2007 was "Year of Social Security". Likewise, Ministry of Public Education declared every year's slogan such as 2005-2006 "Promotion of Cooperation between Family, Mahalla and School". Additionaly, 2008 was declared as "Year of Youth", and promote youth education and various policies on youth.

[17] Information obtained through Interview with representative of U mahalla, Mirobod district, Tashkent City (May 16, 2006), Interview with representative of C mahalla, Shaykhontohur district, Tashkent City (May 24, 2006). C mahalla has sports facilities which set up many training machinery, soccer field, tennis courts etc. Representative of this mahalla highlighted that C mahalla most actively conducts sports within 49 mahallas of Shaykhontohur district.

[18] Material of SOS Children's Villages. SOS-detskie derevni Uzbekistana, *Informatsiya o detel'nosti assotsiatsii*, 2008. Who We Are-Roots, Vision, Mission and Values of SOS

Children's Villages, Information obtained through Interview with educator of SOS Children's Village in Tashkent (March 13, 2008).

[19] Tashkent State Institute of Oriental Studies separate from Tashkent National University, and it is college that specialized in humanities and social sciences. Department of literature, department of linguistics, department of international relations and department of international economics are opened at the institute. On the other hand, University of World Economy and Diplomacy is differ from other university that 4 years academic year. Basically, other universities are administrated by Ministry of Higher and Secondary Specialized Education, however University of World Economy and Diplomacy is had responsibility by Ministry of Foreign Affairs. This university is foster future elite of Uzbekistan.

[20] Questionnaire survey at Tashkent State Institute of Oriental Studies and University of World Economy and Diplomacy were conducted few times from March 15 to April 15, 2008. On the other hand, same survey at Kazakh National University in Kazakhstan was conducted on February 27, 2008, and survey at Kyrgyz Turkish Manas University in Kyrgyz was conducted on March 2nd, 2008.

Final Chapter

Educational Role of Mahalla in Uzbekistan

1. Relationship of the Educational Role in Each Institution

In this book, I have discussed what the purpose of education policy related to mahallas is in modern Uzbekistan, how mahallas are treated in school education, how mahallas and schools cooperate, how the educational activities in mahallas are carried out, what kind of role they plays in education for children and the youth, and what the cooperative activities between mahallas and NGOs, youth organizations, and international organizations are. The purpose of this discussion is to clarify the educational role of mahallas in modern Uzbekistan.

First, Chapter 1 indicated the change in the educational aspects of mahallas historically. Here, I mentioned that a mahalla was a local community that was based on the ties of people that existed before the occupation of the Russian Empire. Each mahalla executive had various educational roles and common facilities within the mahalla, such as mosques, which operated various educational activities. Mahalla committees during the Soviet period and after independence started to have a more structured management organization, but they did not have the standard of organization throughout the nation as seen in current mahalla committees. In other words, mahallas was formed based on ethnicity, religion, and occupation, so they had their own educational activities and mahalla residents nurtured their own identities as mahalla residents through those activities. Also, their own educational activities had an important role in the character formation of children.

However, once Uzbekistan was incorporated into the Russian Empire and was later brought into the Soviet Union, mahallas developed a role in supervising and managing residents, giving them the function of nurturing residents into becoming members of the Soviet Union. As the Soviet-style school system which inherited the Russian modern school system diffused, mahalla had activities that held up the ideals of expanding the policy of the Soviet government and communist ideology. For example, *choykhona*, a main place for interaction for people in mahalla, was changed to "Red *choykhona*" and they had literature that worshiped the Soviet government and nurtured residents who would protect the government policy. They also invited teachers that lived in the same mahalla and had lectures. The educational role of mahallas in sharing awareness as a community member and a mahalla member from the mutual relationship of the resident was weakened and instead, the function of nurturing soviet citizen was given to mahalla during this period.

After the independence of Uzbekistan, the government aimed to get out of promoting the awareness of a "Soviet citizen" and change it to the "Uzbekistan nation". Education reform centering on mahalla is in progress as well as the promotion of restoring traditional Uzbekistan and Central Asian culture other than mahalla. In the meantime, governmental functionality of the mahalla committee that existed during the Soviet period is being promoted and the establishment of Fund "Mahalla" and mahalla related organizations are promoted rapidly. Because of this modern background, the current mahalla has a function of forming "the Uzbekistan nation" based on the governmental authority of the mahalla committee, and it is pointed out that it is one of the educational roles of mahalla.

In Chapter 2, the structure of mahalla and the actual situation of educational activities after independence were clarified. After independence in 1991, the government established legal and governmental foundation of mahalla based on national constitution and the law of the Republic of Uzbekistan "On self-governing institution". From the formation of mahalla until then, the legal base for their existence of mahalla was vague. However, it is clearly indicated in the law mentioned above and governmental organization can be established throughout the nation and they can further systemize mahalla.

On the other hand, however, even after the systemization, the tradition, mutual relationship of people, and adult learning that were developed there were not lost. Currently, mahalla have various activities such as resident management, female support, and solving family problems as an end organization for the government, but on the other hand, they have various activities that express the originality of mahalla. Although excursions for residents and sports promotion activities are some examples, they are important places for learning for the adults who live in that mahalla.

Based on the structure surrounding current mahalla, the hypothesis that national "integration" and local residents' "self-governing" are both done in mahalla arises. However, the mahalla committee and residents have self-governing activities within the framework that the government has presumed and, in reality, it is difficult to have activities that are outside of that framework. It is because the source of the mahalla committee fund is from the government and government related organization so the local government and organization such as Fund "Mahalla" are always managing the activities of mahalla residents and mahalla itself. In other words, mahalla's activities have the aspect that it is only to please the government and it is expressed in the opinion of the previous mahalla representative who have said "mahalla does not have many activities unless the people from the government is coming. It is not supporting the mahalla residents".[1] Based on these, mahallas in Uzbekistan are "self-governed" by local residents within the framework of the government, but as a result, those activities that are geared toward national "integration" are enhanced by patriotism through resident management lead by the government and love for their hometown for mahalla. It means that, in mahallas in current Uzbekistan, national "integration" and "self-governing" are not both carried out. This puts mahallas in a stage where self-governing activities of the residents are slowly built into the identity of national integration.

Chapter 3 talked about the socialization and cultural inheritance of children in mahalla and clarified how mahalla is involved in them as well as rites of passage and religious rituals using the examples of *ramazan* and *hayit*. In Uzbekistan, children learn socialization, religion, and traditional culture through various rituals that are performed inside of mahalla. For example, during *ramazan*, they do not eat anything until sunset, and they learn how to pray when they start a meal, what to put in their mouth and what to start eating by copying their parents, grandparents, and siblings. Also, they learn religion and human relationship between different generations through interactions with neighboring residents. Learning for children is the same for the ritual of *hayit*, and they have the opportunity to learn how to associate with neighbors in rituals and mahalla as well as get to know what kind of people live in mahalla through these interactions.

For the rites of passage, religious rituals and life rituals in mahalla, the mahalla committees provide monetary and labor support for families who cannot. On the other hand, they put pressure on a family that is trying to have an extravagant ritual to reduce the scale. Also, the cultural organization "Spirituality and Culture", which has an office at the local government building, gives guidance to mahalla committees on how to perform the rituals. Through them, they promote various activities for diffusing a standardized level of rituals, and they support young families who don't know how conduct those rituals. Activities like "Spirituality and Culture" allow the communication of the common traditional culture of Uzbekistan, Central Asia, and Islamic area across a wide range, but we cannot deny the threat that it may enforce the standard ritual throughout the nation, promoting governmental control through religious rituals. Based on the actual situation of the activities of mahalla committee, it can be said that mahalla occupies both sides; "supporter" and "intervener". In other words, mahalla has the educational role of "supporter" and "intervener" in the socialization of children.

Chapter 4 clarified how mahalla is treated in school education, what the socio-political background is, and how it influenced children as a result of its implementation in school education. Currently, cooperation of mahalla, schools, and families are established by government ordinance and mahalla is emphasized in national construction after independence in a variety of ways, such as the participation of mahalla representatives in school classes. A great example of this is the policy of mahalla implementation to school education. Based on the "National standard" and concept of "Cooperation among families, mahalla, and school in the mature generation's development", which are the framework of education system and curriculum in Uzbekistan, the government positioned mahalla as the "traditional space", "fundamental space for national integration" and "space for mutual help" and implemented it in school education through textbooks, classes, and school events. It was clarified that for its background, they had the aim to get out from the Soviet Union, integration of ethnicities in the country and Central Asia, and the government's plan to expand the new national system. In other words, the implementation of mahalla in school education had the purpose of diffusing the traditional and governmental aspects of mahalla to students and materialized the government plan mentioned above.

Mahalla as a "space for mutual help" is especially emphasized in ethnic mentality and humanity. This aspect of mahalla allows them to reach ethnicities other than the Uzbek people and is viewed as important for promoting community living among residents, assistance for socially vulnerable people, and national integration. Thus, mahallas are implemented in school education.

The influence of implementing mahalla in school education led by the government can be seen in students' reports on mahalla and students' activities in school events during the spring festival *"Navro'z."* Students who write reports that talk about how proud they are of their mahalla and perform a short play on the ritual of marriage in mahalla at school event show that the formation of the "Uzbekistan nation" through mahalla in school education is succeeding. In the current school education, mahalla is implemented as a device to cultivate the awareness of being a nation in students, and national integration is in progress accordingly. However, nation-building centering on mahalla is not on a firm foundation, so it is important to note that students and the mahalla that support the schools have different levels of enthusiasm in the implementation of mahalla in school education.

Chapter 5 clarified one of the educational roles of mahalla from the perspective of school education. In Uzbekistan, after its independence, they are aiming to form "citizens" called "Uzbekistani", an identity which has nothing to do with the ethnicity they are born in, such as Uzbek people, Russian, Tajik people, and Korean. Although the majority of the multi-ethnic nation of Uzbekistan is comprised of Uzbek people, they cannot view other ethnicities lightly in order to avoid disruption of the nation because of ethnic problems. The nurturing of the "citizen" awareness as "Uzbekistani", instead of the "Uzbek people" was valued in order to solve this problem.

The textbooks that are used in the current school education, especially for "Foundation of Spirituality", "The Alphabet of National Constitution", and "Courtesy", use the word "citizen" repeatedly, and it mentions the actions and mannerism as being those of "citizen" and good lifestyles. Also, not just in the textbooks, but in school events such as "memorial day", residents from mahalla that are close to the school are invited and share their experiences of World War II and mahalla during the war. The nurturing of "citizen" awareness through the actual mahalla is significant. The background of cooperative activities between mahalla and school is that by using mahalla, the living area for the students, to nurture "citizen" awareness in school education, the government aims for a "citizen" awareness development that is more real and easily accepted by the students. In addition to nurturing the "citizen" awareness, they are also aiming to restore the history and tradition of mahalla, create abstract love for their home town, and implement mutual help activities that are over the wall of ethnicities, specifically in mahalla. A series of these projects assist socially vulnerable people, creates patriotism and nation-building, and leads to the integration of the nation. Mahalla is a realistic being for students so the government gave them an educational role to supplement the development of "citizen" awareness in school education, and uses that role as a turning point to connect "citizen" awareness to "national awareness".

In Chapter 6, youth education and project of assistant activities using the cooperation of mahalla, NGO, international organizations, and other institution were clarified. Recently, the cooperative activities between mahalla and *Kamolot*, youth organization and international organizations like UNICEF such as youth initiative center "Voice of the Future" are being revitalized. International organizations not only improve the hardware in the social infrastructure and school environment, but also support material principles such as the youth and the empowerment of specialties that support the youth.

Especially, the examples of characteristic of the cooperative activities are strong network among mahalla, youth organizations, NGO, and international organizations and openness of the activities through international conference and each event. Each institution views mahalla as a place with the functionality to conduct cooperative activities.

However, the results of questionnaire survey done at two universities in Uzbekistan, one in Kazakhstan and the other in Kyrgyz, show that students do not participate in local activities very often, and participation in local activities is decreasing compared to students in elementary and secondary education. Although young people in Uzbekistan see a certain value and expectation in local community activities, there are few people who participate and they gradually stay away from mahallas along with the change in living environment. When we develop youth education in cooperation with mahalla, NGOs, and international organizations in the future, we must consider the fact that, and causes of, young people are detaching from mahalla, as was indicated in the research results. Also NGOs in Uzbekistan are governmental NGOs and often have a base in each city, and manage the NGO in the capital and rural areas. In other words, the unique activity of NGO is that it's actually a governmental NGO, so they are supervised by the government. It also shows here that the development of youth leaders through mahalla and NGOs has government oversight.

Based on what was clarified in each chapter, the government's perspective on the educational role of mahalla is the place for nation-building, from the perspective of mahalla; it is a place for mutual help among mahalla residents, and place for activities for youth organizations, NGOs, and international organizations. In other words, they have various educational roles based on various views of mahalla such as "mahalla for us Uzbekistan nation", "my mahalla", and "Uzbekistan's mahalla" from the outside view such as those of international organizations.

It was also clarified that the three educational roles of mahalla indicated above; nation-building, mutual help among residents, and a place for activities from the outside organization, are independent, but they have a relationship where they affect one another. For example, nation-building starts from mahalla residents helping one another and recognizing the awareness as a member of a local community. The activity of developing youth leader from each institution leads to nurturing young people to become members of the local community or a nation.

Mahalla, the government, NGOs, and international organizations have a relationship that reflects the relationship of mahalla's educational role, so they sometimes have a cooperative relationship, guiding one another and accept it and lead one another. The examples of this can be seen in the relationship of various actors' view of mahalla and idea on the significance of each actor seen in various scenes such as the guidance of the "Spirituality and Culture" organization on circumcision, exploration for a solution for channel for support activities by international organizations in mahalla, pressure from mahalla committees against extravagant weddings, and the prevention on residents' divorce by mahalla women's committees.

2. A Community That Educates

Mahalla's educational role involves a relationship based on various actors, and we cannot overlook the fact that the supervision and management of the government is everywhere. The current educational role of mahalla is based on traditional mahalla from a long time ago, but stays within the range that the government approves. In other words, three educational roles of mahalla, nation-building, mutual help of the resident, and activities of each institution, are summarized in the educational role of nation-building in the end. As Fichte explained, nation precede the state, nor do they exist prior, but must be created through education,[2] the education in current Uzbekistan has a role in creating new state and new nation. And through that process, mahalla serves as a community that "educates" people to be "the Uzbekistan nation". In order to prevent a difference in education between people who received the old school education and people who received the current school education after the foundation of the new state mentioned at the beginning of this book, mahalla is acting as a community that "educates", enabling it to be an organizational body that communicate the ideology of the new state equally to various generations. In current mahalla, the educational role held up by the government and the educational role in the independent educational activities by the residents are competing with each other, so how the balance changes in the future could change the education for children, young people, and adults in the area as well as the relationship between mahalla and the state.

In addition, the educational role of mahalla is influencing the view of mahalla held by individual people. How these views are formed and how they are related depend on ethnicities that make up mahalla, ethnic, religious, and regional traits. In other words, what kind of educational role people give to their mahalla is largely influenced by the ethnic, religious, and regional traits as well as the historical background of the mahalla.

In current Uzbekistan, national construction using the subsuming characteristic of mahalla is in progress, so for that reason, mahalla is included in school education, and the management of residents done by mahalla. Changing from "subsuming the characteristics of mahalla" to "subsuming the characteristics of the state" directly connects to the danger of belonging to an individual community which is connected to belonging to the standard state as pointed out by Takeo Matsuda in the area of social education. From the perspective of Uzbekistan, mahalla is used to change the sense of belonging for the residents. The "community value" mentioned by Matsuda is a concept that is controlled by the government when it is adapted to the situation of mahalla in current Uzbekistan, and it can be said that "from the outside, it is mahalla value but in reality, it is national value".

Since current the mahalla is reconstructed politically with such concept as a foundation, there is a possibility that the traditional ethnic, religious, and regional traits of the mahalla are being neglected. Instead of a nation integrated by the subsummation of the characteristics of mahalla in regards to ethnicity, religion, and region, a local government that respects the freedom of activities for education and community building by mahalla residents is desired. In order for that to happen, it is needless to say that spontaneity and independent activity of mahalla is required.

Conclusion —Future Views and Challenges—

For this book, research of laws, official documents, and fieldwork was conducted in order to research the educational role of mahalla in Uzbekistan. However, there are clear limitations to researching the educational role of mahalla just by researching literature and limited fieldwork. This is because the view of mahalla, and the view of its educational role, is different depending on each ethnicity and area as it was indicated in Chapter 2.

In order to solve this problem, knowing how each ethnicity that lives in the five countries of Central Asia, including Uzbekistan, understands their local community and how they accept the policy of the local community. To understand what substitutes for mahalla where there is no traditional local community like mahalla in Uzbekistan is critical in discussing the view of the various ethnicities that live in Uzbekistan.

The five countries in Central Asia are largely categorized as countries with the historical background of settlers and nomadic people. Uzbekistan and Tajikistan, belonging to the settler group, developed traditional local communities like mahalla. On the other hand, Kazakhstan and Kyrgyz, belonging to the nomadic group, and Turkmen, half nomadic and half settler, had strong traits of traditional tribal systems.

However, in Tajikistan, which is categorized as a settler nation among the five countries of Central Asia, has Kyrgyz people, nomads, living in the country, so each area has a versatile ethnic construction. On the other hand, research clarified that Kyrgyz, which is categorized as a nomadic nation, has an area where many Uzbek people live in and there are mahallas with committees that have various activities similar to those in Uzbekistan.

For example, in a mahalla for Uzbek people located in Osh, the second largest city in Kyrgyz, "International women's day" was cerebrated in the whole mahalla and various member of women's council participated in the activities. There was enthusiasm for local management organization to celebrate "International women's day" as a whole mahalla and trust from the residents who were trying to cooperate with them. On the other hand, in the apartment area with mainly Kyrgyz people, a woman representing their women's council visited homes to celebrate "International women's day". There was a request from the residents that "we want to celebrate 'International women's day' like the mahalla of the Uzbek people" but there were no residents who would cooperate other than the representative, so she bought presents such as perfume and handkerchiefs with her own money and visited their apartments.

As it was mentioned earlier, the activity of women's committee in each ethnic community is different depending on the view of that local community. This is an example of how it influences the activity of women's committees, and this is a qualitative difference that does not appear in numerical values or public documents. This exemplifies the danger of doing research by simply categorizing the five countries of Central Asia into nomads, settlers, and nations with a certain ethnicity.

The future endeavor is to explore the image of local communities and the view of community that each ethnicity has by analyzing and discussing comparisons among, and within, the five countries of Central Asia instead of just focusing within Uzbekistan. When we clarify the awareness of the local community and community view of each ethnicity, the educational role of mahalla discussed in this research and new aspects of mahalla in Uzbekistan will be better understood.

Notes

[1] Information obtained through Interview with the former representative of a mahalla in Tashkent (June 7, 2007).

[2] Johann Gottlieb Fichte, "Doitsu kokumin ni tsugu (Addresses to the German Nation)", *Kokumin towa Nanika (Qu'est-ce qu'une nation?)*, Kawadeshoboshinsha, 1997, p.76.

Selected Bibliography

Ablimit, Rizwan, "Uighur no kodomo no hattatsu ni okeru mahalla (chiiki kyoudoutai) no yakuwari (The Role of the *Mahalla* in the Development of Uighur Children)", The Japanese Society of Life Needs Experience Learning, *Seikatsu Taiken Gakushu Kenkyu (The Journal of Life Needs Experience Learning)*, Vol. 1, 2001, pp. 39-47.
Alistteres, A., Karis., "Rekishi kyoiku ni okeru jiminzoku chushin shugi no jojutsu to 'yoroppa' no jigen (Description of ethnocentrism in education of history and 'European dimension')", Roland-Lévy, R. and Ross, A., eds., *Oushu Tougou to Citizenship Kyoiku—Atarashii Seiji Gakushu no Kokoromi (Political Learning and Citizenship in Europe)*, Akashi Shoten, 2006, (Original: Stoke on Trent: Trentham Press, 2003).
Ardendt, H., *Ningen no Joken (The Human Condition)*, Chikuma Gakugei Bunko, 1994, (Original: The University of Chicago Press, 1958).
Dadabaev, Timur, "Chuou ajia shokoku no gendaika ni okeru dentouteki chiiki shakai no arikata to yakuwari – Uzbekistan no 'mahalla' wo chushin ni (Ideal existence and role of traditional local community in modernization of Central Asian countries: Focusing on 'mahalla' of Uzbekistan)", *Toyo Bunka Kenkyusho Kiyou (The Memoirs of the Institute for Advanced Studies on Asia)*, Vol. 146, 2004, pp. 253-280.
Dadabaev, Timur, "Uzbekistan no chiiki shakai 'mahalla' kara mita jinken no hogo・kakuho (Protection of Human Rights from perspective of Uzbekistan's Local Society *Mahalla*), Slavic- Eurasian Research Center, *SRC Occasional Papers East Europe and Central Eurasian's Modern Period and Nation III*, No. 95, 2004, pp. 27-41.
Dadabaev, Timur, *Mahalla no Jitsuzo : Chuou Ajia Shakai no Dentou to Henyou (Mahalla)*, University of Tokyo Press, 2006.
Dadabaev, Timur, *Shakai Shugi go no Uzbekistan—Kawaru Kuni to Yureru Hitobito no Kokoro (Uzbekistan after Socialism)*, Ajia Keizai Kenkyusho, 2008.
Ebihara, Haruka, *Teisei Roshia Kyoiku Seisakushi Kenkyu (Historical Research of Education Policy in the Russian Empire)*, Kazamashobo, 1997.
Educational Board of Shinagawa Ward, Creation of *"Shiminka"* Curriculum section, Set of unified elementary and Jr. High school education *Guide of Instruction of "Shiminka"*, Kyoiku Shuppan, 2006.
Egami, Namio, eds., *Chuou Ajia Shi Sekai Kakkoku Shi 16 (History of Central Asia The World History 16)*, Yamakawa Shuppansha, 1987.
Fichte, Johann, Gottlieb, "Doitsu kokumin ni tsugu (Addresses to the German Nation)", Ernest, Renan, Fichte, Johann, Gottlieb, Romains, Jules, Balibar, Etienne, Ukai, Satoshi, *Kokumin toha Nanika (Qu'est-ce qu'une nation?)*, Kawadeshoboshinsha, 1997.
Fujimoto, Toko, "Kazakhstan / Kodomo no seichou girei ni miru Islam (Kazakhstan / Islam through Rite for Children's Growth)", *Ajiken World Trends*, No. 85, 2002, p. 18.

Fuwa, Kazuhiko, eds., *Seijin Kyoiku to Shimin Shakai—Koudouteki Citizenship no Kanousei (Relationship between Adult Education and Citizenship)*, Aoki shoten, 2002.

Giddens, Anthony, *Daisan no Michi—Kouritsu to Kousei no Aratana Doumei (The Third Way : The Renewal of Social Democracy)*, Nihon Keizai Shinbun Sha, 1999.

Hahn, C., "Kakkoku ni okeru 'seijiteki ni naru' to iu koto (Becoming political in different countries)", Roland-Lévy, R. and Ross, A., eds., *Oushu Tougou to Citizenship Kyoiku—Atarashii Seiji Gakushu no Kokoromi (Political Learning and Citizenship in Europe)*, Akashi Shoten, 2006, (Original : Stoke on Trent : Trentham Press, 2003).

Hamada, Masami, *Chuou Ajia no Islam (Islam in Central Asia)*, Yamakawa shuppansha, 2008.

Harada, Shiori, "Shinagawa ku 'Shiminka' kyokasho no seijigaku teki bunseki (A political analysis on textbook of 'Shiminka' of Shinagawa Ward)", *Gakusei Hosei Ronshu*, No. 4, Kyushu Daigaku Hosei Gakkai, 2010, pp. 101-117.

Hasumi, Jiro, "Eikoku no citizenship kyoiku – Keii·Genjo·Kadai – (Citizenship education in England : past, present, and future)", *Seiji-Kenyu*, No. 55, *Seiji-Kenkyukai* (Institute for Political Science), Kyushu University, 2008, pp. 63-92.

Hirakata City Education Board, *Social Education of Hirakata*, No. 2 ("Social Education for all Citizen"), 1963.

Hiwatari, Masato, "Uzbekistan no kanshu keizai : Mahalla no kyoudoutai teki kinou no kentou kara (The Customary Economy in Uzbekistan : A Study of the Community Function of Mahallas)", Japan Association for *Asian Studies, Asian Studies*, Vol. 50, No. 4, 2004, pp. 79-97.

Hiwatari, Masato, *Kanshu Keizai to Shijou·Kaihatsu—Uzbekistan no Kyoudoutai ni Miru Kinou to Kouzou (The Customary Economy and Economic Development : The Community-based Structure of a Mahalla in Uzbekistan)*, 2008.

Inoguchi, Takashi, Miguel, Basáñez, Tanaka, Akihiko, Dadabaev, Timur, eds., *Values and Life Styles in Urban Asia : A Cross-Cultural Analysis and Sourcebook Based on the Asia Barometer, Survey of 2003*, Akashi shoten, 2005.

Japan International Cooperation Agency (JICA), *Central Asia (Uzbekistan, Kazakhstan, Kyrgyz) Report of Research Group on Aid, Present Data Analysis*, Part II Uzbekistan, 2001.

Karimov, Islam, *21 Seiki ni Mukau Uzbekistan (Uzbekistan on the Verge of the 21 Century, Uzbekistan na poroge XXI veka)*, Japan Uzbekistan Committee of Economy, 1999.

Katsuki, Kyoko, "Tajikistan ni okeru josei ni taisuru bouryoku no genjou to NGO no torikumi – Crisis center kara shelter katsudou he (Current Situation of Violence to Women in Tajikistan and NGOs' Efforts : From Crisis Center to Shelter Activities)", Kitakyushu Forum on Asian Women, *Ajia Josei Kenkyu*, No. 15, 2006, pp. 109-111.

Kawano, Asuka, "Uzbekistan no gakkou ni okeru chiiki kyoudoutai (mahalla) no kyouiku – Seihu no mahalla seisaku tono kanren de (Community Education in Uzbekistan in Relation to the Mahalla Policy)", Japan Comparative Education Society, *Hikaku Kyoikugaku Kenkyu (Comparative Education)*, No. 35, 2007, pp. 166-182.

Kawano, Asuka, "Uzbekistan no Mahalla (Chiiki Kyoudoutai) to Kodomo no Shakaika : Islam wo Kaku to shita Shakaisei no Shutoku to Bunka Keisho ni Shoten wo Atete (Uzbekistan's Mahalla (Local Community) and Socialization of Children : Focusing on the Acquisition of Sociability and Cultural Succession Based on Islam)", Graduate School of Human- Environment Studies, Kyushu University, *TOBIUME Bulletin of Education Course Graduate School of Kyushu University*, No. 8, 2008, pp. 17-36.

Kawano, Asuka, "'Shikouhin' wo Oshieru to Iu Koto : Gendai Chuou Ajia no Gakkou Kyoiku ni okeru Cha no Hyoshou to Kokumin Keisei (Teaching 'Tea' and 'Tea culture' : Symbol of Tea in School Education in Post- Soviet Central Asia and Nation- Building)", Reports of Researches by Grand of Zaidan Hojin Tabaco Sougou Kenkyu Center, 2010, pp. 1-22.

Kawano, Asuka, "Gendai Chuou Ajia no Kyoiku ni okeru Cha to Kokumin Keisei ('Tea' and Nation-Building in Education of Modern Central Asia)", Tabaco Sougou Kenkyu Center, *TASC monthly*, No. 433, 2012, pp. 6-11.

Kawanobe, Satoshi, *Soviet no Kyoiku Kaikaku (Educational Reform of Soviet)*, Meiji Tosho, 1985.

Kawanobe, Satoshi, *Kakunenshi/Soren Sengo Kyoiku no Tenkai (Annual History/Soviet Union : Development of post war education*, MTsyutupan, 1991.

Kawanobe, Satoshi, *Rossia no Kyoiku·Kako to Mirai (Education of Russia·Past and Future)*, Shindokushosha, 1996.

Kerkkhofs, Jan, "Yoroppa no kachi to seiji kyoiku (European values and political education)", Roland-Lévy, R. and Ross, A., eds., *Oushu Tougou to Citizenship Kyoiku—Atarashii Seiji Gakushu no Kokoromi (Political Learning and Citizenship in Europe)*, Akashi Shoten, 2006, (Original : Stoke on Trent : Trentham Press, 2003).

Kimura, Hidesuke, Yamamoto, Satoshi, *Sekai Gendaishi 30 Soren Gendaishi II (World Contemporary History 30 Soviet Contemporary History II)*, Yamakawa Shuppansha, 1979.

Kobayashi, Bunjin, Shimabukuro, Masatoshi, eds., *Okinawa no Shakai Kyoiku-Jichi·Bunka· Chiikiokoshi (Social Education in Okinawa : Autonomy, Culture, Promotion of Local Community)*, Eidell Institute, Japan, 2002.

Kodama, Shigeo, *Citizenship no Kyoiku Shisou (Educational Thought of Citizenship)*, Hakutaku-sha, 2003.

Kodama, Shigeo, " Citizenship kyoiku no igi to kadai (Significance and challenges of citizenship education)", Zaidanhojin Akarui Senkyo Suishin Kyokai, *Watashitachi no Hiroba*, Vol. 291, 2006.

Komatsu, Hisao, Umemura, Hiroshi, Uyama, Tomohiko, Obiya, Chika, Horikawa, Toru, eds., *Chuou Yurasia wo Shiru Jiten (Cyclopedia of Central Eurasia)*, Heibon-sha, Japan, 2005.

Komatsu, Hisao, "Kashgar no Andijan ku chousa houkoku (Field Work Report of Andijan District of Kashgar)", Shimizu, Kosuke, eds., *Islam toshi ni okeru gaiku no jittai to minshu soshiki ni kansuru hikaku kenkyu (A Comparative Study of the Islamic City Quarters"Mahalla" and Popular Organizations)*, Tokyo University of Foreign Studies, 1991, pp. 46-56.

Komatsu, Hisao, "Bukhara no mahalla ni kansuru noto – O. A. Sukhareva no Field work kara (Notes on the mahallas of Bukhārā : based on the ethnographical material collected by O. A. Sukhareva)", *Journal of Asian and African Studies*, No. 16, 1978, pp. 178-215.

Kudomi, Yoshiyuki, "Chiiki to kyoiku (Local Community and Education)", The Japan Society of Educational Sociology, *Kyoiku Shakaigaku Kenkyu (The Journal of Educational Sociology)*, No. 50, 1992, pp. 66-86.

Mano, Eiji, Horikawa, Toru, eds., *Chuou Ajia no Rekishi·Shakai·Bunka (History·Society· Culture in Central Asia)*, Hosou Daigaku Kyoiku Shinkoukai, 2004.

Marienko, I. S., *Soviet Gakkou no Dotoku Kyoiku (Ethic Education of Soviet School)*, Meiji Tosho, 1972.

Matsuda, Takeo, " Shakaikyoiku ni okeru community teki kachi no saikentou – Shakai kyoiku gainen no saikaishaku wo tooshite (Reexamination of community values in social education : Through reinterpretation of the concept of social education)", Japanese

Educational Research Association, *Kyoikugaku Kenkyu (The Japanese Journal of Educational Research)*, Vol. 74, No. 4, 2007.
Matsuda, Takeo, *Gendai Shakai Kyoiku no Kadai to Kanousei —Shougaigakushu to Chiiki Shakai (Challenges and Possibilities of Current Social Education : Lifelong Learning and Local Society)*, Kyushu University Press, Japan, 2007.
Minei, Akiko, Kawanobe, Satoshi, *Chuou Ajia no Kyoiku to Globalism (Globalization and Education Reform in Central Asia)*, Toshindo, 2012.
Ministry of Economy, Trade and Industry, Japan, *Report of Study Group on Citizenship Education and People's Activities in Economic Society*, March 2006 (in Japanese).
Mizutani, Kuniko, "Uzbekistan − Koukou reberu no kyoiku kaikaku wo chushin ni − Datsu roshia no tame no jinzai ikusei (Uzbekistan : Focusing on the Educational Reform at the High School Level—Human Resource Development for Moving Away from Russia)", *Science of humanity Bensei*, Vol. 36, Benseishuppan, 2001, pp. 42-46.
Monbusho Chousa Kyoku, Soren to Chukyo no Kyoiku Kaikaku (Educational Reform of Soviet Union and People's Republic of China), 1959.
Murayama, Shiro, *Natsuyasumi Seikatsu Gakkou − Pioneer Kyanpu no 1 Kagetsu (Summer Vacation Living School-One Month in Pioneer Camp)*, Minshusha, 1979.
Murayama, Shiro, Tokoro, Shinichi, eds., *Perestroika to Kyoiku (Perestroika and Education)*, Otsukishoten, 1991.
Nihon Islam Kyokai (Japan Islam Association), *Islam Jiten (Encyclopedia of Islam)*, Heibon-sha, Japan, 1982.
Obiya, Chika, "Mahalla no kurashi − Muslim no nichijou to kinjo zukiai (Everyday Life in Mahalla : Daily Life and Interactions with Muslim Neighbors)", Uyama, Tomohiko, eds., *Chuou Ajia wo Shirutame no 60 shou (60 Chapters for Understanding on Central Asia)*, Akashi Shoten, Japan, 2003, pp. 160-164.
Ohashi, Yasuaki, "Gakkou kyoiku to shakai kyoiku no kyoudou − Koumin bunkan katsudou wo jiku ni (Collaboration between School Education and Out-of-school Education : A case study of activities as a citizen's public hall)", The Japan Society for the Study of Adult and Community Education, *Nihon Shakai Kyoiku Gakkai Kiyou (Bulletin of the Japan Society for the Study of Adult and Community Education)*, No. 37, 2001, pp. 51-59.
Ono, Junko, "Chiiki shakai wo katsuyou shita shiminteki shishitsu・citizenship wo hagukumu tame no kyoiku kaikaku : chiiki no kakaeru shomondai he kakawaru koto no kyouiku teki igi (Educational reform for development citizenship in a local community : The importance of the challenge of teaching local issues)", *St. Andrew's University Bulletin of the Research Institute*, Vol. 31, No. 2, 2005, pp. 99-119.
Osugi, Takuzo, *Jouhou Network de Musubu Silk Road—Kokusai Kaihatsu Kyoryoku ni Miru Gendai Chuou Ajia (Binding Silk Road through Information Network : Modern Central Asia from Perspective of International Development and Cooperation)*, Chugokushoten, 2009.
Osugi, Takuzo, Otani, Junko, eds., *Ningen no Anzen Hoshou to Chuou Ajia (Human Security and Central Asia)*, Hanashoin, 2010.
Otsuka, Kazuo, Kosugi, Yasushi, Komatsu, Hisao, Tonaga, Yasushi, Haneda, Masashi, Yamauchi, Masayuki, eds., *Iwanami Islam Jiten (Iwanami Encyclopedia of Islam)*, Iwanamishoten, 2002.
Roy, Olivier, *Gendai Chuou Ajia—Islam, Nationalism, Sekiyu Shigen (Modern Central Asia—Islam, Nationalism, Oil sources)*, Hakusuisha, 2007.
Sakai, Hiroki, *Chuou Ajia no Eiyu Jojishi Katari Tsutawaru Rekishi (Heroic Epic of Central*

Asia- Transportation History), Eurasia Booklet, No. 35, Toyoshoten, 2002.
Sakamoto, Takao, "Kokumin to minzoku (Nation and ethnicities)", *Readings Nihon no Kyoiku to Shakai (Education and Society of Japan)*, No. 5, *Aikokushin to Kyoiku (Patriotism and Education)*, Nihon Tosho Center, 2007, (Takao Sakamoto, *Kokkagaku no Susume (Encouragement of Political Sciences*), Chikuma Shobo, 2001, Chapter 3).
Sanada, Yasushi, "Toshi·Nouson·Youboku (City, Village, Nomadism)", Sato, Tsugutaka, eds., *Kouza Islam 3 Islam·Shakai no Shisutemu (Lectures on Islam 3 Islam and Social System)*, Chikuma Shobo, 1986, pp. 108-148.
Sasanuma, Takashi, "Shogai gakushu shakai ni okeru gakkou kyoiku no arikata wo meguru ichi shiron : Gakusha renkei·yugou no rironteki kousatu wo kirikuchi ni shite (A Prospect of the School Education in the Lifelong Learning Society : A Theoretical Attempts at the Fusion of School and Social Education)", Center for Education and Research of Lifelong Learning, Utsunomiya University, *Annual Reports of Lifelong Learning*, 1999, pp. 119-131.
Sato, Katsuko, *Shougai Gakushu to Shakai Sanka-Otona ga Manabu Koto no Imi (Lifelong Learning and Social Participation : The Meaning of Adult Learning)*, University of Tokyo Press, 1998.
Sawano, Yukiko, "'Shimin shakai' heno ikou wo unagasu shougai gakushu taikei no kouchiku − Uzbekistan kyowakoku no kyoiku kaikaku (Constructing the Lifelong Learning System that Promotes the Transition to a 'Citizen Society' —Educational Reform in the Republic of Uzbekistan)", *Roshia·Yurashia Keizai Chousa Shiryou (Vestnik ėkonomiki ĖKS-SSSR, Russian-Eurasian economy)*, No. 798, 1998, pp. 2-13.
Seki, Keiko, "Uzbekistan ni okeru minzoku·shukyou·kyoiku − Ningen keisei no shiten kara no kousatsu (Ethnicity/Religion/Education in Uzbekistan : Consideration from perspective of character formation)", *Roshia·Yurashia Keizai Chousa Shiryou (Vestnik ėkonomiki ĖKS-SSSR, Russian-Eurasian economy)*, No. 812, 2000, pp. 12-27.
Seki, Keiko, *Taminzoku Shakai wo Ikiru − Tenkanki Roshia no Ningen Keisei − (Living in Multi-Ethnic Society − Character Formation in the Transition Period of Russia)*, Shindokushosha, 2002.
Seki, Keiko, *Kokasasu to Chuou Ajia no Ningen Keisei (Character formation of Caucasus and Central Asia)*, Akashi Shoten, 2012.
Suda, Masaru, "'Shimin' tachi no kanri to jihatsuteki hukuju − Uzbekistan no mahalla (The Control and Voluntary Subjection of "Citizens" : Uzbekistan's *Mahalla*)", The Japan Association of International Relations, *Kokusai Seiji (International Relations)*, No. 138, 2004, pp. 43-71.
Suemoto, Makoto, Matsuda, Takeo, *Shougai Gakushu to Chiiki Shakai Kyoiku (Lifelong Learning and Community Education)*, Shunpusha, 2004.
Sumida, Masaki, eds., *Kodomo to Chiiki Shakai (Children and Local Community)*, Gakubunsha, 2010.
Takahashi, Iwane, *Uzbekistan Minzoku·Rekishi·Kokka (Uzbekistan Nation·History·State)*, Soudosha, 2005.
The Society for Citizenship Studies eds., *Citizenship no Kyoikugaku (Pedagogy for Citizenship)*, Koyoshobo, 2006.
"Tokushu : Kankoku 'Heisei Gakushu' no atarashii doukou (The New Movement of the South Korean 'Life −long Education')", "Chugoku no shougai kyoiku·shaku kyoiku (Life-long and Community Education in China)", *Higashi Ajia Shakai Kyoiku Kenkyu (The East Asian Journal for Adult Education and Community Studies)*, Volume 12, 2007.

"Tokushu Shiminsei Kyoiku wo Kangaeru (Special Issue Considering about Citizenship Education)", Zaidanhojin Akarui Senkyo Suishin Kyokai, *Watashitachi no Hiroba*, Vol. 291, 2006.
Tomiak, J. J., *Soviet no Gakkou (Schools in Soviet)*, Meiji Tosho, 1976.
Uyama, Tomohiko, *Chuou Ajia no Rekishi to Genzai (History and Present of Central Asia)*, Eurasia Booklet No. 7, Toyoshoten, 2000.
Uyama, Tomohiko, eds., *Chuou Ajia wo Shirutame no 60 shou (60 Chapters for Understanding on Central Asia)*, Akashi Shoten, Japan, 2003.
Yaguchi, Etsuko, "Ningenteki jiritsu to seinen kyoiku (Human Independence and Youth Education)", *Kouza Gendai Shakai Kyoiku no Riron II Gendaiteki Jinken to Shakai Kyoiku no Kachi (Lecture Theory of Modern Social Education II Modern Human Rights and Value of Social Education)*, Toyokanshuppansha, 2004, pp. 222-236.
Yamamoto, Tsuneo, "Gakusha yugou no shikumi (System of Fusion of School and Society)", *Shukan Kyoiku Shiryou (Weekly Educational Public Opinion)*, No. 489, 1996.
Yamashiro, Chiaki, *Okinawa no "Shima" Shakai to Seinenkai Katsudou ("Shima" Society and Activities of Youth Association in Okinawa*, Eidell Institute, Japan, 2007.
Yano, Shun, *Chiiki Kyoiku Shakaigaku Josetsu (Introduction of Local Educational Sociology)*, 1981.

Alloworth, E.A., *The Modern Uzbeks ; From the Fourteenth Century to the Present, A Cultural History*, Stanford, California : Hoover Institution, Stanford University, 1990.
Alloworth, E.A., "History and group identity in Central Asia", IN Smith, Graham et al., *Nation building in the Post-Soviet Borderlands : The Politics of National Identities*, Cambridge : Cambridge University Press, 1998.
Bohr, A., "Language policy and ethnic relations in Uzbekistan", IN Smith, Graham et al., *Nation building in the Post-Soviet Borderlands : The Politics of National Identities*, Cambridge : Cambridge University Press, 1998.
CONFINTEA VI National Report, Uzbekistan, 2008.
CONFINTEA VI National Report, Uzbekistan, Tashkent Call to Action, 2008.
Coudouel, Aline, Marnie, Sheila, Micklewright, John, *Targeting Social Assistance in a Transition Economy : The Mahallas in Uzbekistan, Occasional Papers Economic and Social Policy Series*, EPS63, UNICEF, 1998.
Critchlow, J., *Nationalism in Uzbekistan : A Soviet Republic's Road to Sovereignty*, Boulder, San Francisco, Oxford : Westview Press, 1991.
Doi, M. M., *Gesture, Gender, Nation : Dance and Social Change in Uzbekistan*, Westport, London : Bergin&Garvey, 2002.
DVV International, *Activities 2007/8*, DVV International, 2009.
Dzhuraev, L., Khan S., Kamalova, L., Hoshimov, U., Ganiyeva, H., Ziryanova, R., Ernazarova, S., Tursunova, T., *Fry High English 5*, Tashkent : O'qituvchi, 2007.
Fane, D., "Ethnicity and Regionalism in Uzbekistan", IN Leokadia Drobizheva et al., eds., *Ethnic Conflict in the Post-Soviet World : Case Studies and Analysis*, Armonk, London : M.E.Sharp, 1996.
Haghayeghi, M., *Islam and Politics in Central Asia*, New York : St. Martin's Press, 1995.
Heynean, Stephen. P., DeYoung, Alan J., *The Challenge of Education in Central Asia*, Information Age Publishing, 2004.
Japan International Cooperation Agency (JICA). *Uzbekistan Country Gender Profile 2005*, 2005.
Jarvis, P., *Adult & Continuing Education : Theory and Practice*, Second Edition, Routledge,

1995.
Kamp, Marianne, "Between Women and the State: Mahalla Committees and Social Welfare in Uzbekistan", *The Transformation of Central Asia: states and societies from Soviet rule to independence*, ed. Pauline Jones Luong, Ithaca: Cornell University Press, 2004, pp.29-58.
Kawano, Asuka, Osugi, Takuzo, Otani, Junko, "Women's Community Activities in Central Asia from Gender Perspectives", *Journal of Asian Women's Studies*, Vol.17, Kitakyushu Forum on Asian Women, 2008, pp.70-81.
Khalid, A., *The Politics of Muslim Cultural Reform: Jaddism in Central Asia*, Berkeley, Los Angeles, London: University of California Press, 1998.
Massicard, Elise, Trevisani, Tommaso, "The Uzbek Mahalla: between state and society", Tom Everett-Heath (ed.) *Central Asia Aspects of Transition*, Routledge, 2003, pp. 205-219.
Matthews, Mervyn, *Education in the Soviet Union — Policies and Institutions since Stalin*, George Allen & Unwin, London, 1982.
Merriam, S. B., *An Update on Adult Learning Theory*, Jossey-Bass Publishers, 1993.
Muckle, James, *A Guide to the Soviet Curriculum: What the Russian Child is Taught in School*, Croom Helm, 1988.
Muhammadkarimov, A., *Tashkentnama*, Tashkent: Yangi asr avlodi, 2005.
Nicholas, Hans, Sergius, Hessen, *Educational Policy in Soviet Russia*, P.S. King & Son, LTD., London, 1930.
Northrop, D. *Veiled Empire Gender and Power in Stalinist Central Asia*, Cornell University: Ithaca and London, 2004.
Otani, Junko, "The Status in Social Development in Central Asia from Gender perspectives", *Journal of Asian Women's Studies*, Vol.16, 2008, pp.57-65.
Shoshana, Keller, "Going to School in Uzbekistan", *Everyday Life in Central Asia Past and Present*, edited by Jeff Sahadeo & Russell Zanca, 2007, pp.248-265.
Sievers, Eric W., "Uzbekistan's Mahalla: From Soviet to Absolutist Residential Community Associations", *The Journal of International and Comparative Law*, Vol.2, 2002, pp.92-155.
Silova, Iveta (ed.), *How NGOs React: Globalization and Education Reform in the Caucasus, Central Asia and Mongolia*, Kumarian, 2008.
Silova, Iveta, Johnson, Mark S., Heyneman, Stephen P., "Education and the Crisis of Social Cohesion in Azerbaijan and Central Asia", *Comparative Education Review*, vol. 51, no. 2, 2007, pp.159-180.
SOS Children's Villages, *Who We Are — Roots, Vision, Mission and Values of SOS Children's Villages*, 2008.
State Committee of the Republic Uzbekistan on Statistics, *Woman and Man of Uzbekistan 2000-2005*, Statistical bulletin, Tashkent, 2007.
The Advisory Group on Citizenship, *Education for Citizenship and the teaching of democracy in schools: Final report of the Advisory Group on Citizenship*, September 22, 1998.
The State Committee of Uzbekistan on Statistics, *Women and Men of Uzbekistan 2000-2005*, Tashkent, 2007.
Tukhliev, Nurislom., Krementsova, Alla, eds., *The Republic of UZBEKISTAN*, Tashkent, 2003.
UNICEF, *Early Childhood Development in the Central Asian Republics and Kazakhstan*, Almaty, 2002.

UNICEF, *Report of Consultancy of Patrice Engle For UNICEF Tajikistan*, June 18, 2007.

Abramov, M, *Guzapy Samarkanda*, Tashkent: Uzbekistan, 1989.
Abdullaev, SH. M., *Sovremennye etnokul'turnye protsessy v makhallyakh Tashkenta*, Tashkent: Fan, 2005.
Akramov, Z.M., *Uzbekistan*, Moskva, 1967.
Al'meev, R.V., *Bukhara gorod-muzei*, Tashkent: Fan, 1999.
Arifkhanova, Z. H., "Makhallya – Traditsionnyi organ samoupravleniya naseleniya v proshlom i nastoyashchem", *Demokratlashtirish va inson huquqlari* (17), Toshkent: Inson huquqlari bo'yicha O'zbekiston Respublikasi milliy markazi, 2003, s.137-140.
Arifkhanova, Z. H., *Sovremennaya zhizn'traditsionnoi makhalli Tashkenta*, Tashkent: Uzbekistan, 2000.
Ata-Mirzaev, A., "Makhallya v zerkale obshchestvennogo mneniya", *Demokratlashtirish va inson huquqlari* (17), Toshkent: Inson huquqlari bo'yicha O'zbekiston Respublikasi milliy markazi, 2003, s.141-145.
Azizkhanov, A. T., Efimova, L. P., *Teoriya i praktika stroitel'stova demokraticheskogo obshchestva v Uzbeskistane*, Tashkent, 2005.
Bendrikov, K.E., *Ocherki po istorii narodnogo obrazovaniya v Turkestane (1865-1924gg.)*, Moskva: Akademiya Pedagogicheskikh Nauk RSFSR, 1960.
Brynskikh, S., *Makhallya zametki pisatelya*, Tashkent: Izdatel'stvo literatury i iskusstva imeni Gafura Gulyama, 1988.
Dzhuraev, L., Khan S., Kamalova, L., Hoshimov, U., Ganiyeva, H., Ziryanova, R., Ernazarova, S., Tursunova, T., *Fry High English 5*, Tashkent: O'qituvchi, 2007.
Dzhuraeva, Z.R., *Russkii yazyk Litsey*, Tashkent: Sharq, 2007.
Dzhuraeva, Z.R., Kucharov, T.U., *Russkii yazyk kollej*, Tashkent: Sharq, 2007.
Forum Zhenskikh NPO Kyrgystana, *K pobede zhenshchin na vyborakh – Strategiya uchastiya zhenshchin v politicheskikh protsessakh v Aziatsko-Tikhookeanskom regione*, Bishkek, 2007.
Gafurov, B. G., *Istoriya Tadzhikskogo naroda 1*, Moskva: Gosudarstvennoe izdatel'stovo politicheskoi literatury, 1949.
Gody, lyudi, fakty..., Chast' tret'ya, Samarkand: Zarafshon, 2003.
Grazhdanskii kodeks Respubliki Uzbekistan, 2003.
Ideya natsional'noi nezavisimosti : osnovnye nonyatiya i printsipy, Tashkent: O'zbekistan, 2003.
Istoriya Tadzhikskoi SSR, Dushanbe: Maorif, 1983.
Istoriya Uzbekskoi sovetskoi literatury, Moskva: Nauka, 1967.
Karabaev, U., *Etnokul'tura*, Tashkent: Sharq, 2005.
Karimov, I. A., *Turkistan nash obshchii dom*, Tashkent: O'zbekistan, 1995.
Karimov, I. A., *Izbrannyi nami put'-eto put'demokraticheskogo razvitiya i sotrudnichestva s progressivnym mirom*, Tom11, Tashkent: O'zbekiston, 2003
Karimov, R. KH., *Istoriya Uzbekistana (1917-1991gg.)*, Tashkent: Sharq, 2005.
Khakimov, R., *Detstvo : Problemy i perspektivy*, Tashkent: Uzbekistan, 2006.
Konstantinov, N. A., Medynskii, E. N., Shabaeva, M. F., *Istoriya pedagogiki*, Moskva: Gosudarstvennoe uchebno-pedagogicheskoe izdatel'stvo ministerstva prosveshcheniya RSFSR, 1959.
Konstantinov, N. A., Medynskii, E. N., Shabaeva, M. F., *Istoriya pedagogiki*, Moskva: Prosveshchenie, 1982.
Konstitutsiya Respubliki Uzbekistan, Tashkent: O'zbekiston, 2003.

Kostetsukii, V. A., *Azbuka etiki 2 klass*, Tashkent: Natsional'noe obshchestvo filosofov Uzbekistana, 2004.
Kostetsukii, V. A., *Azbuka etiki 4 klass*, Tashkent: Natsional'noe obshchestvo filosofov Uzbekistana, 2007.
Kostetsukii, V. A., Chabrova, T., *Azbuka konstitutsii 2 klass*, Tashkent: Sharq, 2004.
Kostetsukii, V. A., Chabrova, T., *Azbuka konstitutsii 3 klass*, Tashkent: Sharq, 2006.
Kostetsukii, V. A., Chabrova, T., *Azbuka konstitutsii 4 klass*, Tashkent: Sharq, 2006.
Kostetsukii, V. A., Mametova, G. U., Dobrolinskaya, G.V, *Chuvstvo rodiny 5 klass*, Tashkent: Natsional'noe obshchestvo filosofov Uzbekistana, 2007.
Kostetsukii, V. A., Mametova, G. U., Mal'kumova, L.A., Sergeeva, H.I., *Chuvstvo rodiny 6 klass*, Tashkent: Yangiyul poligraph service, 2007.
Kostetsukii, V. A., Mel'kumoba, L.A., Dobrolinskaya, G.V., Sergeeva, N.I., *Ideya natsional'noi nezavisimosti i osnovy dukhovnosti 9 klass*, Tashkent: Sharq, 2005.
Kostetsukii, V. A., Mel'kumoba, L.A., Dobrolinskaya, G.V., Sergeeva, N.I., *Ideya natsional'noi nezavisimosti i osnovy dukhovnosti 8 klass*, Tashkent: Yangiyul poligraph service, 2007.
Kostetsukii, V., Tashpulaetova, M., Asadova, E., *Puteshestvie v mir konstitutsii 7 klass*, Tashkent: O'zbekiston, 2003.
Kostetsukii, V., Tashpulaetova, M., Asadova, E., Tancykbaeva, G., Ashrafkhanova, SH., *Puteshestvie v mir konstitutsii 7 klass*, Tashkent: Sharq, 2006.
Kostetsukii, V., Tashpulaetova, M., Tancykbaeva, G., Asadova, E., Afanas'eva, I., Solov'eva, S. E., *Puteshestvie v mir konstitutsii 5 klass*, Tashkent: Sharq, 2007.
Kostetsukii, V., Tancykbaeva, G., Asadova, E., Afanas'eva, I., Tashpulaetova, M., Solov'eva, S. E., *Puteshestvie v mir konstitutsii 6 klass*, Tashkent: Sharq, 2007.
Kurbanov, S., Seitkhalilov, E., *Otvetstvennost'obrazovaniya v preduprezhdenii i preodolenii vyizovov sovremennosti*, Tashkent: Akademiya, 2003.
Medynskii, E.N., *Narodnoe obrazovanie v SSSR*, Moskva: Izdatel'stvo akademii pedagogicheskikh nauk RSFSR, 1952.
Muminov, I. M. i dr, *Istoriya Samarkanda*, Tom pervyi, Tashkent: Fan, 1969.
Nikolaeva, E.I., Nikolaev, I.S., Lavrinenko, T.V., *Moi Uzbekistan*, Tashkent: O'qituvchi, 1996.
Obshchestvennoe dvizhenie molodezh' Uzbekistana "KAMOLOT", *Programma i ustav (novaya redaktsiya)*, Tashkent, 2007.
Osnoby konstitutsionnogo prava Respubliki Uzbekistan 9 klass, Tashkent: Sharq, 2003.
Prokofieva, M. A., *Narodnoe obrazovanie v SSSR 1917-1967*, Moskva: Prosveshchenie, 1967.
Prokofieva, M. A., *Narodnoe obrazovanie v SSSR*, Moskva: Pedagogika, 1985.
Rakhmonov, E., *Tadzhiki v zerkale istorii*, London&Flint River Editions Great Britain.
Respublikanskii nauchno-prosvetitel'skii tsentr Imama Bukhari, Fond imeni Fridrikha Eberta, *Religiya i molodezh' v sovremennykh musul'manskikh obshchestvakh*, Tashkent, 2007.
SOS-detskie derevni Uzbekistana, *Informatsiya o detel'nosti assotsiatsii*, 2008.
Strategicheskaya programma protivodeistviya rasprostraneniyu VICH-infektsii v Respublike Uzbekistan na 2007-2011gg., Tashkent, 2007.
Sukhareva, O.A., *Kvartal'naya obshchina pozdnefeodal'nogo goroda Bukhary: v svyazi s istoriei kvartalov*, Moskva: Nauka, 1976.
Sukhareva, O.A., *Bukhara XIX- nachalo XXv*, Moskva: Nauka, 1966.
Tashkent entsiklopediya, Tashkent: Glavnaya redaktsiya uzbekskoi sovetskoi entsiklopedii, 1984.

Talipova, R., Salikhova, M., Tsuvilina, E., Niyazova, Z., Nurmukhamedov, T., *Russkii yazyk 2 klass*, Tashkent : O'zbekiston, 2006.

Ukaz Prezidenta Respubliki Uzbekistan, O dopolnitel'nykh merakh po podderzhke deyatel' nosti Komiteta Zhenshchin Uzbekistana, Sobranie zakonodatel'stva Respubliki Uzbekistan, 2004g., No.21, s.251.

Yastrebova, A. V., *Korrektsiya zaikaniya u uchashchikhsya obshcheobrazovatel'noi shkoly*, Moskva : Prosveshchenie, 1980.

Zakon Respubliki Uzbekistan "Ob obrazovanii" 2 iyulya 1992g. No 636-XII

Zakon Respubliki Uzbekistan "Ob obrazovanii", 29 avgusta 1997g. No 464-I

Abdullayeva, Q., Yusupova, M., Rahmonbekova, S., *Odobnoma O'zbekiston Respublikasi Xalq ta'limi vazirligi 2-sinf uchun darslik sifatida tasdiqlagan*, Toshkent : O'zbekiston, 2007.

Ahhmedov, E., Saydaminova, Z., *O'zbekiston Respublikasi*, Toshkent, 2006.

Alisher Navoiy nomidagi Samarqand Davlat Universiteti, *Fuqarolik jamiyati : nazariya va amaliyot*, Samarqand, 2002.

Aminov, B., Rasulov, T., *Vatan-yurakdagi javohir*, Toshkent : O'qituvchi, 2001.

Bakirov, P., *Milliy g'oya targ'ibotida O'zbek xalq maqollaridan foydalanish*, Toshkant : Ma'naviyat, 2007.

Barkamol avlod- O'zbekiston taraqqietining poydevori, Sharq nashriet- matbaa kontsernining Bosh tahririyati, Toshkent, 1997.

Barkamol avlod tarbiyasi, Toshkent : Akademiya, 2005.

Begmatov, A., Rustamova, R., Milliy g'oya targ'iboti va madaniy-ma'rifiy tadbirlar, Toshkent : Ma'naviyat, 2007.

Garmoniya akademik almashinuvi xizmati fridrix Ebert fondi, Gete-Toshkent instituti, xalq universitetlari nemis assotsiatsiyasining xalqaro hamkorlik instituti, konrad adenauer fondi, *Tarix va O'zlikni angrash : O'zbekiston va Geraniya tajribasi*, Toshkent, 2005.

Hasanboyeva, O., Ne'matova, A., Ivragimova, G, *Odonoma 5-sinf uchun darslik*, Toshkent : O'zbekiston milliy enstiklopediyasi, 2006.

Hasanboyeva, O., Ne'matova, A., Turopova, M., *Odonoma 3-sinf uchun darslik*, Toshkent : O'zbekiston, 2007.

Hidoyatov, G.A., Kostetskiy, *O'zbekiston tarixi 9-sinf O'qituvchilar uchun metodik qo'llanma*, Toshkent : O'zinkomsentr, 2002.

Husanov, O., *Mustaqillik va mahalliy hokimiyat*, Toshkent : Sharq, 1996.

Imarov, E., Abdullaev, M., *Ma'naviyat Asoslari*, Toshkent : Sharq, 2005.

Inoyatov, M., *Oila, ijod, tarbiya va ma'naviyat*, Toshkent : Sharq, 2000.

Jalilov, SH., *Davlat kokimiytati mahalliy organlari islohoit : tajriba va muammolar*, Toshkent : O'zbekistan, 1994.

Jalilov, SH., *Mahalla yangilanish davrida*, Toshkent : Mehnat, 1995.

Karimov, N., Normatov, U., *Adabiyot 5-sinf uchun darslik*, Toshkent : Sharq, 2004.

Karimova, O., *Konstitutsiya alifbosi 3-sinf o'quvchilari uchun o'quv qo'llanma*, Toshkent : Sharq, 2007.

Karimova, O., *Konstitutsiya alifbosi 4-sinf o'quvchilari uchun o'quv qo'llanma*, Toshkent : Sharq, 2007.

Mahmudbekov, SH., *Mahallada o'znii o'zi boshqarish tizimi : tarixi va bugungi kuni*, Toshkent : Akademiya, 2004.

Mahmudov, N., Nurmonov, A., Sobirov, A., Qodirov, V., Jp'raboyeva, Z., *Ona tili 5-sinf uchun darslik*, Toshkent : Ma'naviyat, 2007.

Mallitskiy, N. G., *Toshkent mahalla va mavzelari*, Toshkent: Gafur Gulom nomidagi Adabiyot va san'at nashriemi, 1996.
Mirolimov, SH., *Mahalla mehri*, Toshkent: Navro'z, 1994.
Mirqosimov, M. *Kechik qishloq maktablarida uqitish Xususiya'lari*, Toshkent: O'qituvchi, 1975.
Muhammadkarimov, A., *Toshkentnoma*, Toshkent: Movarounnahr, 2004.
Munavvarov, A. Q., *Oila pedagogikasi*, Toshkent: O'qituvchi, 1994.
Musurmonova, O., Qo'chqorov, R., Qarshiboyev, M, *Milliy istiqlol g'oyasi va ma'aviyat asoslari 9-sinf*, Toshkent: Ma'naviyat, 2007.
Nishonova, S., Musurmonova, O., Qarshiboyev, M., *Milliy istiqlol g'oyasi va ma'aviyat asoslari 7-sinf*, Toshkent: Ma'naviyat, 2003.
Nosirxo'jayev, S.H., Lafasov, M.F., Zaripov, M.Z., *Ma'naviyat asoslari Akademik litsey va kasb-hunar kollejlari uchun darslik*, Toshkent: Sharq, 2005.
Odbnoma O'qv dasturi (2-sinf), Toshkent, 2001.
Oxunova, M., *Toshkent ishchilari O'zbekistonda sovet hokimiyatining g'alabasi uchun kurashda*, Toshkent: Fan, 1983.
Qarshiboyev, M., Nishonova, S., Musurmonova, O., Qo'chqorov, R., *Milliy istiqlol g'oyasi va ma'aviyat asoslari 7-sinf*, Toshkent: Ma'naviyat, 2007.
Qarshiboyev, M., Nishonova, S., Musurmonova, O., *Milliy istiqlol g'oyasi va ma'aviyat asoslari 8-sinf*, Toshkent: Ma'naviyat, 2003.
Qo'chqorov, R., Nishonova, S., Musurmonova, O., Qarshiboyev, M., *Milliy istiqlol g'oyasi va ma'aviyat asoslari 8-sinf*, Toshkent: Ma'naviyat, 2007.
Rafiyev, A., G'ulomova, N., *Ona tili va adabiyot*, Toshkent: Sharq, 2007.
Rahmonova, V.S., *Maxsus pedagogika*, Toshkent, 2004.
Saifnazarova, F., *O'zbek oilasi: ijtimoiy va ma'naviy qadriyatlar*, Toshkent: Yurist-Media markazi, 2007.
Sultonov, X., Qarshiboyev, M., *Vatan tuyg'usi o'rta maktablarning 5-sinflari uchun o'quv qo'llanmasi*, Toshkent: Ma'naviyat, 2003.
Sultonov, X., Qarshiboyev, M., *Vatan tuyg'usi umumiy o'rta ta'lim muassasalarining 6-sinflari uchun o'quv qo'llanmasi*, Toshkent: Ma'naviyat, 2006.
Tolipova, R., Is'hoqova, M., Ikromova, N., *O'zbek Tili ta'lim boshqa tillarda olib boriladigan maktablarning 2-sinfi uchun darslik*, Toshkent: O'zbekiston, 2007.
Umarova, M, Hakimova, SH., *O'qish Kitobi*, Toshkent, 2005.
Xalqaro ilmiy-amaliy konferentsiya, *Fuqarolik jamiyatini shakllantirishda yoshlarning roli*, Toshkent, 2008.
Xo'jamberdiev, M. A., Mixailov, A.A., Mamasoliev, N.S., *Ichki kasalliklar bo'yicha tibbiy masalalar*, Toshkent, Ibn Cino nomidagi nashriyot-matbaa birlashmasi, 1994.
Yo'idoshev, Q., Qosimov, B., *Adabiyot 7-sinf uchun darslik*, Toshkent, 2003.
Yusupov, S., *Tarix va adab bo'stoni*, Toshkent: Ma'naviyat, 2003.
Ziyomuhammadov, B., *Pedagogik mahorat asoslari*, Toshkent: TIB-Kitob, 2009.
O'rta maxsus, kac'-hunar ta'limining umumta'lim fanlari davlat ta'lim standartlari va o'quv dasturlari, Toshkent: Sharq, 2001.
O'zbekiston Mahalla xayryya jamg'armasi, *Mahalla*, Toshkennt, 2003.
O'zbekiston Respublikasi Adliya Vazirligi, *O'zbekiston Respublikasining Oila Kodeksi*, Toshkent: Adolat, 2007.
O'zbekistan Respublikasi Konstitutsiyasini O'rganish, Toshkent: Sharq, 2007.
O'zbekiston Respublikasi Oliy va O'rta Maxsus ta'lim vazirligi, Alisher Navoii nomidagi Samarkand davlat universiteti, *Fuqarolik jamiyati: nazariya va amaliyot*, Samarkand,

2002.
O'zbekiston Respublikasi Oliy va O'rta Maxsus ta'lim vazirligi, *Oliy ta'lim me'yoriy hujjatlar to'plami 2-qism*, Toshkent : Sharq, 2003.
O'zbekiston Respublikasi Oliy va O'rta Maxsus ta'lim vazirligi, *Oliy ta'lim me'yoriy-huquqiy va uslubiy hujjatlar to'plami* , Toshkent : Istiqlol, 2004.
O'zbekiston Respublikasi Prezidentining Farmoni, 1992 yil 12 Sentyabr', PF-472 son.
O'zbekiston Respublikasi Vazirlar Mahkamasining Karori, 2003 yil 7 Fevral', 70 son.
O'zbekiston Respublikasi Xalq Ta'limi Vazirligi., *Ta'lim taraqqieti 2 maxsus son*, Toshkent : Sharq, 1999.
O'zbekiston Respublikasi Xalq Ta'limi Vazirligi., Yo'ldoshev, H. Q., *Barkamol avlodni tarbiyalashda oila, mahalla, maktab hamkorligi kontseptsiyasi*, Toshkent, 2004.
O'zbekiston Respublikasi Xalq Ta'limi Vazirligi, O'zbekistan Respiblikasi Ta'lim Markazi, *Odobnoma O'quv dasturi (2-sinf)*, Toshkent, 2001.

Uzbekistan Government
  http://gov. uz/
Ministry of Public Education of the Republic of Uzbekistan
  http://www. uzedu. uz/
Ministry of Higher and Secondary Specialized Education of the Republic of Uzbekistan
  http://www. edu. uz/
State Testing Centre under the Cabinet of Ministers of the Republic of Uzbekistan
  http://www. test. uz/
Ministry of Education, Culture, Sports, Science and Technology in Japan
  http://www. mext. go. jp/
Ministry of Foreign Affairs of Japan
  http://www. mofa. go. jp/mofaj
UNICEF
  http://www. unicef. org/
UNESCO
  http://www. unesco. org/
NHIU Program for Islamic Area Studies, IAS Center at University of Tokyo, Group 2, Database of "Structure Transfiguration of Politics of Middle East", "Democratization of Middle East", Suda, Masaru, "Uzbekistan·Political Party".
  http://www. l. u-tokyo. ac. jp/~dbmedm06/me_d13n/database/uzbekistan/political_party.html
"Report : New Country Programme for 2005-9 signed in Tashkent", Uzbekistan UNICEF
  http://www. unicef. org/uzbekistan/media_2091. html
Kamolot
  http://www. kamolot. uz/
NANNOUz
  http://www. ngo. uz/
Kerajak ovozi (Youth Initiative Center"The Voice of the Future")
  http://www. kelajakovozi. uz/

ASUKA KAWANO (Ph.D. in Education), is an Associate Professor of the Graduate School of Education and Human Development at Nagoya University, Japan. She completed her undergraduate degree in jurisprudence, and received her master's degree in the study of education at Fukuoka University. She was a research fellow at the Tashkent State Pedagogical University, Uzbekistan in 2006-2008 and conducted many field works on education and local communities in Uzbekistan and Central Asian countries. She earned her Ph.D. in education at Kyushu University, Japan. Her main areas of interest are education in Central Asia, social pedagogy, the international cooperation of adult education, community education and lifelong learning.